WINNING WAYS

Secrets to Success in One Design Racing

by Jonathan Weston

with John Bertrand, Peter Commette, Ed Baird, John Kostecki, Dave Perry, Andy Burdick, Annie Gardner, Dave Rink, Cam Farrah, Dick Lamb, Mike Martin, Hal Gilreath, Tom Pace, Scott Steele, Stephanie Taylor, Maru Urban, Paul Abdullah, Robby Wilkins, Alan Taylor, Danny North, Monty Spindler, and words of wisdom from 4 x Gold Medalist, Paul Elvstrom.

Copyright ©2025 Jonathan Weston.

All rights reserved. No part of this publication may be reproduced, distributed, or transmitted in any form or by any means, including photocopying, recording, or other electronic or mechanical methods, without the prior written permission of the publisher, except in the case of brief quotations embodied in critical reviews and certain other noncommercial uses permitted by copyright law.

For all requests, write to westonimages@gmail.com

ISBN 979-8313276106

B&W Interior

Cover Photo: Morgan Kinney, Courtesy Melges Boat Works

Imprint: Independently published

Back cover: Rick Saez of the author, SF BAY, Elvstrom-Zellerbach

Cover Design: Jonathan Weston

Thanks to all the wonderful parents who sent their kid(s) to a sailing camp.

Secrets to Success in One Design Racing

TOKYO OLYMPICS GOLD Courtesy Int'l 470 Class Association ALeN Photography: Nikos Alevromytis

John Cole Photography

Photo: Weston

Photo: Deb Fewell Durbec

Photo: Will Keyworth

Photo: Bryan McDonald

Table of Contents

INTRODUCTION	1
POWER OF PREPARATION	21
THE START	93
KNOWING THE RULES	133
STRATEGY AND TACTICS	145
BOAT TRIM	234
SAIL TRIM	243
BOAT HANDLING	257
CREWING	279
FINAL WORD	290
ACKNOWLEDGMENTS	292

INTRODUCTION

Sailboat racing is one of the most dynamic sports under the sun, requiring well-honed tactical skills and a vast knowledge of hydrodynamics, aerodynamics, wind, currents and rules of the game. While there are no shortcuts to One Design success, there are many actions you can take to accelerate your progress, preparation being high on that list. While most of us don't have the time and resources pros do for championship level preparation, to develop winning ways, you will need to immerse yourself as best you can. Become a student of the game: read books, watch videos, attend clinics, and most importantly, get out there and race. Similar to learning a language, immersion is key; use it or lose it.

I recently ordered take out. The food? Inedible and horribly expensive, but the message inside my fortune cookie was priceless.

> *"There are three kinds of people: Those who make it happen. Those who watch it happen. And those who wonder what the heck just happened."*

You might be one of those who make it happen on the club or even district level, searching for ways to take dinner off the pro's table in the big events (a Peter Commette line). Prepare to eat up the advice, tips, and priceless knowledge from some of the most successful sailboat racers of our time, even if it's just inspiration, a build of confidence.

Perhaps you're one of those who just watch it happen. You're so busy observing what the keen racers are doing; you can't get a feel for how it's done. You're flat out stuck in mid-fleet mediocrity. Not five minutes after the start you're back in your usual place battling it out with the same sailors who still can't figure out how to put into practice all that knowledge every pro is preaching. While reading this book and attending clinics won't like instant grits place you on top of the podium, tapping the knowledge within these pages into well organized and group practice certainly may.

If you're new to racing or have been at it for a while and can't even crack the mid-fleet code, this book was created for you. After reading it, hopefully you will no longer wonder what the heck just happened. And, if you're a kid who's picked up this book instead of your phone, I applaud you.

SECRETS TO SUCCESS

Spoiler alert: There are no secrets to success. The formula is fairly simple: *Fail less. Go fast. Win you will. (Yacht Yoda)*

Hi, my name is Jonathan, and I have a dinghy racing problem. I've been racing boats and boards for longer than I care to count, yet I have still gained valuable insights from the contributors on these pages. In this sport, you never stop learning, and that's one of the reasons I do it. We know the other one; it's a blast!

I didn't come from a sailing family, nor grow up in a junior yacht club program. Like most kids from Atlanta, I played basketball, football, and baseball. At age 12, my parents sent me to Camp Morehead, a sailing camp in North Carolina (Mike Martin, 505 World Champion started sailing here as well!). I did not know what sailing was, nor did I care to. Homesick for the first few days, all I could think about was what I was missing out on: swim meets, Little League Baseball, and going to the Braves games to watch Hammering Hank hit another home run. All dreams of playing First Base for my home team came to an abrupt halt when I took that first ride on a Sunfish, capsizing into the Nueces River. It was a thrill beyond belief. I can still taste the clams we baked after sailing down the Intracoastal on Flying Scots.

I swam so much after my boat that summer, when I got back home, I won States in my age group. But after joining my first regatta with the Barefoot Sailing Club up on Lake Lanier, I realized how much I had to learn about sailboat racing. How I wish I had this book when I was that age.

When I was learning to race, many of the books were far too advanced; much of the information flew right over my head. The greater the complexity, the less likely for learners to absorb, to apply in practice. When sails are presented with too much wind, the boat capsizes. Brains capsize, too! There's a cap to how much information one can absorb; even with this book, resist the temptation to binge read it (as much as you want to).

Rather late in life, I earned my BA in Creative Writing at Oregon State and a Masters in Instructional Design at Purdue University. My goal in doing so was to learn how to not only tell a great story, but to break down complex information; to present it in the most digestible manner. In this book, One Design complexities are broken down with a step-by-step journey, telling stories along the way. Storytelling sticks! It's enjoyable learning, and within these pages, these stories are told by some of the greatest our sport has ever known.

I'd already enjoyed a long career as photographer, filmmaker, and writer for the sport of windsurfing, winning NPPA Sports Photo of the Year (Sports Illustrated), yet my passion for One Design racing has transformed into top 5 Worlds in Windsurfing, multiple Laser District Championships, major Thistle regattas, a USYRU O'Day SE Regional and Southern Collegiate Championship, 2nd Senior Games, 3x West Coast, 2x Midwinters and 2017 Weta National Championship.

A little book I wrote about windsurfing.

I don't kid myself. I'm no Tom Slingsby, can't even carry his blade bag. That's why I've corralled some of the greatest sailors of my generation to contribute their wisdom and stories to this book. Their combined accolades include America's Cup trophies, countless World and National championships.

Through reading their accounts, I can't promise that you'll win any major regattas, but it sure won't hurt. You've got to really want it. Learning the ropes is one thing; getting between them is another. With experience comes an innate ability, an almost sixth sense for the wind. Your mind sharpens, quickly solving whatever problems are thrown at you. The more often you experience those spicy situations, the more intuitively you react. As Peter Commette says, *"If you've taken the time to contemplate whether you should tack, the time to do so has already passed."*

Within these pages, our attention will be placed on boats that require mental reflexes, decisive tactics, critical balance, and physical conditioning. It's a complex game. There is no myth, no black magic. There is, however, a lot to it. Whether you're a casual racer or competitive, my hope is that these pages will prepare you mentally for that moving chess board we call sailboat racing.

Sailing is a lot like life and life is a lot like sailing. We are constantly given multiple choices. In life, it is choices of education, career, partner, finances, living and even sport. On the racecourse, it's pin end, starboard end, or somewhere in the middle (with clear air!). Which side of the course? Do I tack or duck, jibe or stay the course, take risks or play it safe? Even the best sailors don't always get it right. It's how they react when getting it wrong that sets them apart. Do they take a flyer and hope for a lucky shift, or stick to their strategy and wait for others to make mistakes? You win some, you lose some. It's how you pick yourself up after those losses that makes a difference.

There is truly no other sport like sailing. Before I had discovered the sport, my idols were Babe Ruth, Mickey Mantle, Ty Cobb, Ted Williams, Honus Wagner, and the like. I read every biography about them. When I began sailing, I searched for similar book written by the legends of wind. The first book I discovered that would make a big impact on my racing progress was Paul Bert Elvstrom (25 February 1928 – 7 December 2016). I hope this book makes a big impact on yours.

ON PAUL ELVSTROM

Paul Elvstrom to me, the greatest sailor of all time. A bricklayer from Denmark, he won four gold medals over 8 Olympic games, and 20 world championships. It is the principles that Paul lived by that sets him apart. All in all, no one can fill Paul's sailing shoes. His preparation and dedication to the sport is in my book, second to none. Though Paul has passed into the great hall of sailors in the sky, fortunately for us, Dave Perry was able to capture the great wisdom he has left behind during one of Paul's final clinics.

You probably are not aware of Paul's innovations you use every sailing day. His biggest contribution to sailing was popularizing the boom vang. There are other large innovations, such as the hiking strap and the self-bailer. He also built a sailmaking empire, Elvstrom Sails, that is still sewing today. Rounding gate marks? Paul Elvstrom. But his biggest contribution was in sharing knowledge. Before Paul, sailors kept secrets. Unfortunately, many still do!

As a baseball fanatic, I tore through the pages of every biography written by the greats: Babe Ruth, Ty Cobb, Mickey Mantle, Ted Williams. It was only natural that when I took up sailboat racing, I would read Paul's book, *Elvstrom Speaks on Yacht Racing*, my first shortcut to success. If I could put 1/10 of what Paul put into preparing to win, I would have won a lot more.

There are few regattas I've attended when I have not practiced Paul's mantra of getting out on the racecourse an hour before the start. I did not do well in the one's I didn't. His dedication spent hiking out on the bench in his basement? I've followed that not so much! Yet, Paul's passion for sailing certainly made an impression on me as a young man, as I try to keep practicing what he's preached while not.

Photo: Christophe Favreau . International 505 Class

Mike Martin and Adam Lowry on form winning a fifth 505 World Championship.

WHAT SOME THINK SUCCESS IN ONE DESIGN RACING LOOKS LIKE   WHAT SUCCESS IN ONE DESIGN RACING REALLY LOOKS LIKE

PATH TO SUCCESS

As sailors we know well that success doesn't travel in a straight line. One must play with great skill puffs, lulls, headers and lifts. The faster one is able to react to these variances is one thing; learning from your mistakes when too slow yet another. You need to own up to those mistakes by thoroughly analyzing them (race debriefings). In doing so, you will avoid repeating them, hopefully less than others. I believe greater progress is made from losing a tight battle than pulling a horizon job on the fleet.

Recently, I was having difficulty in a Learn to Sail class to instill basic knowledge to a youngster that to get to the weather mark, it was not possible to point the boat straight into the wind. His sharp reply, "Oh yeah? Watch me!" While I appreciated the gumption, his attempt was repeatedly met by luffing sails. Maybe one day he would learn that to be successful in life, he would have to play by the rules of the wind. To be successful as an instructor, I would need to learn how to better teach, or get sprayed by the kid on his jet ski.

Soak up good knowledge and you will soak VMG on that downwind leg. Attend clinics, prepare well, and follow an organized practice regimen. In due time you will begin to read patterns in the wind, currents, weather, as well as the strengths and weaknesses of your opponents. When presented with similar situations, you will subconsciously react in a timely, winning way. The main thing is to keep at it, have a positive attitude, and enjoy the ride. The most successful racer is the one having the most fun. Before lifting the NBA trophy 6 times, Michael Jordan said,

> "I've missed more than 9,000 shots in my career. I've lost almost 300 games. Twenty-six times I've been trusted to take the game-winning shot and missed. I've failed over and over again in my life. And that is why I succeed."

I'm sure I've blown more tacks than Michael's missed shots, so in this book I share some stumbles and kicks of the rock, with high hopes that you won't have to.

Successful people ask intelligent questions, and as a result, take better actions. When experiencing a knockdown, lessons learned are lessons earned. Before we get started on those lessons, I'd like to introduce you to the key players in my book, to view what they see as success:

Ed Baird winning 1980 Laser Worlds. Check out that hi-tech boom vang, kids!

I met Ed Baird at the 470 Midwinters in Tampa Bay when we were both about 15. My dad egged me on to introduce myself.

"Hi Ed. Nice racing there. I'm Jonathan. Me and my dad, we're from Atlanta."
"Oh, Atlanta? Nice of you to come all this way. Were you on the race committee?"
"Um, no. Well, we were in..."
"Same time zone? Zip code?"
His friends laughed. Words for motivation.

Few sailors at the time were putting in the same work ethic required to succeed in other sports. But as hard as one trained for dinghy racing, Ed realized early that you still can't get far on your own. I owe Ed any success I had, as we leap frogged at the top of leaderboard, pushing each other to greater success. Ed and I became both friends and competitors, but between the laylines, it was serious business. It was serious fun, too!

After I garnished some success in world windsurfing events, I blasted off to Hawaii to follow my passion for the evolution of windsurfing. Ed kept after it, soon winning Laser Worlds. Sailing then turned pro. Ed, being the consummate professional he is, went on to win more professional sailing events than you can swirl a hiking stick at. As Rolex World Sailor of the Year, it would take ten pages to list all of his accomplishments, in the most competitive fleets, including: TP 52, Soling, World Match Racing Championships, and the Whitbread Round the World Race (now Volvo). After coaching the NZ team to their first America's Cup victory, Ed became the last American born skipper to hoist the trophy for Alinghi, or any AC campaign.

If I had to describe Ed in two words, it would be mental toughness. He is not a guy you'd want to identify as a "Turkey" on the start line. When it comes to luffing battles and tacking duels, it would not be a wise battle to pick. He's a pretty nice guy off the racecourse (nice enough to contribute to this book), but on the racecourse, you're not taking dinner off his table.

Ed Baird: *Defining success. For me, even after reaching the pinnacle of success in our sport, it's still all about improving. Being better than last time. Gaining confidence. I've never defined success as a number or a particular championship. Doing an Olympic campaign in the Soling led to winning the Laser worlds. Racing Lasers showed me how to manage big fleets and got me a J/24 World Championship. Match Racing made me better at close situations, which helped me win multiple TP-52 events and seasons. Racing big boats helped me understand momentum, mode-changing, longer-range planning and teamwork, which led to winning the America's Cup. America's Cup experience taught me about working within teams and managing resources that helped win Maxi World titles. And so forth... Even to this day, the fun has always been about learning how to be better for next time. I love it!*

John Kostecki also believes that to be successful, you have to enjoy what you're doing. During his professional sailing career, he has won 17 World titles including the coveted 2024 Star Worlds and the Volvo Ocean Race. Inducted into the National Sailing HOF, as tactician aboard Oracle Team USA, he helped bring back home the America's Cup. JK (as John is universally referred to) is an inspiration to a wide range of sailors. He's a role model for youth sailors, a guide for emerging pros, and his athleticism throughout his career has allowed him to stay physically and mentally at the top of his game. In this book, he will be featured in an interview by one his great mentors, John Bertrand.

Photo: Gulain GRENIER

WINNING WAYS

John Bertrand winning Olympic Silver in the Finn, 1984, Long Beach CA.

John Bertrand achieved great success as the first to twice win the Laser NA championships ('75, '77), and twice the Worlds, the '77 Brazil Worlds being one of the most competitive events in Laser history. The San Francisco sailor went on to win the Finn Gold Cup in '78, and an Olympic silver medal in 1984. He's been involved in three America's Cup campaigns with John Kolius as tactician, strategist, and later taking over helm: Courageous '83, America2 in '87, and Stars and Stripes in '92. John has also coached a great many sailors, and was the Australian Olympic Finn Coach.

John Bertrand: Today's champions in the Laser (ILCA) class and other dinghy and keelboat classes rely heavily on structured fitness programs. This evolution traces directly back to forward-thinking coaches and trainers like Bill Monti, who saw beyond the boundaries of traditional sailing practice—and embraced methods like ballet. My journey reminds me that innovation often begins in the margins. Bill and I took what was then a cutting-edge approach—combining running, strength work, and, yes, ballet—and proved that it could make a critical difference in a notoriously tough one-design class.

Peter Commette: Sailing Duck Boats in New Jersey at age 6 (winning 8 Duckboat Worlds!), Peter Commette won the US Youth Championships with all firsts, was second in the 470 Worlds at age 19, and the first Laser World Champion in 1974. Still in college at Tufts University, he won the US Finn Trials and represented the US at the 1976 Summer Olympics. He has been a U.S. National and North American Champion in the Laser, Snipe and Finn. Sailing with his wife and daughters, he has finished well in the Snipe Worlds (3,5,7, and 16).

Peter Commette: Success comes from planning well and training hard together with those whom you love to hang out with, building the team (even when singlehanded sailing), executing the plan, feeling like you did all you could, feeling good that you left no stone unturned, and in the process, proving to your team and you that the effort was a success, regardless of the outcome. There is no shortcut. Embrace the process. Put it all on the line. Feeling good that you put it all on the line, that's success.

Mike Martin: One of the most accomplished One Design sailors in our sport, Mike Martin has not only won five 505 World Championships, Mike's the only one to do it as both skipper and crew (for Howie Hamlin). He's also won 27 North American and European championships in 505, Laser, Thistle, and the only American to win the 18-Foot Skiff Worlds, also with Hamlin. If that wasn't enough, he's a Collegiate All-American and Old Dominion HOFer, Director of Rules and Umpiring 34th America's Cup, and 2019 Rolex Yachtsman of the Year. Professionally, Mike is an accomplished engineer having numerous developed mechanical and electromechanical systems for consumer electronics, surgical devices, and the sailing industry.

Mike Martin and Adam Lowry win 505 Worlds again.   Photo: Christophe Favreau

Mike Martin: I think what has brought me success is the ability to get the boat going its optimum speed quickly as conditions change. And conditions are always changing. This only comes from time in the boat and good communication with your training partners. The very success of the SF based 505 fleet is based on regularly shared information. Until we began doing so, it had been decades since a member of our fleet had won a big championship. Since our collaborative efforts, both skippers and crews have produced over 10 World championships. Together as a fleet, we've achieved that success!

Secrets to Success in One Design Racing

Annie (Nelson) Gardner holds 5 world titles and 20 national and international titles including 3x Hobie Women's World Champion. She was the first female pro sailor, 1995 America3 Women's America's Cup Team navigator and trial horse helmsman. A Silver Medalist at the 1984 Olympic Windsurfing Demonstration event, and commentator for the 34th America's Cup and Louis Vuitton Cup in San Francisco Annie is regarded as one of the best female sailors of her generation.

Annie Gardner: I'm not exactly sure why I am different, but at some point in life I realized I am not your ordinary woman/person. Driven from something deep within, I don't give up easily. If there's a goal in sight, I put a lot of attention and a laser focus on it. Whether it's racing or not, I am determined to go after things and I won't stop until I succeed or die trying.

Andy Burdick: As President of Melges Boat Works, Andy Burdick has been a lifelong ambassador and tireless advocate for the sport of sailing. He eagerly shares his vast sailboat racing knowledge, conducting youth sailing clinics and proudly representing 4 generations of Burdick sailors. He has won over 80 championships during the course of his sailing career, spanning four decades in many classes, including the MC, A, E, C and many other Melges Scows.

Andy Burdick: Success for me is setting a goal to compete for a major championship, going through the routine of preparation, practice, logistic and then going to the event and doing well. The journey is the best part, the campaign. If you get the opportunity to win, then that is even sweeter. Accomplishing a well thought out campaign equals success.

Paul Abdullah competes across various one-design and PHRF class platforms and has won 17 National, North American, and World championships, including the 2022 and 2024 Thistle Nationals.

Paul Abdullah: There's a lot of talented sailors that I compete with and against in a variety of classes. I'm always learning to get better. What sets the good guys apart is the ability to not be afraid of being wrong. Some venues are more difficult to predict than others, but if you play the percentages and take reasonable risks, then you'll usually have a good result. There's always a little luck necessary as well, but usually good preparation and having a game plan will win out.

Photo: Deb Fewell Durbec

WINNING WAYS

Dave Perry: Growing up in Long Island Sound, Dave Perry was two-time Collegiate All-American, Captain of the 1975 National Champions team at Yale. His list of sailing victories include winning the US Match Racing Championship 5 times, winning the Congressional Cup twice. Fundamentally, Dave Perry has three attributes: he is a great sailor, is a passionate teacher and one of the top authorities on The Racing Rules of Sailing. He has excelled in all three areas and his seminars have provided unparalleled inspiration to thousands of young sailors. For all his work, US Sailing inducted Dave Perry into the Sailing Hall of Fame.

Dave Perry: I love leaving no stone unturned. It is tedious and boring sometimes, but I love the process. There is no Silver Bullet. You have to put in the time in the Preparation phase. If you don't prepare to succeed, you are preparing to fail.

Dave Rink started racing as crew for one of the top Flying Scot sailors, Sean O'Donnell. After becoming an arduous student of the sport, he soon began taking the trophies away from Sean (see below!). Most recently, he has won many district events and was the 2023 Atlantic Coast FS Champion.

Dave Rink: Success is having fun. Think about this. As amateurs, to go racing, we take time off from work and pay money to play. Doesn't that sound like a vacation? Vacations are fun! The pros, I don't envy them. We show up to the club and socialize a few hours before leaving the dock. We're on water racing a few hours, and then we're back at the club socializing again, drinking beer, swapping war stories, and eating. Sounds pretty fun to me! It's important not to let anything that happened on the water negatively affect the fun you're gonna have on shore. You're on shore twice as long as you are on the water!

Hal Gilreath Jr. was just a toddler when I was working for Harold Sr. at his dinghy and sailmaking shop in Atlanta. Following in his father's footsteps after sailing for the Naval Academy in Annapolis, Hal has enjoyed much success in the Snipe Class, winning numerous regional regattas, the Snipe Midwinters, and Military World Championships.

Hal Gilreath: I've made transitions in life and sailed several other classes (Farr 395, J70, M24, IC37, Laser Masters, Sunfish…). In each class practice structure, critical feedback, emotional discipline and fitness has proven effective. Each transition brings on new challenges and new friends. Look forward in sailing and life, while pursuing your sailing goals. Get out and practice and use your time effectively. For those of you who want a challenge, accept the risks of failures and enjoy the journey and achievements racing one-design sailboats to grow, prosper and build lifelong and rewarding relationships.

Photo: Deb Fewell Durbec

Secrets to Success in One Design Racing

Photo: Mark Wharton Reid

Cam Farrah represents the foiling youth of our sport. Showing talent early in her years at Fort Walton Yacht Club, she has won everything under the Florida sun, including the A Cat North Americans and WetaFest. The first woman to win both the A Class Catamaran Midwinter Championship and Admiral's Cup, she is the A Class Woman's World Champion. As strategist for Jimmy Spithill in SailGP, Cam is well on her way to sailing success.

Cam Farrah: Whether Im racing a Foiling A-Class Catamaran, F50 in SailGP, F18, Vx One, or even a Collegiate 420, I've learned that every race presents opportunities for comebacks. It isn't over until it's over.

Robby Wilkins began sailing in Columbia, SC, where he has been very successful in the E Scow class, as well as in many other boats. After moving to Annapolis, he was fortunate to have sailed with and served as tactician and trimmer for some of the best in the USA, including Dave Ullman, Bob Johnstone, Major Hall, and many others.

Robby Wilkins: Sailing E Scows is good fun! Not just the sailing, but the great fellowship between competitors. For this championship, we were fortunate to have Chloe, a Julliard trained dancer from Paris on board. She had so much fun, she even skipped dancing in the Olympic closing ceremonies to race with us! Time in the boat is a commitment from your crew to do as many regattas as possible and this develops your team into the best team. You learn more when you are sailing outside of your

Monty Spindler Monty Spindler is every bit as good of a sailor as he is sailmaker. With a longevity few can match, he has designed sails for more brands than any other. The young needle spiker started sailing on the lakes of Detroit at 4 years of age in Optis, his commitment to the sport advancing with a move to Annapolis at age 13. It was here that he met future Olympic Silver Medalist, Scott Steele. Scott and Monty were teammates and All-American sailors at St Mary's College. As a member of the USA Olympic Sailing Team, Monty took 6th at the Laser Worlds in 1977, and second at the Finn North Americans in 1981. Living in Tarifa as a successful windsurfing sailmaker, he is still winning races in Lasers and big boats.

Monty Spindler: Enjoying racing is success in itself. After race overview, identifying the error(s) made in the race, is a direct path to success. Reading the wind on the course is critical! Taking a good look upwind is crucial for tactical initiatives.

WINNING WAYS

Scott Steele grew up on the Naval Academy grounds and was 2x All American sailor at St. Mary's. In 1984, he won a Silver medal in the first Olympic event for windsurfing. Inducted into Severn High School HOF, St. Mary's HOF, and the Windsurfing HOF, you might say Scott is a solid steel Hall of Famer! 2024 Grand Master National Champion in the popular Melges 15 class, Scott still gives the young bucks a run for their money.

Plan ahead and stick to the plan when you can. If not, improvise, but don't wait too long to correct your course. Stay out of the dead zone, and never fall to leeward of a big train coming behind you. If one boat rolls you from behind, aggressively come up and defend the train, or jibe to the favored long tack (only if clear to do so and the wind pressure is there)! Think ahead and focus on maintaining fleet positioning until the opportunity presents itself for gains. While quick decisions can be crucial, patience can be your friend as well.

Tom Pace has earned most of his success as a professional windsurfer and later in the Kona One Design Class. In boat sailing, he has raced with many a fine sailor in the top classes, and lesser ones, claiming the obscure yet fascinating Fish Championships! As Commodore of the Pensacola YC, he was responsible for reeling in bigger fish to their camp, *American Magic*. (Tom pictured on left)

Tom Pace: Success is not just winning. Success is doing what's necessary to give yourself the very best opportunity to sail your best. Think of any given race from prestart to finish as an almost unlimited opportunity to gain advantage... every single tack, jibe, and mark rounding can be critically important, where you can gain leverage and race positions. Boat Handling is easy enough to understand, but getting into and out of a rounding clean, fast, and on better angle than the boats either behind, ahead, or both can mean a win or a mid-fleet finish.

Maru Urban is from the Salvador Coast of Brazil. He helped the US Sailing Team with local knowledge of the tricky waters for the Rio Olympics. An avid Snipe sailor, he placed 2nd at the Worlds, and coach at San Diego YC, Coconut Grove YC and Waterfront Director at Lake Geneva YC. His Opti and ILCA Clinics have become popular due to his excellent data driven coaching strategies with the use of drones and Vakaros.

Maru Urban: We don't just coach sailing. You can be a great tactical sailor, but if you don't have the conditioning, and more importantly for kinetic-driven boats, the flexibility, you're going to fall down the leaderboard as the regatta goes on. Light air can be just as physically demanding as heavy air, so we coach on nutrition, providing drills and exercises that increase endurance and agility, not just going to the gym and lifting a bunch of weights. It must be fun as well, or they'll lose interest.

Photo: Hannah Lee Noll

Dick Lamb: Raised on Annapolis waters, Dick was in the first junior program at Severn Sailing Association. He raced Cadets, Snipes, I-14's and Mobjacks, winning the Snipe Chesapeake Bay Championship several times. He was RC Chairman of the first Windsurfer Worlds while on staff at the NA Sailing Center at Association Island in 1974. Hooked on windsurfing, he finished second in his weight class in 5 NA Championships and was Windsurfer Class President during the explosive growth period of the sport, 1976 - 1983. He then became President of Windsurfing Hawaii, Inc. for another 8 years. He was a Judge at numerous NA and World Championships and was elected to the Windsurfing Hall of Fame in 2024.

Dick Lamb: Dinghy sailing and windsurfing are joyful sports. You don't have to race to have fun, but the heart-pounding ecstasy of racing well is worth the effort. Work on speed, boat handling, mark roundings, tactics and learn the rules well enough to apply them instantly on the water. But for me, the very best result of my racing career is the life-long close friends I have made. I'm still in contact with fellow sailors from Association Island (US Sailing Center, NY) 50 years ago.

Stephanie and Alan Taylor: Alan Taylor began sailing as a teenager when his father brought home a boat, turning it into a shared passion during those formative years. After college in North Carolina, he towed his Taser across the country and spent about 30 years racing a variety of boats, including Lasers in San Francisco. A versatile competitor, Alan has won the Isotope Nationals, consistently reached the podium in the Weta and Windmill classes, and even competed in the prestigious Champion of Champions regatta.

Stephanie Taylor discovered sailing later in life after sustaining life changing injuries from a car accident. Recognized as a natural talent, she explored more than 20 different boats in her first year before finding the Weta Trimaran as her perfect match. She has since gone on to win the Double-handed Weta North Americans twice.

After meeting at a race committee training, Alan and Stephanie quickly decided to team up for the World Masters Games in Auckland, New Zealand, sailing a Weta. Little did they know, a year and a half later, they'd be on their honeymoon, competing in the week-long event. As a team, they secured a rare Gold for USA down under!

Stephanie and Alan: When we race together, we're so in sync that we can almost read each other's minds. Our mantra is to keep grinding, one race at a time. When we make a mistake, we shake it off and stay focused. It's not over until it's over. Beyond the thrill of being on the water and disconnected from the world, the greatest joy in this sport is the community or going to a regatta and making new friends.

Dave Berntsen rocking the bay. Photo: Rick Saez

WETA GUY: As I got older, Master's Laser sailing in the bay and all those death rolls started to add up. I'd always wanted to Hunter S. Thompson "slide into home plate with all the body parts used up." But at age 55, I wasn't quite ready for home plate, just to hang up my Laser cleats. Then one day as I was kicking rocks on the bay shore, the NOOD event was happening. I couldn't help but watch these cool looking waterbugs flying around the city front. I had no idea what they were but it sure looked like fun.

I called my friend, Joe Cool, who always had a pulse on the scene. After being asked about the unidentified water object, Joe said, "You know Davo, right? Everyone knows Davo." I kind of remembered him from my 20 year vacation on Maui, a pro windsurfer. "Well, he's here in the Bay now, and he's the Kingpin, the Boss (the dealer actually). They're called Wetas." "What a's?" "Wetas. It's a Kiwi waterbug. Try one out." Try one out I did. It would take me a while to get up to Davo's speed on the Weta. He had won that NOOD regatta by a city front mile. But I knew on first sail, in a blustery StFYC Spring Dinghy, I'd found the right boat for me. Hiking was optional, done from the comfort of the ama (outrigger thingy).

Davo and I had a lot of fun battles. Even after an hour of racing, it would come down to a photo finish. Without guys and gals like him, fleets go belly up. Davo and I would practice by sailing from Richmond YC through the Golden Gate and back. During the America's Cup, the was wind was over limits, the only entertainment in the grandstands was Davo and I in a tacking and jibing duel. I think they were cheering for Davo, you know, being the underdog. Note the Kiwis far behind!

Photo: Gordon Lyon

While I was doing reconnaissance of the racecourse, Davo would be helping people with last minute riggings. That's the kind of guy he is. Instead of looking for an edge to win, he'd be picking up fish hooks off the beach. He didn't think he was on the level as the some of the other guys in this book to contribute writing, so he helped me land some guys that were (Kostecki and Martin). But I can tell you, his level is high in more regard then sailing. You can probably catch him out on any blustery day under the Golden Gate Bridge, under a ray of sunshine. What a guy. A Weta guy.

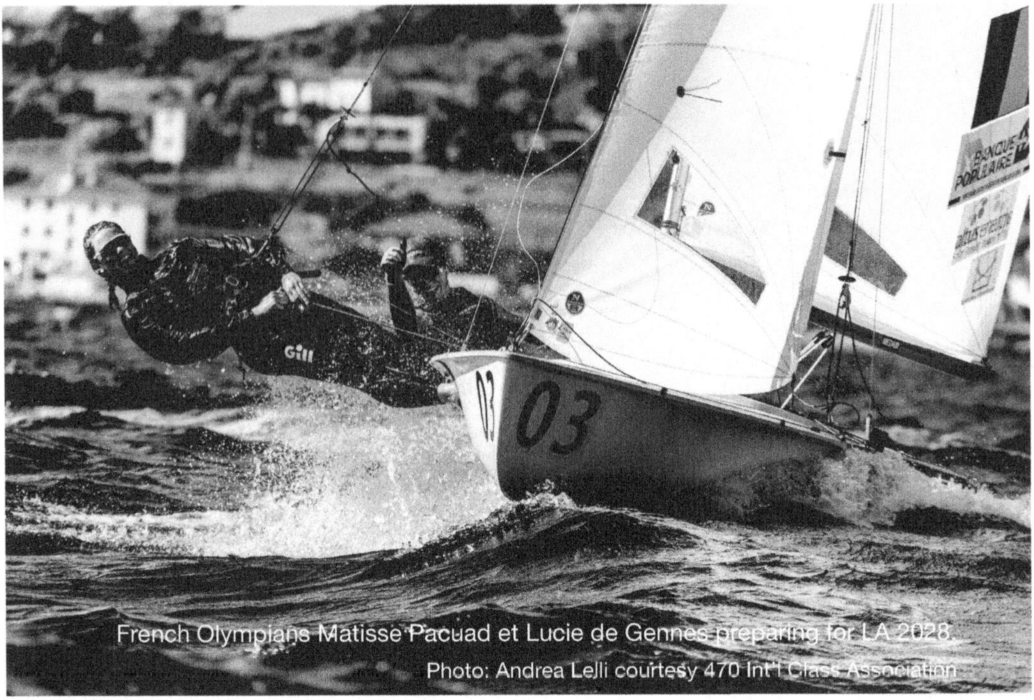

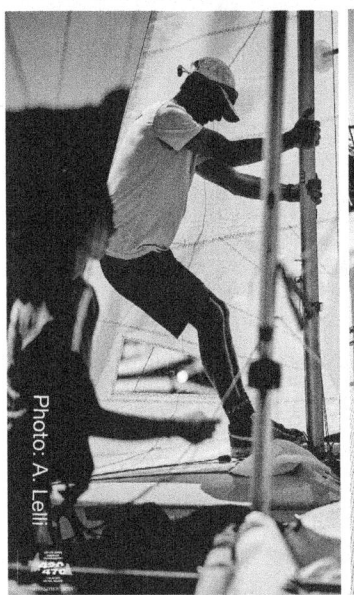

French Olympians Matisse Pacuad et Lucie de Gennes preparing for LA 2028.
Photo: Andrea Lelli courtesy 470 Int'l Class Association

Photo: A. Lelli

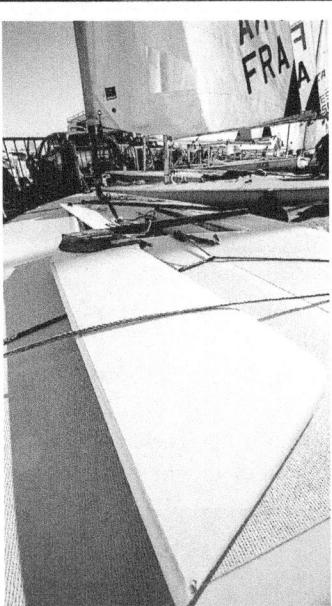

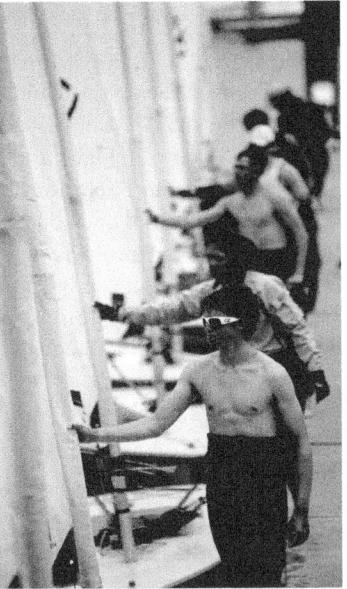

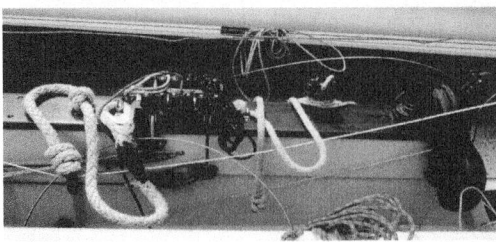

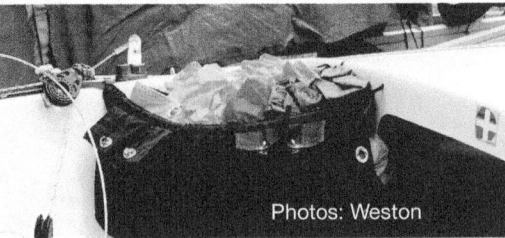

Photos: Weston

TIME SPENT IN PREPARATION

```
                                                    TOTAL DEDICATION
    DONUTS FOR DINNER   DOG NEEDS WALKING
                  MORE BEER                        TRAINS LIKE ARNOLD
       GETS OUT ON THE WEEKEND    WORKS TOO MUCH    SAILS EVERY DAY
              JUST THERE TO PARTY
                        EATS McDONALDS              FISH AND SALAD
UNSURE WHAT TO DO
                                    FAMILY DUTIES   BEN AINSLIE MINDSET

 NOVICE      ROOKIE      MID-FLEETER      SEMI-PRO           PRO
```

THE POWER OF PREPARATION

P6 = Proper Prior Preparation Prevents Poor Performance.

The amount of preparation that goes into a successful sailing campaign depends upon where you are on the "Preparation Spectrum." The novice and rookie will not yet understand the amount of preparation it takes to win. The mid-fleeter may understand, but lack the dedication. They may just be there for the enjoyment and recreation. Many of the best sailors would be considered semi-pro only because they have pursued different careers. Their livelihood doesn't depend on sailing. The pro will be all in on preparation.

> *"Preparation is the most important thing, because only when you are 100 percent sure you know everything and have forgotten nothing, can you concentrate on starting in the right place and using tactics."* Paul Elvstrom

Pro sailors arrive at a regatta with a boat that has all the kinks worked out – brush, tooth and comb – they are brimming with confidence, ready to rumble. Their boat has all the go fasts; as fast as legally possible under One Design class rules, with no excuses to rely upon. Body; a model of fitness, top shape. Mentally; Psyched to win, armed with a vast knowledge of the local conditions.

Those hedging the left end of the spectrum occasionally show up on weekends completely unprepared due to other commitments; a job, a family, life stuff that gets in the way of the most important thing… racing sailboats. They compile a list of excuses: "Had a rough week at the office," "Need new sails," or, "Didn't read that cool new book, *Winning Ways!*"

Al and Alice, typically never even make it to the starting line on time; they're in a last-minute panic to borrow a forgotten part. Most likely, they won't make it through every race, at least not within the time limit. But Al and Alice still enjoy sailing and the process. One day, they'll have their act together. Hopefully, they will arrive at the next regatta more prepared, having read this book!

Most racers lie somewhere in the middle, between being Amateur and Pro. You're reading this book because you want to gain an edge in the club races or climb the regional regatta rankings. Preparation is key. Just ask Tom Pace, one of the most prepared professionals on any racecourse.

Tom Pace: *You may be better than me, more experienced and on a faster craft... but what I can control isn't you nor the others in the fleet. The one I can control is ME. If I do my best prep, get good starts, play the tactics best I can that day, then whether I won or not isn't the take-away. I did the best I could. And, if I did NOT prep well enough (and we all know our own truths!), then that becomes the first steps to take before the next regatta. Successes have to build along the way to becoming those wins on a racecourse.*

Photo: Tom James

It's difficult to explain to anyone why anyone would prepare so diligently, often spending half their paycheck on boat stuff. We tinker away all week in the garage, visit the gym, hit the bike and train hard for just a trophy, or these days, just a trophy hat. My kids think it would be easier to just go out and buy one. But that would be nowhere near as much fun. Races always start with preparation; days, sometimes weeks before the gun goes off.

I like to break preparation down into five things:

Boat Preparation • Physical Preparation • Mental Preparation • Organized Practice • Knowing the rules

Let's first examine the fun and fiddling part:

BOAT PREPARATION

Whatever strategical skills one may have, they won't pan out if the halyard breaks, the centerboard gets stuck, the kite flies upside down. A lot of this can be resolved with boat preparation.

Preparation for a boat begins with the trailer. Without the trailer, you're not traveling it to any regattas. A thorough check of the tires, alignment, bearings (grease is the word!), trailer hitch (put a lock in the pin, make sure it's seated dummy!), spare tires, lights, sufficient covers and padding so all that wet sanding of the boat with 600 grit isn't wasted.

Did I mention wet sanding the boat? At least give it a good washing. Serious racers will wet sand the boat and blades before every regatta, filling and sanding any ding they may have been gifted the previous battle. In some classes, that's not legal. No altering of the blades, not even filling in that shark bite.

Then you want to check the boat over from stern to bow. Are the gudgeons screwed in tight? Anything with a screw should be checked and perhaps reapplied with silicone. Anywhere possible, suggesting replace rivets with bolts.

Ed Baird: *Preparation and might I add, practice, helps reduce the pressure of the moment. But good practice with others of your ability also keeps a certain pressure on. Even during minor events you feel pressure, so practicing under pressure gets you ready for the big events, where the pressure is really on. If you're looking to improve, there is always the need for great preparation. Your boat is calling; rig up.*

Peter Commette also knows that practice and how you practice are key to preparation. *"Preparation brews confidence, and preparation and confidence are the keys to achieving success."*

MAKE A LIST

Peter Commette

In the Laser, Finn and E Scow (my main boats), I had something similar, but in the Snipe, I have five specific measurements to guide me to success. The measurements have to do with rigging and how I color code things. I'll make marks on lines, black being the base and green being for heaviest air (Green for Go!), with other colors covering lesser wind increments.

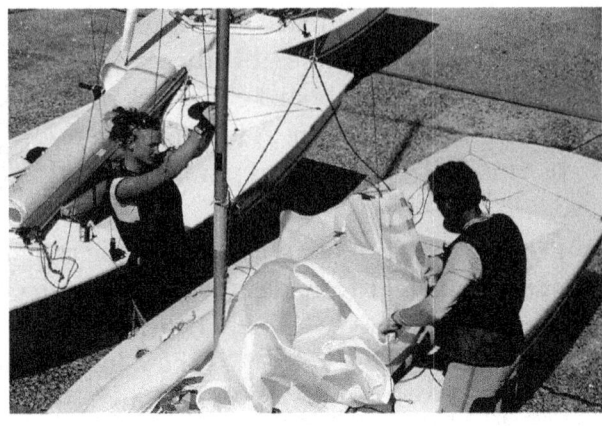

Mark your lines, set tape for markers, measure, measure, tune and tune. This gets you in the ballpark. But the real speed lies between the numbers. The more you sail, the more you are able to peg that minutia that makes a difference between finishing fifth (on the numbers) or first (sailing between the numbers).

I have a bunch of rules I try to live by not only when tuning a boat but also in sailing it around the racecourse. Basic ones. Be in the middle of the line at two minutes, stand up and look for wind, see the first shift or pressure coming down, choose the 2/5ths of line to that side. Another is not tacking more than three times in the first five minutes, and three is only if I have a bad start. When I don't race enough, I live by those rules. When I'm well practiced, I trust in myself more. I can trust myself to innovate. I break the rules. But until you get to the point where you've practiced and raced enough to feel confident and, on your game, so that you can break the rules, I stick to them.

WINNING WAYS

For me, I call being prepared; being at that point where I am sailing between the lines. There are books and articles on competition, books and articles on racing, online seminars, gathering and assimilating tuning guides, talking to the sailors who are training and sailing all the time about what they are doing currently to go fast, comparing regatta and training photos and videos, YouTube, every aspect of winning.

And then there is my on the water list. This list covers every leg, breaking each leg down into sections. I have noticed that my sailing lists grow in disproportionate amount to my time spent on the water! Don't know where I'd be without the lists.

Here is the author's list. Some of it is Weta specific; most applies to all boats:

Blocks running freely? Cleats good? Spray with McLube if not.

Kite furler bearings stuck? Take it apart or replace. If you're not able to easily furl or unfurl the kite, race over.

Frayed lines? Replace them.

Mast track free of blemishes?

How about the rails? Any cracks? Seal them with epoxy (inject with needle if damage has been done).

Are the ports lubricated? Do they leak? Replace. Add a handle to them if used on Weta to flood ama hull's and then drain water after a capsize.

Check the centerboard trunk. Is it solid? Does the board need shimming?

Flip the boat, check the gasket. Does it need replacing? Sometimes Dacron tape will extend its life.

You rang? Check all ports as well for O ring lubrication. A dry O ring is a leaky O ring.

Unfurl the sails (hopefully you washed and dried to prevent mildew). Did you look to see if any battens were shattered or broken? Always carry spares. Never store sails where rats can eat them.

Check the hiking straps. Nothing more fun than going overboard when a strap line breaks. Same goes with the tramp lines if you have a Catamaran or Trimaran.

Not in the maintenance sense, but for preparation, make sure you have a nautical flag chart stickered onto your boat. As well, print out a course chart from the SI's, place in quart Ziplock and tape to the boat.

Velcro or bag a dry erase grease marker to your cockpit. Use it to write down the course before every race, as well as any other things such as avoiding a restricted start/finish line.

Make sure your start watch works. If you're smart enough to carry a flare, make sure it and all other safety equipment such as a radio are charged and in working order. If on a John B. Sloop, don't forget a paddle and anchor as well.

This was just my list. Every boat will differ, so make yours.

BOAT TINKERING

Boat tinkering, aka meditation, is a required practice for even the casual racer. I'd accurately call myself a boat tinkerer, particularly in my Weta "adult" years. With the Weta, I wasn't really tinkering for an edge as much as ways to just make handling the boat easier, which in fact does give one the edge. I once tinkered up some pool noodles to stuff in the akas to keep water from gushing into the main hull. Within days of posting this online, there was a run on pool noodles.

There were a couple of times when I regretted those innovations; for example, when I put a swivel cleat on the base of the mast to easily lower and raise the furled kite (screecher). I had only done it, at least originally, for safety reasons, as during the StFYC Elvstrom Zellerbach regatta, wind speeds kicked up to near 40 knots. It was brutal. Nobody would be able to race in these conditions, but when I tried to head upwind just to tuck tail it back to the yacht club, the kite kept unfurling. I'd have to head downwind, refurl, head back up and repeat.

It seemed it was happening to everyone, and not really a fault of the boat. On rare occasions, the forces of nature trump normal boat operations. This was one of those. I headed to the lee shore of Alcatraz, as Dave Berntsen and one other guy still standing followed. Out of the wind, we took down our furled kites and stashed them as best we could, then made it back to the yacht club safely.

This got me thinking about adapting the cleat from a hitch T cleat to a swivel cam. Ronstan made them, so it was only a matter of installing it and class legal. But what changed everything, was that during the next regatta, I took the furled kite down on the upwind leg. It didn't make a big difference, but since I was far ahead at the weather mark, people thought it did and followed suit. It had been much easier to just furl and unfurl the kite, but now you had to raise it coming around the weather mark as well. The swivel cleat also served to foul up the jib sheets.

The only memory I have of ever passing Randy Smyth downwind, two-time Silver Medalist in the Olympic Tornado Class) was in a big regatta (2018 USYRU Multihull Championships), held in the Weta Trimaran at Fort Walton YC. Randy had lowered the kite on the windward leg and had a slight lead at the weather mark. The fun came when things got tangled; See Randy ahead, trying to raise kite. Hey, I created that disastrous moment for him, advantage *moi*!

The best innovation I came up with was for safety. Whereas other boats will stop when capsized, trimarans just keep on trucking. A Weta sailor will wear some type of web harness tethered to the same D Ring that anchors the hiking strap. The location keeps you with the boat, but not on the boat. During the Elvstrom-Zellerbach, Gordo (real name Gordon Lyon, but we like to think we are full-blooded Hawaiian, so we call each other like Dano,

Davo, Jono...), got knocked off the boat by a breaking wave, right near the GG Bridge. He got dragged behind the boat in cold water for a good half hour. I'm not sure how he survived that.

The innovation was to place another D ring further forward by the centerboard trunk. With this setup, you couldn't get knocked off the back or fall off the sides. You could, however, get trapped under the boat if you could not unclip, so Weta sailors should have an easily unclipped tether to their harness. Or don't flip (I never have!).

Another safety device is the rope ladder, which some people tape to the back of their boat so that they can easily get back in. Here's a funny story I found online from an interview with Hal Gilreath.

"The most bizarre thing that happened in a regatta? Getting washed out of an intercollegiate 420 as it planed down the East River. I was hanging onto the transom and the tiller. My crew was yelling "Hey, what are you doing? Get back in the boat!"

I was like, "Sure, no problem."

Leo Boucher, Photo Allison Chenard

WINNING WAYS

Ava McAliley and Christine Brown   Photo Int'l 420 Association Looma Pictures

Stu McNay and Laura Dallman-Weiss   Photo: Lexi Pline

LOWELL NORTH
BOAT TINKERING INNOVATOR

by Danny North

I'm proud to say that my Dad is Lowell North. It was in Point Loma that, with my grandfather, he built a Star boat in their basement. That's what you did back then. You didn't go out and buy a boat, you built it. I think they chose the class because at the time it was by far the most competitive and interesting class in San Diego. It was a boat you could tinker with. They went well in it. What a lot of people don't know, is that in 1945, 17-year-old Malin Burnham took the 15-year-old Lowell North with him on a train to Long Island Sound where they won the Star Worlds. It was right at the end of the war, with no gas to get back.

Lowell majored in engineering at UC Berkeley. It was not surprising that his engineering mind would explore sail design. Back then, there were only cotton sails, a black art of design rather than an engineered evolution. Needing to be stretched into shape, the cotton sails had a lot to be desired. Lowell looked at them with an eye for improvement, cutting and re-cutting again.

But then Lowell recognized Dacron to be a much superior fabric; stiffer and more conducive to proper design. With that innovation, Grandpa helped Dad set up a loft where they made the first North Sails. Before then, there was really only Murphy & Nye. Lowell was the first to cut shape into sails, and I'm pretty sure he was the first to use computer-aided design to shape and manufacture sails with the advent of plotters. We were still doing the actual cutting of the sails with scissors on the floor up until 1983, but the designs themselves were computer-generated from consensus, from a brain trust of what were now North Sails designers.

WINNING WAYS

As for tinkering on the Star boat hull, Dennis Conner, Mr. America's Cup – he won it four times using North Sails – will tell you that there were more holes drilled in the deck of Lowell's boat than just about anything. That's because Lowell was moving tracks, moving jib leads this way and that, right up until the boat left the dock.

In a recent interview, Dennis said of Dad, "When Lowell got involved in the class, he was creative, and so bright. He started making sails with broad seams, as opposed to just a flat piece of fabric. When he put the broad seams in the right place, the sails were wonderful. And they really sped up the starboard."

In Havana, 1957, Lowell won his first star-boat world championships as skipper under a bit of duress, so that probably had to be one of the most memorable. It was the eve of Castro taking power in Havana. There was fighting in the streets, lots of armed guards outside the Yacht Club. It was a year before I was born, so I can't speak for that.

His last victory as Skipper was at San Diego YC, which was fairly memorable because the last race was held in the fog. Several boats got lost. Davey Miller ended up anchored off Ocean Beach about three miles away on the other side of Point Loma and had to swim ashore. He called his wife from a pay phone to come pick them up. Lowell, I don't know how he did in that foggy race, but he had put a compass on his boat and won the regatta, It was his third Star boat world championship as skipper and now everyone has a compass on their boat. The rest is history.

Dennis Conner added, "Wow, all I can say is, what a guy. He's our best sailor, the best we've ever had in America. But to make a long story short, Lowell took his beginnings with the Star to victories in the SORC and to all sorts of big boats, which dominated the sailing world for years."

Lowell Orton North (December 2, 1929 – June 2, 2019) received a gold medal at the 1968 Mexico City Olympics in the Star class with the boat North Star, together with Peter Barrett, and a Bronze in the Dragon class, 1964 Tokyo Olympics. He sold North Sails in 1986.

THE PREPARATION OF STUART WALKER

by Dick Lamb

Dr. Stuart Walker was one of the most renowned dinghy sailors ever to hoist a mainsail. He was the driving force behind the creation of Severn Sailing Association in Annapolis, an Olympic sailor in the 5.5 meter class, author of ten widely read books on sailboat racing, and winner of numerous International 14 and Soling championships. He was known and feared for his incredible preparation: of his boat, his crew, knowledge of the racecourse and the weather.

"Cross 'em when you can."

One of Walker's proudest feats was becoming the first American to win the I-14 Prince of Wales Cup, held in 1964 in Lowestoft England. Dr. Walker was one of a handful of Americans in a highly selective and mostly British fleet that would be appalled if a Yank won what was considered their National Championship. The Brits also knew intimately the tricky conditions at Lowestoft, making Walker's victory comparable to the US winning the soccer World Cup in Brazil.

The I-14 was an ideal class for Stuart and his crew, Stovy Brown, as it placed a premium on boat development. He was an inveterate tinkerer. He complained to a friend after a race in which he had noticeably improved boat speed, that he couldn't figure out which of the five modifications he had made before the race had made the difference.

Stuart and Stovy spent several days thoroughly researching the Lowestoft racecourse from a high hill overlooking the racecourse, acquiring local knowledge from watermen, and charting the results. The course was five times around an equilateral triangle of one-mile sides, the first leg a beat. The local sailors almost always bet on heading out to sea on port after the start, instead of hugging the shore to stay out of the adverse current, in search of the stronger wind and summer sea breeze that came in daily when it wasn't storming.

During a practice race the day before the 1964 POW race, Stuart fouled out just after the start. In those days, if you fouled someone or hit a mark, you left the racecourse immediately – there was no penalty turn exoneration. Stuart and Stovy sailed to shore and climbed the hill again, spending the day observing the race's progress, noting what paid off and what didn't. They concluded that staying inshore on the first lap, then heading out thereafter, would likely pay off.

I remember Stuart's description to the sailing class at SSA. The wind was light to moderate with an adverse current of a couple of knots on the upwind legs. They got a good start near the port end and headed inshore on starboard tack, while most of the big guns tacked out for the slightly stronger winds offshore. He hugged the shoreline, pulling up his centerboard as they neared the shore to get as far as possible out of the current. After a series of short tacks up the shore, they headed out and had a sizable lead when they hit the starboard tack layline for the first mark. His boat speed was unsurpassed, so they cruised to the win. Stuart was so elated he backflipped overboard as he crossed the finish line – another first for the Prince of Wales Cup!

The moral of this story is that champions don't merely have a good day, they spend years preparing themselves and their equipment for competition. Stuart Walker didn't leave anything to chance. Sure, he was born gifted, but so are many of his competitors. For those of us privileged to know him well, he continued to be an inspiration that we have carried with us for whatever endeavors we undertook. – Dick Lamb

Maru Urban Clinics — Photo: Hannah Lee Noll

PHYSICAL PREPARATION

Photo: Hannah Lee Noll
Maru Urban Clinics

There's no better way to prepare the body for sailing, than by going sailing (and windsurfing, which last I checked, was sailing!). But the wind doesn't always blow, so if you're not on the Pro end of the spectrum or don't live in a year-round sailing area, you'll be tasked with creating your own training regimen. You'll be headed to the gym or a home workout area. In that case, you'll have to devise a sailing specific workout; one that mirrors the act of sailing.

At Maru Urban's clinic's they give provide attendee's with all kinds of specialized training routines to not only increase strength, but agility, balance, and endurance. You might think that racing in heavy air is the most taxing on the body, but it's the light air drifters that do me in. Being cramped into a pretzel up against the mast, that's when balance exercises, squats, and stretching pays off.

Maru Urban Clinics — Photo: Hannah Lee Noll

CROSS TRAINING

While fitness and a healthy heart are key, keeping a well-stretched muscular body is also important on agility required boats. Probably the best cross fitness training for sailors is running, swimming, paddling, In-line skating and biking. Anything beats the hiking bench.

Skiing is also good for building up the quads. Snowboarding, good for tearing off the shoulders. Many of the Laser and Finn sailors in the SF Bay Area put in some serious miles on the road or mountain bike. I lean toward mountain biking, as it requires quick accelerations and varied forces, similar to high wind sailing. If hard to get out to do anything, you would be wise to follow something like the Peloton program. During long winters in Germany, they play a lot of squash, and then smoke and drink *ein alt bier* or *ein alt pils*. Whatever works.

Phil's Trails, Bend — with Amanda Weston

I wondered what training regimen John Bertrand went through, when he won what I consider (with great bias since I was there to witness his stern), one of the most competitive and physically challenging regattas of my time. This was before One Design racing and its peak competitors splintered off into so many different wind sports (windsurfing, kiteboarding, kitefoiling, wingfoiling, parawing foiling...).

BEND IT LIKE BARYSHNIKOV

by John Bertrand

I remember the summer of 1976 vividly. I was coming off winning the Laser Class World Championship, but I felt there was another level waiting for me—something I hadn't yet tapped into. The Laser Class was now beginning to attract the best sailors from every class in the world, and word on the water was, we would all be converging at the next Laser Worlds in Brazil. To win again, in what I knew would be taxing conditions, I would need to up my game.

Like most singlehanded sailors, I did my best to stay fit: I jogged occasionally, did some basic calisthenics, and spent hours on the water. However, I had no structured training program beyond typical on-the-boat drills.

That was when I crossed paths again with my high school physical education teacher and good friend, Bill Monti. Bill was one of those rare individuals who saw the big picture in athletic development. Although he knew little about the specifics of dinghy racing at first, he understood the physical demands and mental endurance required for top-level competition. He approached me with a concept that would revolutionize my preparation for sailing: cross-training.

The Genesis of a New Approach

Bill and I began by analyzing every aspect of Laser sailing. On the surface, it's a straightforward, singlehanded dinghy. But those who have raced a Laser know how punishing it can be. You need the agility of a gymnast, the endurance of a marathon runner, the balance of a surfer, and the strategic thinking of a chess player—all rolled into one. We broke down these components:

1. **Endurance** – The sustained hiking positions and long regattas demanded more cardiovascular fitness than I had ever realized.
2. **Strength**—Although the boat is "simple," controlling the sail and hull through waves in a strong breeze taxes the arms, legs, and core muscles.
3. **Agility and Flexibility** – Tacking and gybing in a tight fleet or big breeze can be akin to a dance routine—one misstep, and you're in the drink.
4. **Mental Toughness** – Inevitably, your mind becomes as tired as your body. You need focus to make tactical decisions at the end of a four-race day.

Bill's vision of cross-training was structured around these fundamentals. Instead of only relying on time in the boat for practice, we would develop a comprehensive routine combining running, cycling, swimming, and resistance exercises to build a well-rounded athlete capable of withstanding the Laser's rigors.

Early Skepticism and Breakthroughs

At first, I was excited about breaking new ground but nervous about spending more time training outside the boat than on the water. When Bill mentioned Ballet as a core component of the training, my commitment to the project was tested until I saw how many pretty girls were in the class! But Bill kept me focused on keeping meticulous track of my metrics.

We measured heart rate, recovery time, flexibility, and perceived exertion during workouts. Over a few weeks, I began to see patterns emerge. My heart rate recovered more quickly after intense drills on the water. I could hike longer before my legs started trembling. My shoulders felt stronger when pulling in and adjusting the sheets in gusty conditions. Suddenly, the rationale behind cross-training became crystal clear: I wasn't just developing general fitness; I was building sailing-specific stamina.

Incorporating Ballet Training

One of the most surprising but effective components of my cross-training program was ballet. While it might sound like a strange pairing—ballet and Laser sailing—ballet actually bolstered several attributes essential for top-level dinghy racing. Under Bill's guidance, I decided to give it a try, and it quickly became a necessary piece of the puzzle.

Balance and Core Strength
Ballet places a tremendous emphasis on maintaining balance and alignment through the core and lower body. Every position—whether a plié, relevé, or arabesque—demands that you strengthen and stabilize your midsection. On the racecourse, I found this paid dividends when shifting weight to keep the Laser flat and fast upwind and maneuvering through tacks and gybes.

Flexibility and Range of Motion
From deep knee bends to graceful leg extensions, ballet stretches muscle groups that traditional workouts can sometimes overlook. This extra flexibility allowed me to remain comfortable in the contorted positions one often finds oneself in during mark roundings or sudden weight shifts.

Body Awareness and Grace
Laser sailing may not look "graceful" from the outside, especially when you're drenched and hiking hard, but the precision of your movements truly matters. Ballet taught me to be conscious of every part of my body—hands, arms, hips, legs, and especially my feet. Subtle shifts in body position translate directly into boat handling efficiency.

Discipline and Mental Focus
Ballet is highly technical; it demands unwavering concentration and repetition of the same moves until they're second nature. That mental focus transferred seamlessly to the racecourse. I became more locked in when under pressure, whether it was navigating a crowded starting line or making tactical calls in fickle breezes.

"At first, I endured some good-natured ribbing from fellow sailors about my "pirouettes," but the results soon spoke for themselves. My posture improved, and I felt more in tune with the demands of a strenuous, ever-changing environment on the water."

Designing a Sailor's Training Program

Bill and I put together a World Championship routine that I followed religiously :

WINNING WAYS

1. **Running (3–4 days a week)**

- Interval Training: Short bursts of high intensity followed by active recovery. This mirrored the high-output efforts needed when rounding marks or accelerating off the start line.
- Long Distance: To build endurance, I would do a longer run one day a week.
- Running (1–2 days a week)
- It was a tremendous full-body workout that honed my breathing control, which is key when you're at the edge of your oxygen capacity on a windy downwind leg.
- Strength Training (2 days a week)
- Core Work: Planks, sit-ups, and balance exercises to maintain proper hiking posture.
- Upper Body: Pull-ups, push-ups, and light weights with high repetitions for muscle endurance.
- Legs: Squats and lunges for hiking strength and stability.
- Ballet Sessions (6 days a week)
- Focusing on balance, flexibility, and precision of movement is crucial for boat handling and tactical agility.
- On-the-Water Practice (2 one-hour sessions a week)
- Nothing replaces time in the boat. Short and sharp sessions fine-tuning boat handling—tacks, gybes, and mark roundings—while applying my newfound fitness and balance skills.

The Road to the 1977 Laser World Championship

As the 1977 Laser Worlds drew closer, I felt a sense of confidence I hadn't experienced before. My energy levels stayed high throughout back-to-back practice sessions, and the precise movements honed through ballet training helped me maneuver the boat more fluidly. I could push aggressively on the start line, knowing I had the stamina—and balance—to handle the physical demands of the race.

Bill's presence as a motivator and strategist was invaluable. If I felt tired, he was there to remind me of the greater goal. He would say, "Laser sailing is about discipline—not just in tactics but in personal preparation."

Those words became a mantra, especially as the training sessions became more intense.

SETTING TARGETS

There's a saying, "If you don't know where you are, you won't know where you're going." My mantra, inspired by Robby Naish, is, "You have to know where you're going. You have to set a target."

I go with three targets: one is an event, such as a triathlon. The other is on someone's back. The third is time. How much time am I going to commit to that target? And then once I set a target, I make no excuses to not hit it.

Event targets

Aside from going windsurfing to keep fit (the wind is not always there), when I was younger, I trained for the Ironman. Sometimes, the training can be your undoing: Biking up Haleakala good; crashing into a cow on the way down, bad. In-line skate training was the best, till I skidded out on Cannery Row, broke my back and arm in three places. I've even crashed in a helicopter.

Peter Commette uses the lesser events for testing rig settings, building fitness levels, trying new things out, and honing his mental focus for the targeted event. In Peter's words: "Some competitors try to win every event. Not me. I circle the one that's most important and build up to it." He targets.

Sailor Targets

Training can be monotonous. It helps to have some sort of mantra, a target on somebody's back. When I was a younger, it was, "Beat Ed Baird" and when I got older, "Beat Dave Berntsen." You should be realistic on whose back you place circles, so if you've been mired in mid-fleet mediocrity, "Beat Bob Baconmaker" might help you take it one target at a time.

WINNING WAYS

Don't be shy when in the rigging lot. If you've got a target, drill them for go fast secrets, just like I've grilled a lot of great sailors in this book! Some will be helpful, some won't. When sailing in a class of boat new to me (Flying Scot), I targeted one of the champs of the lake, Sean O'Donnell. "How are you able to point so damn high?" I asked Sean. He responded, "Because I'm a better sailor than you." Very helpful! But I wore him down, and eventually learned enough "secrets" to at times cross ahead.

Time Targets

In training for Triathlon events, Chad Hawker, 13x Half Ironman Champion, gets up at 4 AM, swims in Monterey Bay, bikes up the hills, runs along the beach, and that's all before breakfast. Then he swims in the pool, works out in the gym, does an hour of Yoga, and goes into recovery mode. I'm all for just doing the last bit; hot stones and massage. While that kind of training takes a professional time commitment, you do what you can do. Go sail!

My youngest daughter, Holly, takes it to another level. She works as a Barrister by day, and as a training fiend when not. She is an Adventure Racer, completing several grueling events in NZ including God Zone, a 666k non-stop "adventure" of trail running, mtn biking, kayaking and mountaineering. My triathlon participation may have inspired her at a young age, but she took it to an ungodly level, so no excuses with the time crunch.

Team Vertigoats on the 38k biking leg of NZ God Zone (666k). One team member broke their bike and had to run the entire biking leg, the rest of the team carrying his bike! Carry on, Vertigoats!

Less Excuses

If you're like me, you do what you can. Yet, realizations eventually come into play. Like the great pro sailor turned photographer Will Keyworth once said: *"The brain is writing checks the body can't cash."* Nevertheless, arrows have been drawn toward a positive journey. As I say, *"The gudgeons may be rusty, but the bones race till the tiller falls off!"*

WELL STRUCTURED PRACTICE

by Hal Gilreath Jr.

If one is going to practice, time is the primary constraint. Go to practice with a plan as time is a constant constraint. In the early part of a season, we worked on the basics and re-familiarized ourselves with boat handling, and time/speed distance. As the season progressed, we focused on boat speed and tactical situations (starts, mark roundings, boat to multi-boat interactions…). Toward the latter part of the season, practices focused on different areas depending on regatta results. Across all the practices we worked on decision making and control of emotions. Critical feedback, whether from coaches, teammates or self-introspection, was essential.

Through a good mix of talent and hard work and over four years, we achieved both team and personal recognition worthy of being at the top of intercollegiate sailing. These rewards came through hours of practice and maturation of tactics. More importantly, this period of sailing imparted upon us the practice structure ability to make critical decisions while under physical, mental and emotional pressures. Little did I realize how valuable these experiences would prove to be.

I went off to Naval flight school and embarked upon a new learning and practice structure. I learned flying is very similar to sailing as it is multi-variable decision making in a dynamic and stressful environment. One can't stop a plane and think about a decision. Nor can one dwell on a mistake. One must continue to think ahead, communicate with crew members and focus. Flight school itself trained us through a combination of ground school, simulators and flights; all with highly critical feedback loops. Throughout training we built confidence in our abilities, teamwork and communications to earn our wings. The structure, intensity and time management translated well to sailing and training.

After surviving three years flying in the EA-3B Skywarrior I rotated to Arlington, VA and was welcomed to the Severn Sailing Association Snipe Fleet. This phase of sailing was highly competitive with goals of doing well nationally and internationally. We found ourselves behind the power curve initially with a long way to go to achieve our goals. Once again practice, emotional discipline and fitness factors came to the fore. I met, sailed with and sailed against great sailors, extending my sailing community internationally. We practiced quite a bit, the fleet worked as a team and kept ourselves in shape. Unintentionally we followed a similar structure to what we used at Navy. We did more boat speed practice since racing was on longer courses. Even so, we tailored our practices and regattas to more mechanics in early season moving to boat speed and large fleet tactics as the season progressed. This led to the successes we achieved in the World Championships, while enjoying the social aspects of a strong fleet. There were disappointments (breaking a mast at the Pan Am trials, losing our drain plug and falling out of contention at the Snipe Nationals....) and satisfying moments (winning the Snipe Midwinters, Military World Championships, finding my lifelong partner....). Each of these became building blocks of enjoying life, dealing with setbacks, and looking forward.

I've made transitions in life and sailed several other classes (Farr 395, J70, M24, IC37, Laser Masters, Sunfish...). In each class practice structure, critical feedback, emotional discipline and fitness has proven effective. Each transition brings on new challenges and new friends. Look forward in sailing and life, while pursuing your sailing goals. Get out and practice and use your time effectively. For those of you who want a challenge, accept the risks of failures and enjoy the journey and achievements racing one-design sailboats to grow, prosper and build lifelong and rewarding relationships.
– Hal Gilreath Jr.

DIET

Along with getting a good night's sleep, you need to fuel your body well, not just eat donuts. I'm no nutritionist, but the one thing I do eat or should I say drink daily, particularly before a long day of racing, is a fruit/veggie smoothie. I don't go for any of those expensive powders. I sub out almond butter for my protein intake. Here's what else goes in my Vitamix blender: spinach leaves, bananas, shredded coconut, apples, strawberries, an orange, flax seed, blueberries, garlic (5 cloves) and when good, a bit of honey or coconut sugar.

I down a real meal of something like fish and maybe a vegetable if I can stand it for my meal of the day. Other than that, I believe it's a good idea to drink a lot of water, stored in a good Yeti thermos bottle on board. If the forecast is for big breeze, go ahead; eat 'em while they're hot! Notice in the photo on the right a requirement for heavy air success, catching donuts like popcorn.

WHAT TO WEAR

Preparing what you're going to wear out on the water is as important as a good ski jacket and pants for the slopes. Whatever you wear sailing, make sure that you have everything in one bag, ready to put on between the RC meeting and leaving the dock, if not before. Keeping it all in one bag might prevent you from leaving something at home or hanging to dry in the last yacht club's locker room! Doh! Bag check.

Of course, what you wear depends on the weather forecast, water temps, the type of boat; in other words, your expectations of getting cold and wet. What is essential gear? Those with a long history of racing have all that worked out; which brand works and fits for them.

Here's what this no worse from wear seasoned sailor has worked out:

Sailing gloves: all seasons, full fingers for winter, ¾ fingers for all other seasons. Gill's grip the best for me. Make sure you have at least two pairs, as sailing gloves don't dry quickly.

WINNING WAYS

Spray Top (Smock). Mostly used over anything else in spring, fall, winter: Zhik and Slam, Gill, Helly Hansen, Henri Lloyd, or Ronstan; you can't go wrong with any of these brands. Whatever you do, don't show up to a race wearing a down jacket.

Undergarment: Under the Smock, I will wear a Gill rash guard type of shirt, long or short

Dave Berntsen Photo: Rick Saez

depending on the season. If cold, I'll wear fleece. Wetsuit: If in cold waters, and any risk of capsizing, I'll wear a wetsuit underneath. O'Neill tends to make flexible ones, but Xcell, Body Glove, Sooruz (Europe) whatever you can find will work. I like the Ronstan wetsuit pants as they have a good seat and knee reinforcement/traction, paired with a thin Xcell top.

Hiking shorts: Summer, or to wear over your wetsuit. Zhik makes the awesome wetsuit overalls with Power Pads I really like because it has reinforcement in the right places. Traditional hiking shorts are fine for Laser sailing, like Magic Marine hikers. I slide my weight fore and aft a lot, and bang my shins aplenty, so I'll supplement the shorts with some thin knee pads. The knee pads and reinforced seat have served me well. They pay me nada to endorse. I have some SLAM hiking shorts I picked up in France that have a thinner padding but feel and make me look cool. That's a hard thing to accomplish. On some boats, it's easier to sail by the seat of your pants if you have thinner hikers. But I like to use Zhik hikers on a Laser when I have to hike long and hard. A good set of knee pads is in my bag as well, particularly when sailing Lasers.

Neckie: Summer. Put ice in your neckband to stay cool during hot summer drifters, and another to cover your face. That's Peter and his daughter, who spend a lot of time under the sun in the water.

Overalls: When I'm in a boat like a Flying Scot and don't expect to go swimming, but it's windy enough to get plenty wet, I go with my Helly Hansen overalls. With these overalls and the smock covering my chest and arms, I'm high, dry, and feeling country. West Marine also makes a less expensive version. You won't cry if you leave them in a locker room in a YC galaxy far, far away.

Wetsuit booties: If you're in a hiking boat, you need a good pair of booties with some decent grip. Zhik makes good ones, but they take a bit of lacing up. I just use zip up ones from Ronstan. Just make sure that your booties cover where the hiking strap would rub your legs raw. On boats that don't have hiking straps, I use these leather Topsiders. There's also no shoe with better deck grip that I've come across (doesn't mean they don't exist).

Just a shirt: I wear a long sleeve nylon shirt hoodie in the summer, so I don't get burnt. The jury is still out whether sunscreen is good or bad for you, so a 50 SPF shirt reduces my use of it. I use sunscreen on my nose and ears.

Hat: Don't forget the hat, and a retainer to keep from losing it in the breeze. Within that hat, don't lose your head, or your cool.

Sunglasses: Wrap around sunglasses with Croakie are essential when on a boat with lots of spray. I tried putting RainX on mine. Bad idea!

Trapeze Harness: If you're in need of one, I would look at the European models.

Water: Back in the day, we used to wear water bottles for leverage. Glad to not have to recommend any of those, but bring some time of type of cooling thermos bottle with plenty of water. It should be part of your kit to ready.

MENTAL PREPARATION

Visualization is key in many sports such as slalom skiing or bobsledding. In no sport is this less true than racing sailboats; there are too many variables at play. Let's hear from Dave Rink how he went from Zero to Hero without the aid of simulators and other expensive technology.

STUDENT OF THE GAME

by Dave Rink

I think what sets me apart from most racers is that I "study". I'm not sure what else to call it, but it feels like I'm doing fun homework. Hard to call anything "work" when it's your passion, but this work goes a long way in developing confidence.

The work starts with reviewing every racing picture taken at a regatta. Of course, I look at pictures of my own boat in action, but I also look at other winning boats. I try to identify the differences between them. Is it sail trim, weight position, angle of heel? If someone was faster than me, why was that? I "study" the pictures and I'm critical of myself. I want to get better.

I didn't grow up sailing, so I've never had a coach. Just going to regattas, you learn so much. YouTube videos have been a godsend. There's lots

Drone footage: CJ LaCour

Flying Scot Fleet 48, Lake Norman YC, NC

of instructional videos out there and some from national champions giving great advice. A couple of those I've watched a dozen of times. I study the gybing technique, roll tacking, sail trim, the hand-switch when tacking, etc. If those experts are going to be gracious enough to make the videos, the least I can do is try to put those tips into practice. Drone videos have really become a great tool as well. They can really help with the postmortem after regattas. How did boat XYZ get so far ahead or so far behind. Mostly they help with more basic things like: how to round a mark; boat-on-boat tactics; and starts.

Every time Dave Dellenbaugh or Dave Perry has an online webinar I try to attend. It's like you're back in college attending a lecture. In the beginning much of what they said went over my head, but eventually that stops. We're at the other end of the spectrum now. Much of what they say we've heard before or we "think" we know. However, it's still great to hear an expert say something out loud that you've kinda known for a while. Just like hearing the same concept again but explained in a different way. It reinforces that concept and helps solidify it into your long-term memory.

The last form of '"studying" is taking comments from other good sailors seriously. Here's an example. A national champion sailor made a passing remark to me that I "sure was in a hurry to cross the boat on a tack." I really had no idea what he meant so I went work asking others and researching on YouTube. Sure enough I was tacking all wrong. I wasn't staying low long enough. I wasn't letting the boat load up on the new tack before trying to flatten or "squash" it back down.

Dave Rink recording David Ame's start seminar.

The key to this is that I heard it while I was "at a regatta". You don't get those nuggets of gold by staying at home. We probably race more regattas a year than anyone in our fleet, but we don't stop there.

We still participate in club racing and teach sailing classes. Surprisingly, teaching classes can really help instill what you know to be true and give you confidence in your technique. The point is, you're learning every time you get on the water. The more you get on the water the more you'll learn.

– Dave Rink

OWN YOUR MISTAKES

Part of a resilient mindset is being able to let go. Own your mistakes so you don't repeat them. Sometimes, you can sail your best race and get beat. There's always someone faster out there. Knowing that by getting beat, through "failing gloriously," that you will be better next time. I've said it once and will say it again, that there is more growth to failure than success. Like sailing on an offwind leg (or any leg), success is never achieved in a straight line. It's a squiggly line of failures leading up to it. How you handle those failures is paramount to your success. Fail you must. Yoda.

SET REALISTIC EXPECTATIONS

It's important to realize that by attending bigger regattas, you're going to go through a long phase of losing before you ever raise the trophy hat. That's why it's also important to attend lower end regattas and more informal club racing, where they don't even keep score. It's like kid's soccer. Everyone goes home with a happy meal.

If you do attend large fleet races, don't try to swallow the whole fish at once. Look at the earlier regattas and see who finished just in front of you. That's your race strategy: baby barbecues. Don't try to swallow the whole hog.

Because, if you go in thinking you're going to get on the podium right away and don't make it, you'll be hammering in that Loser attitude. Instead, you won. You beat *Barely a Wake*. Next time, you'll beat *Rock Lobster*, all the way until one day, you'll be in the *Love Shack*.

BUILDING CONFIDENCE

As a CBS Sports and NBA TV Producer for the Orlando Magic and OKC Thunder, I've been fortunate to have videotaped or filmed a lot of winners in life, including Kobe Bryant. Kobe's success was fueled by an unrelenting desire to win. During an interview before a game with the Thunder, I began to ask about how he thought he would stack up against Kevin Durant and Russell Westbrook. I got out, "How do you think —" before he interrupted, *"Gonna kick their @ss."* Kobe did work harder than others. His desire was greater. He inherited a high basketball IQ. But he also had that *"it"* factor one can't explain.

A lot of people want something, but some want it more than others. They think, *some people are just born to win sailboat races and others like me aren't.* You'll never find out which one of these you are until you give it your all. I'm guessing that if you're reading this book (good start), you've grown tired of going home from the trophy ceremony empty handed. You want it more than others. Call it drive or determination, ambition alone is a good start.

You can have all the ambition in the world, but you still have to put the hours in on the water. Reading is just a prerequisite. Racing Clinics and seminars are good shortcuts to success. Yet, you can't only practice. You need to get to the regattas and *race*. Nowhere is immersion more important than in overcoming fear. Fear to get up on the line, fear to fight for room at the mark, fear to sail in heavy air. It's all about immersion. Like learning a language, you have to immerse, to throw yourself into the deep end, tread some rough waters, get outside your comfort zone.

Harry Melges IV & crew winning E Scow Nationals Photo: Morgan Kinney

Paul Elvstrom preached that if you work hard enough, winning races will come easily. If you put in little effort, it will become difficult. "Why show up? Go do something fun with your life!" While some do just come to the races for the party, there is only one way to become a champion. You have to put in the effort, but the process with group practice can be quite enjoyable.

Paul Elvstrom: *I love to sail. I feel well in a boat and if I'm not sailing, I don't feel well. That brings me to a very good point. Now you are all young, but young people can have problems, too. And if you have problems — business, education, family — give up racing because you will be bad. And I went into business problems, and I knew I was out of racing, and I love racing, but I was bad. I couldn't concentrate, my preparation was poor. I didn't work hard enough, and yes, when the race started I gave everything I had. But I knew I had lost before I started. I then get angry at myself when I make a mistake I should have seen, because I like to do it perfect. If I lose because of bad luck, then I don't do anything, but if I lose because I have been stupid, then I'm angry.*

Paul Elvstrom, forever the Opti-mist!

IT'S YOUR TIME

by Peter Commette

At the Snipe Don Q championships in Miami, the biggest regatta other than the Nationals, a soon to be iconic Snipe sailor named Ernesto Rodriguez came up to me and made a bold (at the time) statement. It was many years ago, but I remember it like it was yesterday. Up until that point, I had been beating him regularly, or maybe it was starting to be pretty even between us by then, but, clearly, he had gained a lot of confidence, and we were tied going into the last race of a no drop race series. In the parking lot while rigging our boats for the last race, Ernesto said to me "You had your time. It's my time now." We were then and still are close friends; he could say

Ernesto Rodriguez, 7-time US National Snipe   Photo: Natalie Bailey

that to me. I love throwing down the gauntlet. My teammate and I won that day, but he was right. His timing was a little off; that's all. He's now won the Snipe Nationals six times, gold at the Pan-Ams, the Snipe Western Hemispheres and second at the Worlds. It's been his time ever since, but that boy has a lot of confidence, well deserved and born from a tremendous work/practice ethic.

Confidence. It's bred and manifested in so many ways. I heard a guy talking to friends in the parking lot while unrigging from a day of racing. He was saying that he consistently beat certain sailors who were pretty good, because he believed he should beat them. The flip side I heard in my head, was that he wasn't beating others, because he believed he couldn't.

So, it comes down to confidence, and confidence and can only be born from preparation. That's where I'm having trouble now as I'm older because I don't sail very often. My confidence has taken a hit. You know, it's funny, you get out there on the water and all those years of competing kick in and there's no throttling back. Then I get tossed into a position where I'm in the noise, where making intuitive, split decisions make or break you, and… I hesitate. No confidence. I dip back into my rules. The moment is lost. A good finish but not a great one.

The Flying Commette's

If you haven't done it for quite a while, you start thinking about what you're going to do next instead of just doing it. "Tack! But I don't, and that window closes. I can still sail up near the front because I have all these little rules tucked inside my brain. But to win, you need to prepare, and practice is a big part of preparation. You need to build confidence to pull the trigger. The more you compete, the more you place yourself in the noise, the greater your confidence becomes."

MENTORS

As a young sailor, what I lacked in coaches was made up for with mentors. A mentor might be a coach, but it can even be a competitor. It can even be somebody you've never met; in my case, Paul Elvstrom. He was my imaginary mentor. I suggest you find not only a coach, but a mentor. Real life mentors included Harold Gilreath, Dick Tillman, Johnny Sinclair, Lee Estes, and my Dad.

Dick Tillman won major championships in Snipe, Finn, Sunfish and Laser, but was mostly known for just being a great guy.

Seeking out a good mentor or two is never bad advice, but sometimes, they come by happenstance. You can't force someone to mentor you. To be worth their wisdom, they first need to believe in you. Whether they are a sailor or from some other endeavor, just make sure they are genuine in their intentions, particularly when being a woman. There are life coaches and specific sport coaches. The experiences they share can be invaluable. If only for an evening's seminar, there are mentors out there for the taking.

PREPARE TO TAKE RISKS

One thing you should mentally prepare for as part of your strategy, is how aggressive you plan to approach the race. Are you going to take every chance in the book? Or play it safe, and watch the jackals win? What's your game plan? When there's a tight crossing, are you going to duck, tack to lee bow, or will it be in your risky playbook to try to cross? If you're like Mike Martin, far ahead of the fleet, you won't have to take risks. I'm going to take a wild swing and guess you're not.

Therefore, as part of preparing your strategy, you need to dial in how calculated are your risks.

LOSE THE LOSING ATTITUDE

If you win, are you going to be humble? If you lose, are you going to let it get you down? Sailboat racing of any kind is about going fast, but also much about minimizing your mistakes, or at least making fewer than your competitors. Turtle and the hare! Hare today, upside down tomorrow! You must own up to every mistake. I just love the guy that comes in from a day of racing and needs to announce to everyone in the parking lot that the only reason they lost the race was because they tried a new go-fast doohickey that didn't work out. You lost because you were foolish to try something new during a regatta.

That's what debriefings are for; to not only attribute to successes but to air out mistakes, so that you and others can learn from them. Every regatta is an opportunity for growth. When that opportunity to attend a regatta knocks, you need to answer it.

ENJOY YOURSELF

There's a fine line between being overly competitive and having fun. The key to success in sailboat racing for me, particularly as I age down the rankings, has been to approach it for what it is: a game designed for pleasure, for having fun. I'm going to go out on a limb here and you're not getting paid to do this. In the end, nobody really cares how you've done. Your loved ones care about whether you came home safely from the adventure. And that's about it. Strawberry fields forever.

Looking back on big races I've won, I was really just out there having fun, wasn't I? Unless poorly prepared, I was. But iff winning is not your goal, then why are you racing? The entire uphill process of learning how to race was a ball, as long as I didn't remain in the back of the fleet forever. Dick Tillman was in the last place for his first two years! Back of the fleet forever is no fun, I don't care how many beers you drink. If you have Back of the Fleet Paralysis, you who do nothing to prepare for the race other than replace that moldy boat cover, your low ambitions are most likely across life. Elvstrom would say, "Time to get a move on!"

But what's worse: low achievers or the guy or gal that is so intent on winning that they spoil the fun for everyone else by being so downright serious and mean about it? Tomorrow could be your last race. Win, lose, or draw, enjoy the heck out of it.

Cooking along in a Lake Norman Community Sailing Social Sail with son David and his girlfriend, Daisy. The whole time I was saying, "tack", she thought I was saying, "attack!" And so we did.

ZEN AND THE ART OF SAILBOAT MAINTENANCE

A narration of a summer motorcycle trip undertaken by a father and his son, *Zen and the Art of Motorcycle Maintenance, by Robert Persig*, is a philosophical adventure riding on the fundamental question, how to live. That excellent book is not so much about motorcycle maintenance as one man's reconciliation of science, religion, and humanism. Resonant with the confusions of existence, this classic is a touching and transcendent book of life.

While this book comes nowhere near its success, there are some parallels to motorcycle maintenance sailboat racing. A boat does require maintenance. It does require somewhat of an odd relationship to make the boat an extension of your being, and if kept well, it will bring much happiness. To come to a race completely prepared; boat, fitness, and particularly in the head, will more often than not place you in a Zen state. Your nerves are calmed, you're in tune with the shifts, and you handle adversity like a pro.

You can't always prepare well and expect great results. Look at Steph Curry; he carried the Olympic team on his back with a performance for the ages. Yet, sometimes he's not firing on all cylinders. Just the other night, he scored 0 field goals. That's rare, but you'll have regattas like that. You just have to shake it off, own up to whatever it is that led to such a dismal performance, and live to hopefully win another day. Sometimes, it's up to the will of the wind. Most often, it's not. You've buggered it up.

As a lesson learned, when I was in my early twenties, I was racing every weekend both collegiately and in regional regattas. At the time, I was winning quite regularly, often sailing in what some might call a Zen state. I got to a point though, that when I'd win, I didn't feel like I had faced stiff enough competition. After I'd lose, whatever mistake I made, the loss would eat at me like worms in an apple. I stopped having fun, so I took off to Hawaii and went windsurfing. When I came back to the "Mainland," I got back into racing boats again in Laser Masters. I lowered my expectations, and while exceeding them, began to have fun again.

LOSE THE BATTLES, WIN THE WAR!

Dave Rink: *A common mistake fueling mid-fleet frustration? Fighting battles while losing sight of the war. Luffing competitors up at the start will often result in a bad start for you. When sailing downwind, don't try to roll over the top of someone, or you both end up sailing a longer distance while losing boats. Unless the regatta is being decided by who beats whom, sail your own race and sail it fast. Going into a regatta with a clear mindset of letting these small battles go... will go a long way toward helping you win the war.*

TOKYO OLYMPICS   Int'l 470 Class Association   ALeN Photography, Nikos Alevromytis

Paul Elvstrom:
If there are good fast people in front of me on the reach, then I will follow, but if it is people I can easily pass by planing, I will go up. But I will wait until they are in a bad position and slow, so they won't luff me.

Mike Martin: *We try to avoid tight battles, If we are sailing our best race, we are in the lead with no one else close to us. If not, we are looking at the big picture trying to get to the front of the fleet.*

THE WINDSURFER

At one of the early 470 Midwinters, I discovered what would be my "cheat sheet" to get after it; a long plastic object with colorful sail and teak booms, traveling in the cockpit of Dave Ullman's boat. You guessed it. It was a Windsurfer. Dave had no clue how it worked, nor did his crew who owned the contraption. As a result, I could have very well been the first person on the East Coast to windsurf, or at least to try. I eventually got the hang of it.

With the money I saved up from working at the only small boat sailing parts store in Georgia, Harold Gilreath's Marine, I bought one. It was like Henry Huggins and the Paper Route. I did that, too. I was getting after it.

There were only a handful of Windsurfers sold at the time and those who bought them weren't particularly good at racing, but my crew, Chris Downing, and I had fun racing each other. Windsurfing was fun (it still is!), but there was no real game to it. Yet, the cross training proved to be quite valuable, as the increased feel for the wind saw our results quickly go from back of the pack to mid fleet. We pretty much stuck right there. I started using excuses, like not living in Florida and being in a yacht club program.

BREAKING THROUGH

It wasn't until the 470 Midwinters that we managed to break through. As the Red Tide moved in on Tampa Bay, dead fish were floating everywhere on the first day, bloated on the second, and by the third day of that event, the fish started exploding. We started the race yet decided to head in when flying fire ants started attacking us on the boat. The harbor was upwind to the right. About halfway there, the breeze filled in nicely on the right side of the course. Not only did it serve to stem the ants from attacking, but as dumb luck had it, we were the first to reap its benefits.

Chris, having gone from sitting on the lee side of the boat to out on the wire said, "Hey, man. Don't look now but do. We're about a mile closer to the weather mark than the entire fleet!" "Whaat? No way!" "Way! What do you say we at least cross Ed Baird's bow."

Heading for the weather mark, that lead, however exaggerated, quickly evaporated. Dave Ullman was charging toward us like a rocketship. We "let him" pass, then followed Dave closely, quickly taking note of his sail settings, and held our own from there. For the first time, we did cross Ed's bow. All Ed's cronies had to say back on shore was, "Better to be lucky than good."

True, that was a pure stroke of luck, but even though it was just one race, it served to let us know that we were in the game. We could do this! What happened next was clearly chalked up to destiny. A week after I got my license, I was driving back alone from a multi-class regatta in Alabama, where I couldn't find a crew. Heading up a blind hill on a one lane dirt road, I collided with another car trailering a Hobie. The 470 mast went through my back windshield and knocked my skull clean to Mississippi. When I came to, the two survivors from the other car helped pull me out of a smashed window.

LASER FOCUS

Out of that disaster, with the boat insurance money, came the purchase of a brand-new class of singlehanded boat. It was called The Laser. Maybe Dad got a new car out of it as well, but that wasn't as important as getting a new Laser. Chris, having been abandoned, started working at Gilreath's and bought a Laser too. It was like Oprah... a Laser for you! A Laser for you! Pretty soon, everybody had a Laser, even Dad.

During my first days of making real headway, I simply got out on the water with Chris and we put in the practice time. It was an easier thing to do back then, eager as a beaver to chop down the leaderboard wood. Once I had my license, after school I'd drive up to Lake Lanier 4-5 days a week. Gas was 19 cents a gallon, so I could do that!

Before we did this Laser and Windsurfing training, we were average, mired in mid-fleet mediocrity. But after a few years of training against each other, making the other faster, we were able to win some.

BIG STAGE MINDSET

There's a case to be made that some people are wired to win District events and some World. You could also attribute championship success to conditioning and mental fortitude. A District event lasts 2 days, whereas National and World events run 5 or more. And for the Olympics, focus in a highly distracting environment needs to be maintained for weeks on end.

Being adaptable to all conditions is required to win big. Is your mind wired to sail in light to medium air, or heavy air? When the wind kicks up its heels, the sailors who have immersed themselves in heavy stuff will shine. At the same time, many of those sailors will falter when the drifter strikes. That's why, if your sights are set on winning on the big stage, traveling to areas outside of your comfort zone is so important. To win on the world stage, you need to compete in Europe as well, subjecting yourself (and crew if applicable) to not only a wider range of conditions, but elevated competition.

It's unknown here if you as a reader will ever ascend to the top of the leaderboard in a big event, or whether you even aspire to. But it's fun reading into the minds of those who have! To ride that wave in any sport, one must be wholly prepared, have nerves of steel, ice water in their veins.

My first big event was the most competitive and challenging of any event I've experienced, the Laser Worlds in Cabo Frio, Brazil. To qualify, you had to either win your country's championships or your district in the USA, your district. I had won and qualified in 4 different District championships, I was still completely unprepared in every way for the level of competition and conditions I was about to face.

To get through the event without health issues was probably the bigger challenge, with most of us getting food poisoning. Looking back at the results, as

NAME	SAIL NO.	RACE 1	RACE 2	RACE 3	RACE 4	RACE 5	RACE 6	RACE 7	T
1) John Bertrand	US 7	12	(19)	2	1	2	3	1	2
2) Peter Commette	US 25	(36)	2	21	3	6	5	9	4
3) Mark Neeleman	H 76	(26)	17	9	2	7	13	6	5
4) Tim Alexander	KA 2	(63)	14	5	19	19	7	10	7
5) Gary Knapp	US 55	43	5	(64)	9	4	11	4	7
6) Monty Spindler	US 92	6	6	15	4	15	36	41	8
7) Cam Lewis	US 61	(73)	59	7	8	1	21	3	9
8) Warwick Phillips	KA 83	(77)	68	1	11	5	4	11	9
9) Craig Thomas	US 98	14	11	3	(46)	28	15	30	10
10) Manfred Kauffman	BL 53	7	15	(61)	16	3	37	25	10
11) Eric Braathen	N 15	(71)	20	11	21	10	28	18	10
12) Gastao Brun	BL 21	39	37	4	5	11	(46)	16	11
13) Andrew Foulkes	KA 34	8	(56)	20	17	21	42	7	11
14) David Perry	US 81	15	(76)	44	24	17	17	5	122
15) Ed Adams	US 1	29	41	6	23	16	(88)	19	13
16) Svend Carlsen	D 23	31	36	(50)					

mediocre as mine were, I was still excited that I beat Paul Cayard! Then John Bertrand told me that Paul got gangrene, what an excuse! I still managed to finish top half and beat Paul in most races as well as Gold/Bronze medalist Jonathan McKee overall. Finishing top half of the fleet in Laser Worlds these days would be great for an American, but back then, USA was boss. What happened? Like in the NBA, I suppose world competition happened.

I remember breakfast on day 3 when they announced who was leading the event. The whole room went "Whooooo." I will keep referring to this event, as it was the Who's Who of small boat sailing at the time, before short board windsurfing scattered the party. It wasn't such a shock that an American was on top of the leaderboard, but nobody expected it would be the little unknown stud, Monty Spindler. Let's hear his side of the story:

BIG TIME DISTRACTIONS

by Monty Spindler

As a competitor at the 1977 Laser World Championships, Cabo Frio, Brazil, I put everything I had into preparing for it. Placing my university studies on hold to train for the event, I put in max time on the water, as well as physical preparation. This included putting in a lot of miles on land as well, running long distances every day in Annapolis. I even built a hiking bench, gained a few pounds, feeling my preparation was complete. I was right on track, but was I mentally prepared? That was something I had not considered.

Most of my training had taken place on my own. I had some good results in a few USA national Laser events, but very little experience on the International level. When the USA team arrived (late) in Brazil, one person representing each district of the country, you couldn't help but notice how well the European teams were sponsored.

At the time, we from the States were all amateurs, while the EU team training was on a professional level. We were impressed, if not a little intimidated. They were running around the marina, doing push-ups and sit-ups, everything but the New Zealand *Haka*. There was only one sailor there from NZ, so kind of hard to pull that off on his own.

It was a deep fleet; full of talented sailors from around the world. Even today, you look at the entry list and see that it was a star-studded field. I thought to myself, "Monty, you are prepared. Go for it!" I entered that event a blind optimist.

The early races went well enough. Like I said, the fleet was tough, and nobody had managed to win more than one race, much less finish top ten. I didn't really check the standings, just focused on sailing one race at a time. But then, as everyone stayed in the same hotel and ate breakfast together, it was announced that after four races, I was atop the standings! Microphones approached; cameras buzzed... a golden moment for this aspiring helmsman!

The golden moment turned optimism to distraction... did not "prepare my head" for the position I found myself in, lost focus in the last half of the event and dropped to sixth John Bertrand won the event, making an enormous impression on me with his physical and mental strength. My lesson: Serious training produces results; be comfortable up there; mentally prepared to enjoy results under pressure.

– Monty Spindler

After taking second place at the Finn North Americans, Monty worked as a sailmaker for Ulmer and Hood sails in Annapolis. Along with Scott Steele, he was an All-American at St. Mary's College. He soon turned his focus to windsurfing and became a sailmaker for Neil Pryde, Art Sails, and now his own brand, Loftsails. Monty was inducted into the Windsurfing Hall of Fame.

I would argue that though Monty's expectations were high, a 6th place finish was still very respectable. Perhaps it had nothing to do with buckling to pressure. The conditions had changed. In the beginning, the wind and sea state were very Annapolis like. But then the wind and waves approached top end, victory at sea, with fifteen-degree shifts experienced at the top of waves. Boats disappeared between waves! Marks disappeared between waves! Just ask Peter Commette. While leading the race, he couldn't find the mark.

Maybe they flew the change of course flag at the previous mark, maybe they did not. It was difficult to make anything out at all.

If you had not immersed yourself in those conditions, you were not winning this event. I'm not sure if anyone was quite prepared for such large, open ocean swells, but training in San Francisco would certainly have given John Bertrand the edge needed. You could say that to hang in there for the long run was key. Consistency in all conditions wins big championships.

This is what the Change of Course flag looks like, Flag C. There will be a + or – chart, meaning longer or shorter, and usually a compass direction and whistle tweets.

YOU WIN SOME....

by Dave Perry

We went out to the last race of the 1984 Soling Olympic Trials in first place. The winner of the Trials goes to the Olympics. Our friends Robbie Haines, Rod Davis and Ed Trevelyan sailed a better last race and won the Trials. I was gutted and bitterly disappointed.

I stayed off high bridges for the next two weeks and put my sharp letter openers away. I had trouble sleeping, eating, and even breathing. Then I went to one of my best friend's wedding in San Francisco and ran an awesome youth clinic in New Jersey. I started to feel better. Robbie asked me to come back out to Long Beach to help them tune up for the Games.

They won the Gold Medal at the Olympics, and I felt proud that I had been able to help them prepare, and then I felt even more pride in our Olympic effort, realizing that we were right there at the top of the game. I got married that Fall to my now wife of over forty years, and we have raised two wonderful kids. And I just became a grandfather. Life is good!

I was a high school athletic director for twenty-one years, and I shared my story of disappointment with countless kids who were experiencing their own disappointment. It always seemed to help them. I began to realize that every experience shapes us into the best form of ourselves. As Mick Jagger has been saying for years, "You can't always get what you want, but if you try sometimes, you just might find, you get what you need!"

The legendary sailor and author, Stuart Walker, wrote once: "Winning is the object of the game; but it is not the object of playing the game." We play the game of sailboat racing because we love it! We love everything about it. Being outside and on the water, doing it with our friends, getting away from the screens, confronting challenges from all sides and trying to navigate the best path through them, being active and feeling alive. Sure, the occasional pickle dish is nice, but it's not what keeps us coming back. I've been doing this a long time. And I am still racing as much as I can, and with my wife which makes it even more special!

Every great sailor has experienced some bitter disappointments in their career. That comes with the territory. In fact, the disappointments often are the building block to even more successes. The Kiwis have a saying: "Don't lose the lesson in the losing." There's a reason they are among the best sailors on the planet. As I always write in the front of my book Winning in One-Designs, "Hike Hard, Sail Fast, Be Smart. And when all else fails…Bang a Corner!" It's a game. A great game, win or lose. Always Enjoy!

Dave Perry, with Yale Sailing Team, after winning Collegiate Nationals in 1975. Dave was Captain and two time All American. Left to right: Peter Isler, Steve Benjamin, Ginny Hopkins, Peter Bowe, Dave Perry, Susan Daly.

–Dave Perry

USYRU SINGLEHANDED CHAMPIONSHIPS

I would use my gloriously failing Laser Worlds experience to propel me at this penultimate event of singlehanded sailing. To make it to the finals, you had to be one of the eight top singlehanded sailors in the nation. Each year, it was held in a different class of boat, but in 1978, it was held in Lasers. That meant only one thing; the stakes were raised.

In Santa Cruz, pumping and rocking to initiate planing were legal, as the wind was in the 25-40 range. Seas were like giant mountains rolling through. The wind was so strong and swell so great they closed the harbor to all other boats. Only us 8 O'Day Finalists and the RC boats were allowed to leave harbor. You didn't need to pump, rock, or ooch. You just needed to keep the boat upright and from breaking.

Getting around the racecourse in one piece was not going well for me. These were Hot Donut conditions, yet when it came to heavy breeze, I was still half-baked. Living in the South, I had done all of my sailing in winds under 25 knots. Aside for the guy from Navy that would win, the entire army of other racers struggled to cross the finish line in one piece. My poor girlfriend was on the RC boat, emptying her stomach of the fine farm fresh Santa California dinner we'd eaten the night before. What a waste!

Then, as I was just getting the hang of things and in second, the mainsheet block pulled out of the boom. Continuing on with my no DNF's mantra, the boom then snapped in half, shattering the radial head in my elbow, later requiring surgery. That ended my championship run.

I must add to the lore of this Santa Cruz story, the proving grounds for high wind sailing! Years later, racing a Laser Masters event, I was a full baked donut and doing very well. And then the boom snapped in half. Flailing in 35 knots of wind, twisting the mainsheet up in knots, I freed the sheet and turned the boat dead downwind to keep that action away from my face. The Coast Guard tried to tow me. a good twenty-foot swell running against us and the boom making nice cuts to all parts of the old cold cruller, I untied the tow line. I still bleed. Sure, I could have flipped the boat and tried to untangle the mess in the high seas, fended some Great Whites off (we were right in the heart of the Red Triangle), but I decided to head downwind toward a beach and try my luck at surfing the boat in. The Coast Guard told me I couldn't do that, it would be a disaster. I yelled, "Watch me!"

Approaching the beach halfway to Capitola, this looked doable. Managing to position myself perfectly in a lane to safely steer between waves, or so it seemed, a monster wave leaped up above my mast, cascading like right onto my head. As I hung onto the hiking strap, the boat shot out ahead, then flipped on a rail as I scooted my way up onto the sand like Hunter S. *Safe! With all parts used up.*

THE OLYMPICS THAT WEREN'T

I was wondering what Major Dick Tillman was doing at the O'Day Finals. As it turned out, as Captain of the US Olympic Sailing Team, Dick was scouting for a crew for his Flying Dutchman to go for Gold at the 1980 Olympics in the USSR. Well, we trained pretty hard in a military manner for Tallinn. Dick had tracked for a cold front for a promising training ground. Ice froze in the water bottles for added weight to my trapeze harness. The Flying Dutchman has big @ss genoa jib, so the extra ballast was needed. Dick had gone to England to get the previous Gold medal winning F2, a classic wooden Hoare. "Ever ridden a Hoare?" Dick asked. "Excuse me?" I replied. "What? No, it's the make of the boat, a classic. Just as demanding, though."

After going through a gazillion tacks and jibes, we could see some dark clouds rolling in. "This is good," Dick claimed. "Good for what?" I asked. "Good for training. We could get this in Tallinn, you know." I had never been on a boat going that fast. Then lightning bolts started flying. "Hey Dick, are we going to get those in Tallinn, too?" Dick grinned. "Maybe. You think the Russians are going to call a race over a few little lighting strikes?" "Whaat?" I could no longer hear him between the roar of the wind, the chilly water splashing my face, and the thunder. The lightning!

"Woohoo!" Dick, yelled. We were certainly blazing along now on a reach, the jib and kite still in my hand. I figured I might show off my high-flying trapeze act when CRACK! The mast broke. The boat went one way, and I went flying the other. Somehow, the jib had wrapped around my ankle like a serpent in Star Wars, dragging me and my water bottles backwards, the entire Intracoastal Waterway going up my nose. From the pain, my ankle may have snapped as well. With the wind still catching the downed sails, the boat was pulling me backward like a human sea anchor. This was some E ticket to ride. Would the Olympics be worth it?

Then I got the call from Dick. We weren't going. So if you're ever disappointed that a race got canceled due to bad weather, think about that.

Then

These are the Brits who were to be our biggest competition in the Flying Dutchman class at the 1980 Olympics. They also had a classic woody built by Bob Hoare.

FACILITATION FOR THE WIN

Teaching and running clinics can also improve your own sailing. In Instructional Design speak, we call this Facilitation. When you teach something, you really have to study up on the subject or be embarrassed by someone raising their hand to tell you you're an idiot. I've even taught myself something here. I've never drawn the course on my boat before with a grease pencil, but I think I will from now on. Were we allowed to go through the start/finish? Oh yeah, it's written down right here. How many laps? With hands full, this information can be written right in front of you.

When I was just 17 year old, Major Hall, one of the brightest minds in One Design sailing, brought me onboard as an apprentice coach during my last summer at the US Sailing Center, Association Island, NY. My job was to coach the women's team from Newport Beach, Maureen O'Hora and Stephanie Elliot. I suppose I coached them well. Held in 470's, they won the Women's World Championships, held in 470s.

Regardless, I patterned the facilitation of my own seminars and video talks after both Gary and Major's clinics, sharing many of the same techniques with others at my own seminars over the years, including coaching the Cayman Islands Olympic team. Now that's a good gig with benefits!

One of the outcomes of my own teachings is that others in my fleet soon adopted strategies and used them against me. For example, my strategy (or borrowed strategy from numerous clinics attended, books read, videos watched), was being borrowed by everyone who had watched one of my videos. Hard to find a hole to duck into when the entire fleet is approaching on port with a minute to spare! This was all fine and dandy. Through improving the level of competition, you improve.

Though my memory does not serve me well, I would also owe a lot to Ed Baird's clinics. I suppose this photo taken of me from Ed's coaching boat by one of his many girlfriends proves I was indeed a participant. It's slowly coming back to me, walking into St Pete YC and seeing classrooms with whiteboards and little magnetic boats for demonstrations. Suffice to say during any good clinic, there is always a lot of pushing the limits, rocking the boat, tipping the boat over.

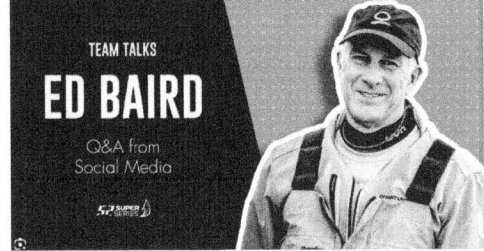

Ed Baird: *One powerful lesson I learned from sailing was that you learn more by sharing knowledge with others than keeping it to yourself. One of the first times I was compensated in the sport was when a group of my Laser buddies convinced me to host a 2-day clinic and work with them on how to sail their boats better. It was a low-stress, action-packed weekend of trying new things. I challenged my friends to experiment and share their results. Each sailor was asked to put themselves into*

unfamiliar situations and try find a way to come out of it well. Then they had to describe what happened and how they could do it better next time.

Not every attempt at something new worked, but failure at a particular thing meant learning for the future – a good thing – as evidenced by Jonathan Weston's reaction to capsizing during a drill. But there were no racing results to worry about, so everyone was free to explore new ways to get around the course. Back on shore, we all talked about what we learned each day – and here's the important part – we ALL got better. I was excited that, as the coach, I got as much out of the process as anyone. It's amazing how describing how you do things can actually help you improve how you do that thing!

At Randy Smyth's clinics, he shares invaluable knowledge that helped him win two Olympic Silver medals in the Tornado class. With Randy, there are also a great deal of boat handling practice drills. He among many other things, line sighting techniques to avoid being the victim of line sag. This is all done on his home waters at Fort Walton YC. He teaches you all about how to be a pirate on the

Photos: Weston

starting line, and take home the treasure.

Though I would never wear the title of COACH on my back, I began teaching sailing at an early age (15), beginning with a job as Sailing Instructor/Camp Counselor at Camp Morehead. We would just throw the kids into the water, sink or sail. The thing I most remember about that summer was taking the boats out at night and sailing up the Intracoastal Waterway to Atlantic Beach. I'm sure the camp owner, Captain Purcell, just rolled over in his sea grave.

Right after graduating high school, I got a summer job at the US Sailing Center running the rigging shop, fixing boats for some pretty awesome sailors at night, while crewing for top racers in big time regattas by day. I also landed a gig as a Coaching Apprentice under Major Hall. That was major!

Along with that stroke of luck, for my 18th birthday, Major gave me an assignment to coach the California team during the Women's Worlds Championships (held in 470s). The skipper was a mature 16, who, I didn't realize at the time, had been dating Gary Jobson. She introduced me to Gary as her new boyfriend. I guess he was okay with it. He didn't put up any kind of fight, not like he did while winning the America's Cup as tactician, with Ted Turner as skipper. She was probably too young for him anyway.

I followed that girl to California, where Gary showed me what a good sport he was by allowing me to take his clinic in Newport Harbor for free. I had just placed third in the US Youth Series at Association Island. Commette was first, Johnstone second, and when I got home from that event, I was proud to tell Mom and Dad I got third out of 200 other kids from around the country.

Dad was pretty proud, but my mom was more driven. She told me, "You'll do better next time." Well, Jobson's clinic sure helped me do that. After his clinic, I would win the Laser California Championships with all bullets, owing it all to Gary, especially for the girlfriend.

Gary Jobson, AC tactician, keeping a watchful eye.

Gary set short courses, even shorter than the ones I would experience later in college sailing. I remember one drill, where we had to tack or jibe every time he blew the whistle. Blow a tack, and you got an electric shock. Not really.

Practicing starts, mark roundings, tacks, gybes, and capsize drills are common in clinics. But what about some extraordinary training, such as a surfer might do, running with a big rock along the bottom of the ocean? As Captain of the University of Florida sailing team, I would utilize many of Gary's clinic exercises such as sailing without rudders, teaching my team how to steer the boat using only their weight and sail trim, which minimizes during maneuvers, the braking action of the rudder. We'd also sail at night, and if with crew, blindfolded. We did play a mean pinball.

WINNING WAYS

One of Maru Urban's staff experts acting as the clinic role model.

Even back then, there were enough on land and on water coaching sessions which upped my game tenfold. But what really upped my game was not only the organized practices of college sailing, but the responsibility that came with it. Either I coached my team up a few levels or we would get wasted by the other college teams in the South. While our competition was not as lofty as the Ivy league teams up north (Tufts, Yale, Brown, Harvard), there was the rivalry between UofF and FSU. Who was the Captain of FSU? Ed Baird.

Us Gators would win the Southern College Championships when all in one boat, but on Lasers as a team of four, we were no match for the wit and team racing mastery of FSU and Ed Baird. Being good sports, they threw all teams a big keg party (lemonade), where they shared their team strategies in case we ever met again, we could in turn up their game.

College sailing is tops, but the USA is also catching back up to International sailing by traveling to Europe where the real competition now lies.

Secrets to Success in One Design Racing

WINNING WAYS

A NEW DAY FOR CLINICS

Maru Urban Clinics — Photos by: Hannah Lee Noll

Welcome to the 22nd Century for ILCA Clinics. Wait, it's only the 21st, but looking at the technology and use of data incorporated into Maru Urban's clinics, one might question. Back in my day, a whiteboard was the killer tech. No longer so. Pas de tout. Or in Maru's case, since he hails from Brazil, *de jeito nenhum*. It was at the Rio Olympics that Maru helped the US Sailing Team grip the local knowledge, the wild wind and currents that our team (my team, anyway) would face. This knowledge, and the skills Maru exhibited, led to Dave Dellenbaugh suggesting he move to the States, where our young sailors could certainly use a hand up.

As of this writing, Maru is the Waterfront Director for one of the most prestigious Yacht Clubs in America, Lake Geneva YC. Not to be confused with the one in Switzerland, it is up there in Buddy Melgesland, Wisconsin. But a few times a year, our young sailors get the opportunity to participate in one of Maru's clinics. In the past, they have taken place in Key Biscayne Yacht Club, and just before the Orange Bowl in Miami (hey! I won that way back in 77!).

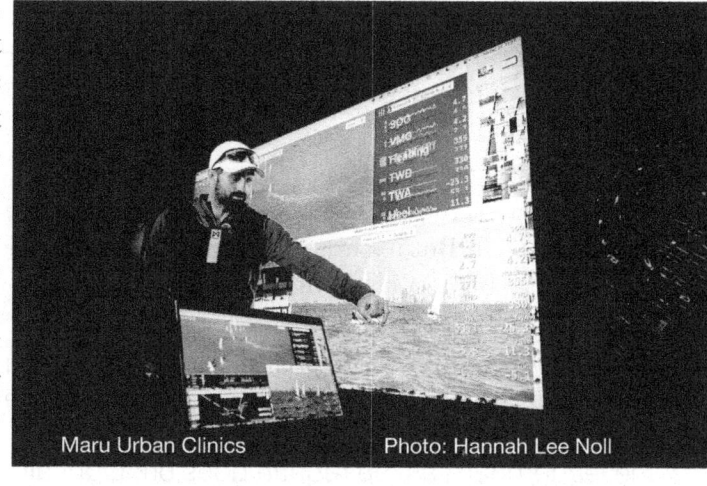
Maru Urban Clinics — Photo: Hannah Lee Noll

What makes these clinics special is not only the expert knowledge and Laser sailing techniques of the instructors, but you guessed it, the use of cutting edge technology. Utilizing the *Vakaros* system, a small device mounted on the deck forward of the mast, each clinic participant's racing data during the

Maru Urban Clinics   Photo: Hannah Lee Noll

clinic is collected. This device tracks heading, speed, and boat heel. Call it Strava on steroids. That data is processed overnight (during the day, in Croatia!). Results are exhibited the next morning at the debriefing, in perfect sync with the drone footage and coach boat footage. How cool is that?

While no other clinic (that I'm aware of to date) takes advantage of this technology, there is more to a clinic than bits and bytes. The coaches coach, and they do it well. But it's not all about tacks and gybes. Let's hear from Maru on what the biggest challenges young sailors face:

Maru Urban: We don't just coach sailing. You can be a great tactical sailor, fast as all get out, but if you don't have the conditioning, and more importantly for kinetic-driven boats, the flexibility, you're going to fall down the leaderboard as the regatta goes on. Light air can be just as physically demanding as heavy air, so we coach on nutrition (no more McDonalds!), providing drills and exercises that increase endurance and agility, not just going to the gym and lifting a bunch of weights. It must be fun as well, or they'll quit and go play with their phones.

But that's the difference between the young sailor and the salted. Their lives revolve around screens. They eat up the technology like there's not tomorrow. Well, there is tomorrow, and it's the end of clinic regatta. They eat that up, too.

We instill in them mental fortitude, giving them examples of top professionals in other sports, like Kobe Bryant. We even give them a book, *Mental Toughness for Sports Kids*.

But then we teach what they came here to learn, and that's how to make a Laser go faster. Boat handling a big challenge, and nothing like a good clinic with instructors capable of demonstrating excellence to make a quantum leap. Yet, it's how to make a Laser go fast downwind; how to play the waves, that the clinic has proven to be of great benefit. It's a real jolt in that regard, a gamechanger as you might say in the US. Learning how to do it right can advance any sailor off onto the horizon.

Maru Urban Clinics   Photo: Hannah Lee Noll

Yet, anyone who expects (parent's mostly) to go out and win a big championship after one clinic has to be dreaming. It's a long process. That said, there is nothing like a clinic to jump start that process.

Look for future Maru Urban clinic dates at UR SAILING Instagram or Facebook page.

Clinics are one way to advance quickly, but if you have the resources, hiring a private coach is another. Let's hear from John Bertrand again, on his coaching philosophy.

THE LEARNING CHANNELS

by John Bertrand

I really enjoy coaching and teaching. I love the process of imparting knowledge to a wide range of people with vastly different skill sets. From the very beginner (no matter what age), to the most seasoned Olympic caliber sailor. I love to see someone improve, learn something new, and reach a goal. It requires an individual and personal approach.

We all learn differently, and there is no one approach that can be applied to everyone. To maximize the experience and overall benefit, it is critically important to determine how an individual processes information to make sure it is delivered and received properly. Finding the right learning channels and packaging the message properly is key. In other words, you've got to speak the language of the student.

The three major learning channels are sensory, auditory, and visual. If someone is a visual learner, you can talk until you're blue in the face, and chances are the message won't get through. If someone's strength is auditory processing, then demonstrating something is not gonna do it. The sensory learner needs to feel it or experience it before they can grasp a new technique. And the challenging part is it could be different channels depending on what is being taught or given different external circumstances. So knowing all that, the best starting point is to deliver the information or lesson in all three channels and be observant to which channels your individual students are picking up.

I had the pleasure of giving private lessons to a local Annapolis Master sailor, Jeff Caruso. It was really enjoyable because of Jeff's enthusiasm and his ability to apply new concepts very quickly. I saw a great improvement in his sailing in only a couple of sessions working with him. The first session was the day before the Chesapeake Masters regatta. He reported seeing a drastic improvement during the regatta from his normal competitiveness. It helped that our first practice the day before the regatta was in similar conditions (extreme) to the first day of racing. A few simple tips kept him on his feet and more comfortable and less energy spent in those conditions.

On the second day in calmer conditions, he was able to focus on applying some new principles and rig settings. It is very satisfying as a coach to hear a report like Jeff's; that at most mark roundings where he normally gets passed by boats, he was passing them instead. Also, after a rather tangled start in one race that put him near last at the first mark, he reported passing seventeen boats during the course of the race.

My analysis of Jeff is that he is able to pick up new techniques and theory very quickly. I think Jeff has at least two channels working, and maybe all three. My first impression of Jeff is that his auditory processing is dominant and well developed. From almost the first moment we met, he asked me to explain what it was we were going to work on for that lesson. And he was very focused on what I was saying and asked quite a few questions to make sure he fully understood the particular concept or subject.

Once on the water it was too windy to talk effectively (and I lost my voice in the process of shouting over the howling wind), so I demonstrated what I wanted him to do. I made him follow behind me and imitate what I was doing. This took a little longer for him to pick it up but he did after a very short time. We were working on sailing the boat super flat. Instead of using the mainsheet, I had him ease the mainsheet beyond the normal heavy air upwind setting and had him sit on the deck (not hiking) and only use the tiller to keep the boat flat. I wanted him to see and feel how the boat was when sailed flat. The other main lesson was the proper body position in the boat. This enabled him to expend less energy and he was able to "relax", even in the high winds. Just a few simple pointers gave him the ability to conserve his energy and increase his overall confidence.

Knowing the right communication channels greatly increases the information uptake and leads to a more productive and meaningful experience for the sailor.

Photo: Weston

In other countries, sailing is part of their culture. While in the USA, every city has an MLK Blvd., in France, you will not find a seaside village without an Eric Taberly. Along the coast, there is a sailing school for all stages every skip of the stone, with racing being a part of life. To be a sailing coach there, you have to complete two years in a dedicated university program.

SAILCOACH ACADEMY

Welcome to the world's first Sailing Academy, where education and competitive sailing are equally important. The SailCoach Academy has been a dream of its founders for many years, and a dream for many kids to go to school and sail in one place! 2024 saw that dream become a reality. The SailCoach Academy believes that the future of sailing lies in combining top-quality coaching with excellent education. Their boarding school program in Malta and Valencia gives young sailors the time and support they need to grow, both on the water and in the classroom, helping them build a strong foundation for success in sport and life.

Photos: SailCoach

From a beginner friendly Sailing School to year round coaching clinics, SailCoach supports sailors at every stage, and have seen its graduates win multiple World championships and Olympic medals. They also provide coaching support at major Optimist and ILCA regattas worldwide and offer full time training at the SailCoach Academy for young sailors balancing school and competitive sailing. Explore at www.sailcoach.com

WINNING WAYS

THE LATE GREAT JOE DUPLIN

Vince Lombardi, John Wooden, Bobby Cox, Joe Duplin.
Until Peter Commette spoke of the legendary Joe Duplin, his Tufts coach, I had never heard of the man, nor been fortunate enough to meet him. Reading of the lore of the Star and all the stars who have raced them, I realize my life is incomplete.

I decided to post this photo of Joe on the Vintage Star group page. Would anyone remember Joe Duplin? Would they ever. Having not only been a great coach, but great sailor and builder of Stars and Etchells as well, a thousand likes and comments Tufts teammates and just from folks who the vintage Star "gets their heart pounding." and Joe So many told proudly of the lore of Joe Duplin, as if he were their own son:
"A two-time Olympics Sailing Coach, Joe Duplin touched the lives of many and helped put us all in "Smart Shoes"!"
Paul Giuffrida

"When you think about the who, what, when, and how of everyone involved, it was an amazing group of friends, many with staggering achievement. The mere presence of talent across the board on Mystic lake those days made it something of a sharkpit, and Joe loved it! He often remarked that you are only as good as your competition, and in that sense, no one was safe!" Fritz Mueller

Some Joe Duplinisms:

"You lift weights and train till you can pull trees out of the ground. Then you can come on my boat."

"There were times when it was tough to put food on the table, but there was always a Star boat, ready to race out in the yard."

"Just open up the bailers, Babe, and let the blood flow out!" (P.C.)

Joseph Duplin passed away on August 7, 2016 at the age of 82.

RACE DAY PREPARATION

All right! You've prepared your boat, your body, your mind, and now you're the first to pull into the yacht club or wherever the next regatta is being held. You've given yourself plenty of time to rig the boat. Better yet, you've arrived the day before the regatta begins and the boat is already rigged. If a major regatta, you're on the spot practicing at least a few days prior, working out any kinks and getting to know the waters. In that case, you've talked to the locals and figured out that where the water turns green is where the current runs swiftest.

I can remember racing Lasers on a lake in Tennessee. There was one man there that looked like Paul Bunyan, with a long beard and drawling voice, chewed tobacco. "You see them cows over there? Them all pointin' their noses into the wind. When you see the herd of 'em turn a bit, well, that's the wind shiftin' might rightily.

Dang if that man wasn't speaking the truth. Nobody ever beat him on that lake. Local knowledge. It's a thing.

CHECK FOR POWERLINES

Before you put the mast up and move your boat,

CHECK FOR POWER LINES!

Dan Wilson and I were at a well-known yacht club in SoCal, together dollying a boat from an outside parking lot to a nearby beach launch, when the boat stopped dead in its tracks. We looked up, saw the power lines swaying, and almost stopped dead in ours. Fortunately for us, they were either insulated enough or just telephone wires, but it sure woke us up.

Others have not been so fortunate. Manton Scott, one of the best small boat sailors in the U.S., was killed when his '470' mast touched a power line at Duxbury Yacht Club (Mass.). Scott had won the 1973 470 Midwinter championship and was preparing to take place in the 470 Worlds. Peter Commette went in Manton's place to honor his friend, instead of going to the Youth Worlds. Taking second, Peter said that proved Manton would easily have won those worlds.

WEATHER APPS

Having been caught in more thunderstorms than you can shake a weather stick at, I no longer rely much on apps. I know sailors who will favor on side of the course over the other because an app pointed arrows that way (okay, guilty, it was me! And hey, it worked!). I rely on Reddit, too, for much of my extended knowledge, and learned that all of these apps you pay money for are simple based on Gribs. I don't know what a Grib is, but if it comes with bacon and toast, I'm all in.

Alexa, what's a Grib? All of the apps use data from gribs, I grib you not! They are the direct output of computer models untouched by human hands. Keep your hands off them gribs! Computer models make necessary numerical assumptions in order to solve equations fast enough to generate forecasts instead of retrospectives. Nanonano. Unfortunately, that means artifacts we really care about are smoothed over. These artifacts include cold fronts and areas of steep pressure gradients. Alexa, put the centerboard down before I port tack the fleet.

All of the apps including but not limited to Windy, Predictwind, and Windfinder are just pretty repackaging of Gribs. They are not reliable predictors of localized short-term weather artifacts like squalls. Generally, the East Coast is much more subject to thunderstorms and tornadoes. In California, you have to worry more about smoke from fires or earthquakes in the lot.

In the long run, you can't beat NOAA and weather radar. Check the maps before heading out from the dock. There have been both minor and major disasters over the years. Boats broken, people perished. Since those events, RC's have sided with caution, and in the opinion of heavy air specialists like myself, too much caution. It's up to the PRO to decide. Expect to race on the top end of the wind in places like Santa Cruz, SF, and Cascade Locks (Columbia River Gorge).

PRE-FLIGHT CHECK

Before rigging the boat, after putting it on a dolly if applicable, I go around and check all bolts, screws, cleats, ports, etc., to make sure they are all tight and watertight. It's always good practice to McLube all blocks and anything else that swivels. I also spray that stuff on my main track and bolt rope, or if on a Laser, I just spray the mast. This helps release the main in light air. I try to not spray that stuff where there is constant contact with the water, using coconut oil instead on the centerboard/daggerboard trunk, and the blade as well, being careful not to get it on the boat, board, deck.

Yet before you get to all that, and the longer you may have traveled to the event, the more important it is to unwind. Stretch it out before you start pulling your boat together, particularly if you've not arrived a day early. Hopefully, you've camped the night before or at least arrived on site by 8am with plenty of time to spare. In the rare case you still need to register and ensure you have the most updated SI's (Sailing Instructions), get that out of the way early, as the first order of business is to get that boat rigged right. Unless you're just here for, you know, the party.

If you haven't had the opportunity, make sure that your cam cleats are angled correctly, particularly if borrowing/chartering a boat. There are few things more capable of hindering your ability to fully hike than a mis-angled cleat. Not being able to cleat or worse, uncleat your sails, will have you coming in off the rail to adjust. Slow. Or flipping if you can't uncleat. Slower.

Your tool bag should include two types of screwdrivers, two types of pliers (vice grip), sandpaper, Quickfix, McLube, silicone sealant, spare blocks and shackles, fasteners, and whatever else you commonly use to fix up your boat. Don't be that cad running around at the last minute asking everyone to borrow a screwdriver. Keep a ditty bag on board with the essential tools, along with rigging tape and cassette tape for telltales on the shrouds, spare line, pins, and rings.

The next choice to be made is what lines you are going to rig; heavy air, light, or medium. If the forecast is in doubt, go medium. If typically light, go light, and use less purchases. If typically heavy, consider using a heavier gauge wire for the shrouds and forestay as well.

RIG TENSION

On simpler boats, the mast just goes in the hole, you put the boom on, and you're good to go eat a donut. On others, there's decision making to do; namely, how tight should your rig be? The conditions will dictate, and those conditions may change, so you need to decide whether to listen to the weather forecast, trust your Gribs, or JimBob with the grub worms down at the bait shed. Quite often, the fishers will be more accurate than that app you paid for.

Mast rake and feel of helm primarily go hand in hand. Generally speaking, by raking the mast forward, you will favor neutral helm and provide your boat with the most power (though giving your jib a fuller, more powered shape through weather sheeting also alleviates weather helm). Raking it back will increase weather helm and "feel" while effectively depowering the rig. In strong breeze, the boat will fly faster, at least upwind. Too much forward rake and you will induce lee helm, which is not a good thing, particularly when heading off wind. Too much rake will be slower in the lulls and add drag to the rudder. In big breeze, I rake back and go forth. Too much rake in light air is slow.

Many boats use a measuring tape and run it up the halyard, taking the measurement at the transom. I'd like to credit my dad for starting that trend (probably D Day and freeing Camp Ebensee were more to his credit). These rake numbers should be published online in your Class Rigging Manual but jot your own numbers down and see what works best for you. It really takes a training partner to use not as a measuring tape, but a measuring stick, to really tell what's working and what is not.

It's difficult to adjust the rig once on the water. On the Weta, most people on the East Coast of USA have fixed length Dynema shrouds. Out in the windy West, particularly in NorCal and The Gorge, where conditions are quite a bit more rough, Davo and I used thicker stainless shrouds and two different sizes of shackles. When it's windy, I would replace the longer shackles with short shackles, made in France. The ones made in China cost $3 each and the ones made in France $40 each. Get the French shackles. Losing your mast in heavy seas is more costly.

Photo: Spinsheet

A lot of boats utilize a Loos gauge, which accurately measures your shroud and forestay tension. I just give it a good shake and know by feel if the rig is too tight, too Loos, or just right. Baby bear it (wiggle to see if it feels just right) if you don't have a Loos gauge or it's somewhere lost under your car seat.

One thing is for certain, you won't be using the same rig tension for light air as for heavy. I actually came up with an adjustable forestay for the Weta, which worked well for me, but did complicate matters. It thought it was worth being able to tension the rig for breeze and big chop, then slack it off if the wind backed off. Illegal during races I only attempted this in-between.

Mast rake is of no concern on a fixed rig like a Laser. Just make sure that the collar rivets are replaced when necessary and turned in the right direction. That's all there is to it, though some of the top sailors will visit the distribution point for the best choice of spars; not bent, most stiff.

Not all masts are alike; nor are One Design sails for that matter. The top guys will test several masts, then buy five suits of sails, keep the best tested ones for racing, one for practice, and sell the others. Beware of buying sails from pros unless they're selling cheap and on a budget. Boats, holes, money.

GEAR READINESS

Once you're all rigged, get your sailing gear laid out in sequential fashion. This should be a routine to minimize last minute panic. Keep your start watch on you. Before the first gun, there's often very little time between the skippers meeting and leaving the dock for an hour of practice and course reconnaissance.

THE SKIPPERS MEETING

Unless the Skippers meeting is mandatory, having read the SI's delivered online, I've often skipped it if the RC schedules the meeting during my Pal Elvstrom designated course reconnaissance time. I'll check the board for fleet start order if a multi-fleet regatta, and to make sure that nothing has changed, but the whole affair for me is better spent with other preparations, like stretching and checking over my boat.

MarkJump Photography

Paul Elvstrom: We come to a big regatta and there's a skippers' meeting, and everybody sits there with the rules, and they're so nervous; and I'm always hoping that there would be a member of the committee who would break this, and try to make even important events fun—everybody smiling and looking forward to going out and competing in the boats and being nice against each other. And when you enjoy yourself sailing in that way, you are sailing much better than when you do something to make yourself nervous. Remember, we are sailing for fun. That's why we're here. We shall not be nervous. That's my experience in my life in yachting.

That said, the Race Committee meeting does serve as a way to recognize all the wonderful volunteers who gave up their time to make it a jolly good show. How sweet it is! With most regattas, there should be nothing to be nervous about. It's sailboat racing.

Will Keyworth Photography

GET A GAMEPLAN

Any extra time you might have, get the local sailors to lend advice. Make them feel like the experts they think they are. "Hey, Linda, you're a smart gal..." Sometimes it's better to ask sailors from other classes in a multi-class regatta, or someone from the RC, rather than a close competitor.

If all else fails, follow in the path of the top locals… unless you find yourself in the lead. Yet, it's no fun being far in the lead, only to see the local sailors lift 30 degrees on a shoreline puff. Tacking right on their wind on the first leg will make you an unpopular patron at the bar as well. It's okay to do it on the final leg and in final races, but you're going to get a lot of payback doing that on the first beat, and piss people off. It's a bit of an unwritten rule of sailing. Maybe I'm just wishing it was, and people would cut that out.

Did I mention how important it is to get out on the water an hour before the start? I learned that from reading Paul Elvstrom's book. In biking, they call it course reconnaissance, and it's done for days ahead of an event. Dedicating one hour to this should be part of the plan.

STRATEGY OVER TACTICS

Peter Commette: *Joe Duplin, my coach at Tufts, taught me something really important: value strategy over tactics. A "strategy" is the overarching plan or vision for achieving your goal that race, or that series, while "tactics" are the specific, concrete actions taken to execute that strategy on a moment to moment basis; essentially, strategy defines the "what" and "why" of a plan, while tactics detail the "how" to implement it. Where, when that gun goes off, are you initially planning to go? What's your goal for this part of the race, for that part of the race? And then all your tactics will fall in place. You can't put tactics over strategy. It must be the other way around.*

Being able to change that strategy on a dime when things change? Well, that comes from vast experience, from sailing often, from practice breeding confidence. The worst thing to do is wind up going against your strategy. Even if you win, you lose confidence in what you're doing.

Joe Duplin was always preaching, "You live by the sword; you die by the sword." And that sword, is strategy. I've died by that sword, but I've won a lot more by it. So, there's your saber rattling for strategy.

Dave Perry: *I have always been a good "flexible thinker." Things don't always go as planned. You can get hit by a lot of unexpected meteor showers. I have always been good at staying in the Here & Now and dealing with what is dealt to me and making the best decisions in the moment.*

I always say, "the game of sailing is played thirty seconds ahead of the boat." If you miss the first shift, you are on the back foot. The lanes going the right way are now filled, and you are forced to go the wrong way, often in bad air. If there is a boat to leeward and ahead of you, the top boats are thinking "when they tack we will _____." The mid-pack racers say, "Oh they tacked...what should we do." And by then it is too late to execute a good plan.

THE GREATEST COMEBACK

Chris Kitchen, Weta Co-Designer Photo: Jennifer Kroon

At the Weta West Coast Championships in Richmond, races had been dominated by Kiwi Chris Kitchen, the boat's co-designer (designed also by his dad, Roger). Chris is a world champion professional on the Australian 18-footer C Tech, so this was one case where us amateurs got to race against a couple of pros. Randy Smyth was also racing.

This regatta took place during the same time the Kiwis were drubbing Oracle Team USA in the America's Cup. Up 8-1, Chris flew a giant Kiwi flag, which had no effect on slowing him down. He was all bullets and led from the gun, so I had basically given up on reading the course chart. Just follow Chris and his George Clooney looks around the racetrack; fight Davo for second place.

But then the wind really kicked up its heels. The Hot Donuts sign was lit! After one lap, Chris and I were neck and neck, with a sizable lead over the rest of the fleet. He was a hard bird to shake, but after a long weather leg, HD managed to put the dough on his wind when he tried to squeeze inside at the weather mark. The bad air and current caused him to pickle fork it, so I finally stretched out a good lead while he unpickled and did his penalty spin.

But when I rounded the leeward gate and headed for the finish line, *record scratch*. Was it two laps or three? If I went through the finish line and it was three laps, I'd be DSQ'd. That's another thing you need to check the SI's for. Is the start/finish line restricted? I knew it was, but oh crap, not

Author   Photo: Rick Saez

the lap count. I had no choice but to heave to and wait for Chris, to see if he was aiming to cross or go around.

While in irons, the ebb tide pushed me to windward. I could see Chris and his obnoxious Kiwi flag flying upwind, but he would have to tack once if he was going to finish. Was he or wasn't he? He was. Time to bear off! But while doing so, a monster gust hit. I was not keeping a clean house. Like a

Star Wars sea monster, the jibsheet wrapped around my ankle. For the life of me, I couldn't shake it loose! This meant I couldn't get out on the tramp and hike, nor could I easily bear off toward the finish! With full weather helm to the point of nearly snapping the carbon tiller, I was cavitating all the way.

It was going to be super close at the finish. I know you're excited as I am now writing about it, but much moreso were the ladies onboard the Richmond YC RC boat. They were jumping up and down, cheering me on, cheering USA on!

But oh nooo! Here comes the Kiwi! I shook my bootie off (the wetsuit boot), and pipped Chris across the line in a photo finish. It was just one race, but it was as if the tables had turned at the America's Cup, which indeed they had! Spithill and Company began the biggest comeback in sporting history, winning the Auld Mug and bringing it back to the USA! Yep, I'm pretty sure I started that comeback.

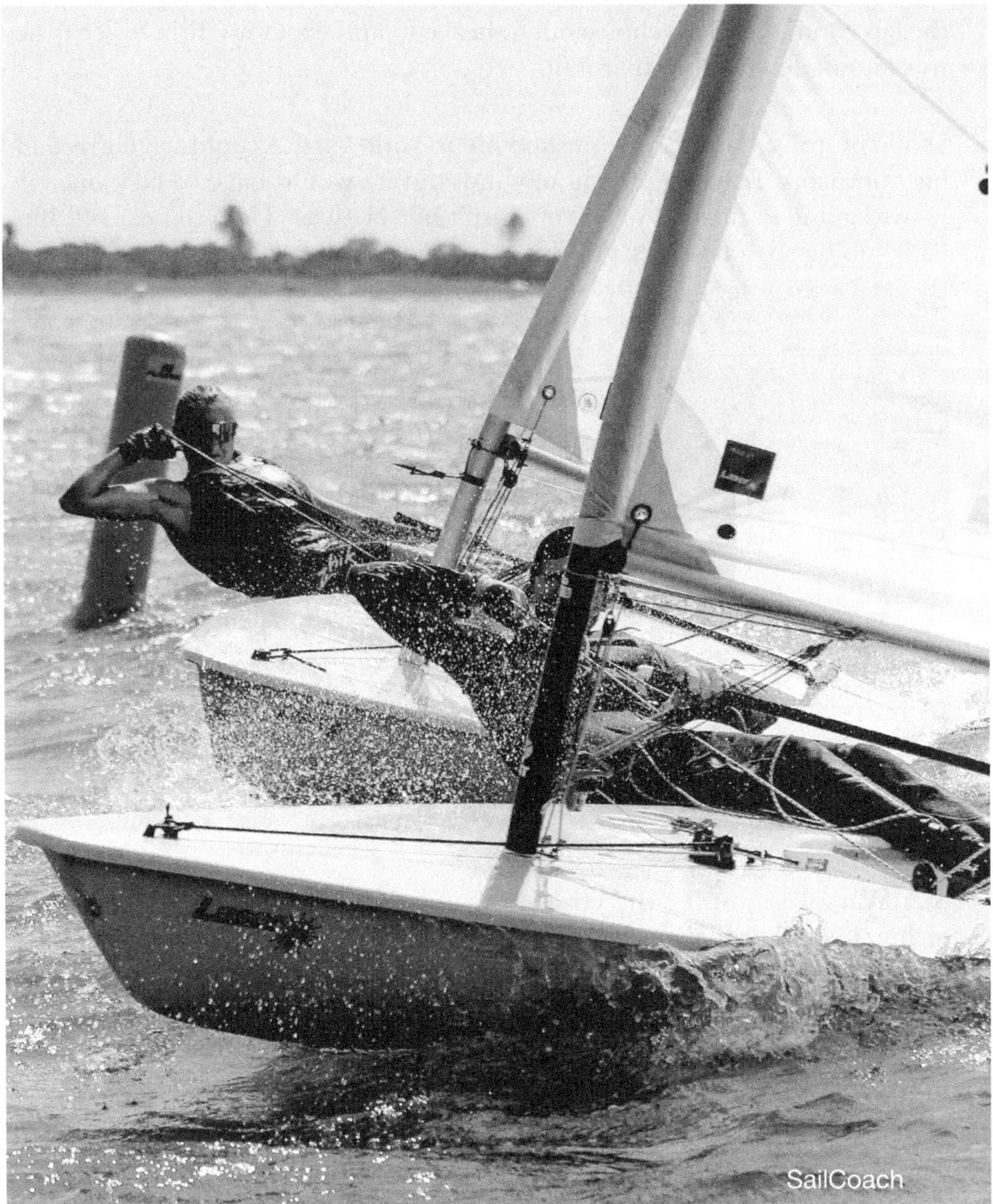
SailCoach

56952
GER
56645
88
43
International 470
Photo: Andrea Lelli

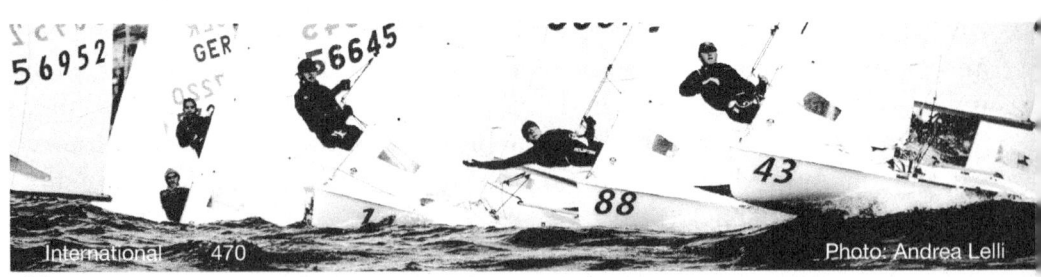

THE START

Have you ever watched an Olympic ski race on TV? They always cut to the skier as they prepare to step up to the starting gate. Their eyes are closed, visualizing every single move they'll make on the course. You probably already know that sailboat racing is nothing like that. It's much more like a box of brownies; you never know what you're gonna get.

The start of a sailboat race typically involves controlling chaos. The more boats, the shorter the line, the more favored one side of the line, the higher the level of chaos. More strategy is applied at this moment of the race than any other. If you start poorly, there will be very little opportunity to apply your pre-race strategy (there is that!) or anything else you will read in this book, so put down the phone and pay attention, class. *Bueller*!

PRESTART PSYCHE

Probably the first rule of starting is to show up on time. Check the race board the night before to make sure the start time hasn't changed, particularly on the following days of racing. The last Windsurfer LT regatta I sailed, I spent a sleepless night working out a strategy needed to win, when I should have been checking online to see if the start time had changed. It had, by an hour. Nothing like pulling into the parking lot ready to execute and seeing a race underway.

The thing that stuck with me the most after reading Paul Elvstrom's book, is to get out on the course one hour ahead of the start. I believe that is the one tip that accelerated the path of my going from mid-fleeter to little hot shot. Getting out there early, I was able to take bearings and more importantly, get warmed up, tuned in, and shake the nerves out.

After checking in at the RC boat, sail to the upwind mark and back down should they have it set (they should!), practice kite launches and take downs if applicable. If you're a by the compass sailor, record your compass headings. If an intuitive sailor, note landmarks. As soon as you get a starboard tack bearing, tack to port and get that heading. Do this again and again to the time the percentage of lift time vs. percentage of header. Which way is the wind oscillating, if at all?

Dick Tillman had once tried to upend Peter Commette's victory at the Laser Worlds by telling a fellow competitor how to get into his head. "Be the first out on racecourse! He hates that!" The fellow asked what time he thought that might be. "6 am! Sunrise! It's the only way!"

One of Peter's friends overheard the conversation, so Peter planned to get out there even earlier. As it were, on his way to the race site, Tillman's spoiler ran out of gas on his moped. Commette had to tow him on his. Guess who won that regatta?

I've witnessed other efforts to psyche sailors out before the regatta even begins. At a 2021 Flying Scot Fall 48 regatta, Lake Norman YC had the sailors on hold, as the wind was gusting to 30 and the water still cold. The eventual winner of that event, Dan Neff and his daughter, Ella, just two up, sailed back and forth in front of the clubhouse, showing how it was done.

Photo: Deb Fewell Durbec

So be like Elvstrom, get out there early. Practice mark and gate roundings. Check your boat speed against any other sailors with the proper preparation mindset (PPM's) to get out there and practice early. Most importantly, loosen up so that you shake any nerves out. We all have them before the first race.

Check the course. It may not be displayed until the Preparatory signal. Write it down on your boat. Get two good watches as well. If no crew, I like to mount them on each side of the mast. Looking down at the start is not the best approach. Ronstan's are large thus highly visible, dedicated to start sequences for sailboat racing. They have an audible signal as well. Some club races use an automatic start horn box, but it's better to rely on your watch, as in a regatta, those audible signals won't be happening.

> This flag means that the course is open. That generally means the line is set. You can get out there and practice whether the course is open or not.

Once you see a yellow and black four square flag flying, sail behind the RC boat and make sure they see your number. Once you've done your reconnais-

sance, hang around the starting line and don't nap. Few worse ways to get off the starting line than by taking a leak off the back of your boat. Keep your eyes peeled to the class flag on the RC boat, as audible signals are hard to hear in breeze. After the first race, you never know what sequence fleets will start. Of course, if it's a one class regatta, that's not a concern, or is it? Keep an eye on the raising of your class flag.

START SEQUENCING

You're probably well aware of start sequencing and if being over early, or On Course Side (OCS), you will need to restart.

If not familiar with how sailboat races are started, I'll quickly clue you in. Whether a three or five-minute start sequence, a race start utilizing Rule 26 is typically made up of three phases;

5 minutes: Warning signal, a Class flag is raised; 1 sound

4 minutes: Preparatory signal, a blue flag is raised (at times with an I or Black flag); 1 sound

1 minute: Preparatory flag is lowered; 1 long sound

Start: Class flag lowered; 1 sound

INDIVIDUAL RECALL

If you've had a clean start, you're off to the races. If hailed over early, you must dip back below line and restart. Typically, there are two or three boats that head over the start line early. It's not required but common for the Race Committee boat to hail them by voice or bullhorn. It's not easy for OCS boats hailed to restart and get back in the race but try you must! Boat speed! Luck! When the RC drops the X flag, that means that all OCS boats have restarted and been cleared.

X flag

GENERAL RECALL

If all of your mates are over early, and you all of a sudden see yourself clearly in the lead, they've all gone back for a restart. You will see this flag flying: there is no penalty given to any boat. If you were over early, you get what in golf they call a Mulligan.

EXTRA PENALTY STARTS

Another way race committees tame the fleet from aggressive starting, is to fly the extra penalty flags. You will generally not see these on the first start of the day. They commonly fly in big fleet starts when the RC gets hungry and would like to get a start off by dinnertime. So, not only do you need to check the course chart, but you also need to check to see which other flags are flying along with your Class flag. Maybe your Class doesn't have a flag, it uses a nautical flag. Again, make a printout of all flags, or you'll be flagging sorry.

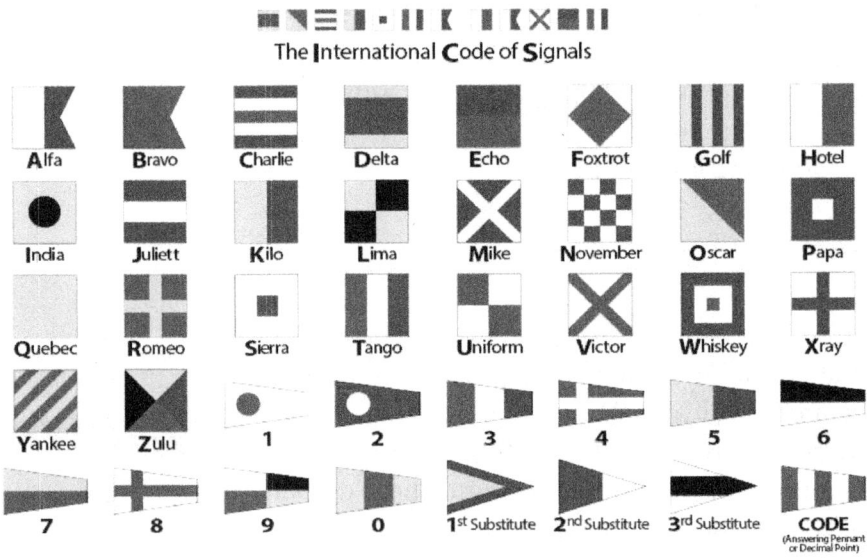

I FLAG STARTS

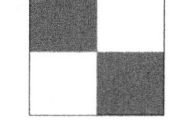

I Flag (Rule 30.1) restricts you from being above the line one minute before the start. . If you are over the line any time after one minute before the start, the only way to exonerate yourself is to round either the pin end or RC boat end.

Not only do you need to check the course chart, but you also need to check to see which other flags are flying along with your Class flag. If your Class doesn't have a flag, it uses a nautical flag and as well for course numbers.

U FLAG

The "U" flag rule, or rule 30.3, is used when the race committee wants to impose stricter starting penalties. During the last minute before the starting signal, no part of the boat's hull, crew, or equipment can be in the triangle formed by the starting line ends and the first mark. A boat that starts within the "Devil's Triangle" under the "U" flag is disqualified and given the maximum number of points (number of entries plus 1)

Z FLAG

The "Z" flag, rule 30.2, is a bit less harsh, giving the perpetrator who infringes on that triangle within one minute before the start, a 20% penalty. I have never seen U or Z flag's flown. Kind of like a freak flag, you never know.

BLACK FLAG STARTS

When the Rule 30.4 Black Flag is flying, you know the Race Committee is fed up with the fleet. It only happens in big fleets, where there are so many recalls that the only way to keep racers behind the line is to impose a severe penalty. A Black Flag means only one thing: if you're over early, you're going home. DSQ. It's very much like the wasp spray, Black Flag. You're so dead.

SITUATION: OCS – No extra flags flying

You are early to the line at the RC boat end, carrying too much speed, on a boat with great momentum. You try to head down the line, but there are boats blocking your way. You think about a quick tack, but you'd be fouling ten boats and be eating that nice yacht club dinner at a table by yourself. You are now ten feet over the line with 20 seconds remaining until the start. Which of the following actions would you take?

- a) Make a quick tack and foul ten boats.
- b) Sheet in and sail over the line far enough to clearly tack and circle around the committee boat.
- c) Push on the boom and sail backwards until you are behind the line.
- d) Pull the centerboard up and sponge the cockpit. Claim you've been hit by a whale.
- e) Head over the line and then reach down until you see some line sag. Dip into that spot with speed, then round up for a good start with great acceleration.

Solutions:

- a: Unless you are in a very small, non-aggressive fleet, tacking on the line is a surefire way to spend that regatta dinner eating alone. Certainly, nobody will be buying you drinks.
- b: Even if by sailing around the committee boat, you cross the line in second row, you can quickly tack away at the start and clear your air. You'll be much better off than being OCS. This approach can also be a good solution with the I Flag in flight.
- c: Push on the boom and sail backwards. This can be a good solution, particularly if you have a crew, and your boat does not carry much momentum. Yet, in this scenario, there are boats behind you, and your boat is not only difficult to stop and send backwards, but tough to get going again.
- d: There are no whales on your lake. Panic is not a good option.
- e: Provided there is enough time to do so, heading over the line and then dipping down into a gap (there is most often always line sag in the middle of the line), and then rounding up with acceleration with five seconds to go… this is most often the best solution.
  - When it's not: Someone who has your number is going to run down the line with you and keep you above the line. Or there is no

line sag for you to squeeze into, there is often going to be a General Recall, but don't count on it.

In Summary: Practice your starts. Know your boat's momentum. Rounding the boat or dipping the line depends a lot on which end is favored. If heavily starboard favored, round the committee boat. If pin, dip the line.

Even if you have a clear path, the likelihood of your timing being perfect depends on how well practiced you are, unpredictable changes in wind speed or direction, and especially current. In an upwind current, getting to the line early and sitting there luffing is a dangerous place to be. Only the most skilled sailors can do it, and if there is current, it doesn't matter how much skill you have, you're going over early, mate. The RC can hail your number if the choose to, they usually will. If all of your mates are over early, and you all of a sudden see yourself clearly in the lead, they've all gone back for a restart. You will see this flag flying: there is no penalty given to any boat. If you were over early, you get what in golf they call a Mulligan.

Situation: Dishing Out a Protest

The preparatory signal has sounded. You are one minute before the start and Alice Aggressor gives you the hook tapping your rail. She's probably angry that you didn't help out with the dishes at the regatta dinner. You thought about yelling, "rubbing is racing!" and, "Have you attended Dave Perry's Rule Seminar for 2025 updates?" but Alice was too busy working on her Phd. Alice yells, "Foul! Do your spins, Bucko!" What do you do?

Options

- A) Ignore her and remember to help out with the dishes at the next regatta.

- B) Do your spin(s) right away, clear of all other boats.

- C) You have to wait until the start gun sounds, then do your penalty turn(s).

- D) You have to wait until the start gun sounds, be clear of all other boats, and then do your penalty turn(s).

Solutions

Which option did you choose? The correct answer was A.

Why A? If Alice does not say the word, PROTEST, she has not properly registered a protest. While it is not required for boats under 6m, it would help to fly a red flag. To make you shake in your Zhik boots over her rules knowledge, she could also cite the rule number of the infraction, and call out your sail number loud and clear. As it was, she did none of the above. You do not have to do a dang thing.

B) Had Alice hailed you properly, and you agree with the infringement, you are still in good shape. Any foul taking place after the Preparatory signal and the start signal, can be exonerated before the start. Did you know that? Unless you've caused significant damage and sunk both boats, you can do your penalty turn (or turns, depending on what is designated in the SI's) even before the start, provided you are clear of other boats and not fouling them in the process. This can be challenging in a tough fleet and with little time left on the clock, but doable. If a serious collision results from the foul, the boat in the wrong is still liable for damages.

C) Bammp. Wrong answer.

D) Trick question, but wrong answer again. It's a trick question because in either case, you need to keep clear of all other boats while exonerating yourself. This includes being over early OCS. If hailed, don't be a kook, just peel off and barrel downwind through the fleet. More fouls will be incurred and new swear words learned.

DSQ at the Barbecue

I learned the I Flag rule the hard way at The Old Goat, Lake Lanier SC, sailing with Lee Estes on his Thistle. Not having had a lot of Thistle practice in the thirty years prior, I misjudged our speed and carried us over the line about 40 seconds before the gun. This was during an I Flag start, and I did not know what the I flag was and had never seen one. We dipped back down where we saw line sag and then rounded back up with a powerful start. What a great race! DSQ.

SITUATION: I FLAG OCS

Situation: You didn't look at the tide charts. You haven't noticed that the tide has gone from with the wind to against it. With an overcrowded line, you got to the line early and sat there luffing, and started to drift over the line, when you look up and notice the dreaded evil I Flag is flying. Oh no!

Mr. Bill! Bailout! 30 seconds still to burn before the start. What to do?

Choose between the following resolutions:

a) Push the boom to go backwards.
b) Sheet in with speed, go over the line and tack. Round the RC boat and hope a gap has opened up.
c) If pin favored and enough time, reach down the line and round the pin. Hope for enough space between starboard boats and shoot the gap. Or, get lucky and port tack the fleet!
d) Start anyway and hope they don't see you over early.
e) When your number is called over early, wait for everyone to pass and restart.

Solutions:

a) Too late. You've already broken the I Flag rule. You must go forward, not backwards. To go backwards, you are only pinning yourself down inside the fleet.
b) This works.
c) This also works. It really depends on which end of the line you infringed.
d) This never works, unless a lot of boats are over early with you.
e) Excuse yourself. It's the last race of the day and your throwout anyway. Bonus, you'll be first to the bar.

BLACK FLAGGED

140garble81…159garblegarble7" came the numbers hailed by the start boat, followed by other sail numbers. Was it me?

In my experience, nobody was better at starting in big fleets, or small for that matter, than Ed Baird. At that time and for many years after, he was about the hardest guy to beat in the world. Tough as nails and tactically smarter than your average Baird, he'd just as well kick sand in your face and have your lunch money.

Ed invited me back from Hawaii to take part in the 1981 Laser Midwinters. I guess he wanted redemption for losing to me at the USYRU Singlehanded Championships. There were 500 boats split into four fleets. We would alternate racing against each group, but as you can imagine, with 250 aggressive little gnats on the line, there were lots of general recalls.

Of general recalls, I'd had my fair share. But the Black Flag, that was a new one to me.

I had been out of the boat for a year while on my windsurfing hiatus, but somehow that worked out well for me in the breezier races. I had scored four straight bullets. Then the wind died and reality kicked in. I scored a 61 and 66. With a throwout, that still put me in the lead, 7 points ahead of Ed. However, one more bad race and I'd cough it up. Would I finally win a National regatta? It was only my second try, so finally was a stretch.

My first Nationals, I won the first race. Beginner' luck, mostly. I still remember that race like it was yesterday, Augie Diaz walking up to me on Ft Lauderdale Beach and slapping me on the behind. "Good going, kid. Guess I need to watch out for you." In truth, he didn't much, not from behind anyway.

The Midwinters in Tampa Bay would be the largest in class history. Like many events, it was about more than good racing. This was a big party; getting together with a bunch of old friends, young as we all still were. Nobody was more surprised than I was when I won those four races. I supposed the windsurfing had really paid off. Maybe I should not have given up sailing, but windsurfing was becoming a professional sport, and sailing was still an amateur one. Oh right, the Black Flag…

On the final day and penultimate race of the Laser Midwinters, the wind kicked up its heels. The Hot n' Now sign was *lit*. But after three more General Recalls, there was that Black Flag, fluttering in the breeze. I told myself to play it safe. I had the boat speed, so all I would need is a middle line start. Let Ed take the advantage. I hadn't taken any ballet, just a year of windsurfing in the big waves of Hawaii. With my 6'3" length and 185 pounds of perfect Laser hiking machine, I felt I could give up a few yards.

Ed, being Ed, was stalking me. I checked the lunch money in my pocket. Then I noticed the St Pete YC gang were on both sides. Ed was just to windward, Rick Merriman to leeward. Was I getting team raced? As the start horn sounded, I thought for sure I had been well blanketed by the fleet, out of the watchful sight of those on that Race Committee boat. There had been line sag, and I was positioned dead in the middle of it. Numbers were being called. No way they could have seen me. Was there someone with binocs on the pin end, who radioed to the RC boat?

WINNING WAYS

Ed pulled off his usual perfect start to windward, but I started with good speed and got a jump on him. I had an instant lead on the entire fleet. Normally, that would be a fine and dandy position to be in, with clean air and a clear path to victory. But now I was sticking out like a sore thumb. *Was* I over early? I sure looked guilty, but was I charged? Like I wrote, it was windy, and the hailing RC boat was too far away to clearly hear. Maybe the numbers even overlapped to magically come up with mine. "159007! Over early!"

Who yelled that? Then, several racers, mostly from that St Pete YC clan chimed in. "159007!" "159007!" "159007! OCS! Clear out!"

Now, I never gave much thought to what I would do if my number was ever called when the Black Flag was flying. I supposed I would just retire, like the rule states. I'm pretty keen on following the rules. Without rules, there is no game. So, when I looked around and saw myself way ahead of the fleet, and hearing my number called, I did something foolish. I cleared out.

When I got back to the beach, I was upset at myself, but not that much. That's racing. You push the edge and sometimes, you fall over it. I guessed I had pushed that edge. Plus, I came into this regatta with zero expectations, perhaps minus zero. My thought was that I was just, for once, going to just sail for fun. And that paid off! Or almost paid off. What happened next though, made my knees buckle.

As I approached the staging area to applaud Ed for winning the regatta, I knew I wouldn't even be standing on the podium, having to now eat another 66 points. But it really was a blast to be racing again. After all, I'd had four more bullets than I'd expected. Then the PRO, the head guy of the race committee, came walking my way, their eyes with a concerned look. Had I done something wrong?

"Are you okay? Did you break down?" The first man asked.

"But, but. You called my number over, right? 159007. I was–"

"No. Nobody called you over early, Son."

Lesson learned: In a Black Flag situation, until a race committee boat rides up and flags you down, keep on racing. You've got nothing to lose.

STARTING IN THE ELECTRONIC AGE

When I was looking for a photo to demonstrate line sag, I came across some photos kindly donated by Melges from their Melges 15 Winter Series. A long line was set, but there was very little line sag! At the Melges Performance Center, they also use the Vakaros system for both clinics and racing; not only on the boats, but on the Race Committee, utilizing Vakaros RaceSense.

RaceSense takes a great deal of error out of OCS call. Both RC and the competitors know right away if they are OCS. It also helps in reducing the number of General Recalls. The system is being legalized and incorporated even in the staunchest of old school One Designs, like the Thistle and Etchells.

There are other standalone devices on the market available such as Velocitek and Sailmon Max, each having their advantages of battery life, ease of use, readability, quick access to data interpretation, and price. Most of them will run you over a grand (though at the Melges events, Vakaros can be rented).

With device alertness, you will become

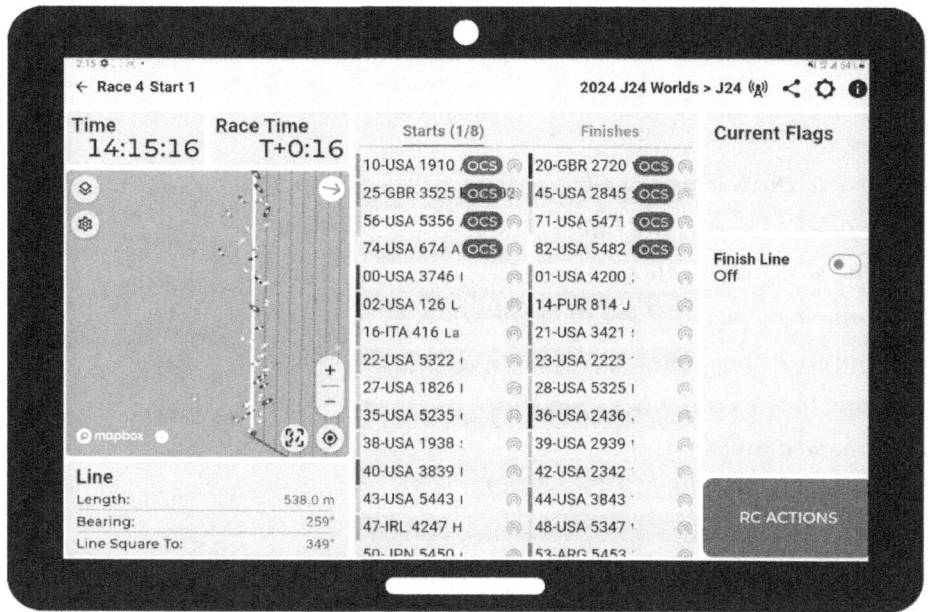

more aware of how close to the line you're approaching. It won't help you determine which "turkey" (as Peter Commette politely puts it) to start next to, nor seat of the pants things; but it goes beyond starts, providing data for both practice and race analysis. If you're new to the game or stuck in the middle of it, my advice is to lose the compass, lose the devices, and get your head the hell out of the boat. But that's me. I'm old school. But I can tell you who I'm looking at now to judge whether I need to get up on the line a bit; and that's kids these days with devices onboard.

BREAKING DOWN THE START GAME

Here's the object of the game when the signal sounds:

Be as close to the line as possible.
Near the favored end of the line.
Next to the slowest people as possible.
With as much accelerated speed as possible.
In as clear air as possible.
On the long tack as quickly as possible.
Headed toward pressure.
With as many beers in hand as possible.

Okay, scratch the last one; it's just what people think we're doing when we're out racing boats. Let's break these down a bit more:

When the start signal sounds, **be as close to the line as possible:**

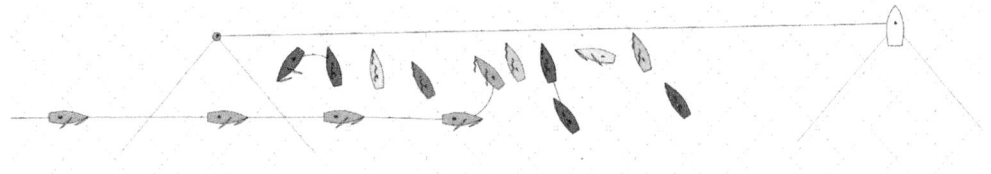

How close and how early to toe that line can be decided by your fleet size, competitiveness, line length, and how fast you can accelerate your boat up to speed. In big fleets, you will see boats lining up even before one minute, ensuring they have a well reserved space. Be careful if the current is running against the wind, or you'll be pushed over early. If there is a small fleet or the line is long, you can time the start so that you are only as close to the line as necessary with a second or two to go before the signal sounds. Some clubs still use a gun for the start and first boat finishing.

When the start signal sounds, be **near the favored end of the line:**

How can you figure out which end is favored? The most common method used is to go head to wind. Whichever end of the line the boat is pointed most toward, is your favored end, at least for the time being.

If an imaginary line is drawn at midships perpendicular to the boat, the side of that imaginary line is either going to point below the RC boat or the pin. If a dead even line, it will

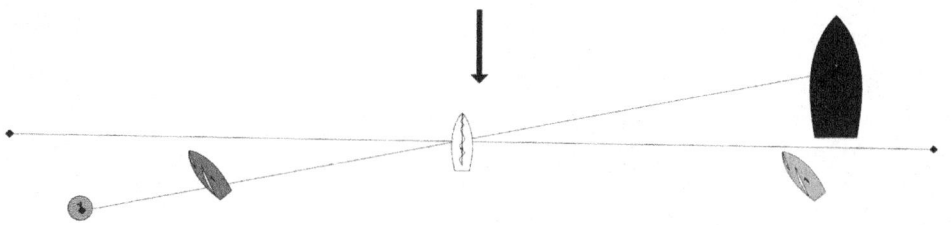

point at both, running parallel to the start line.

Some people use math and a compass or Tacktick electronics to figure it out, others make do without. Doing without means going head to wind, or sailing back and forth along the line, noting on which tack your sails are more closely hauled. The end you're pointing at when more closely hauled is the favored end. Whatever method you use to take these bearings, take them five min-

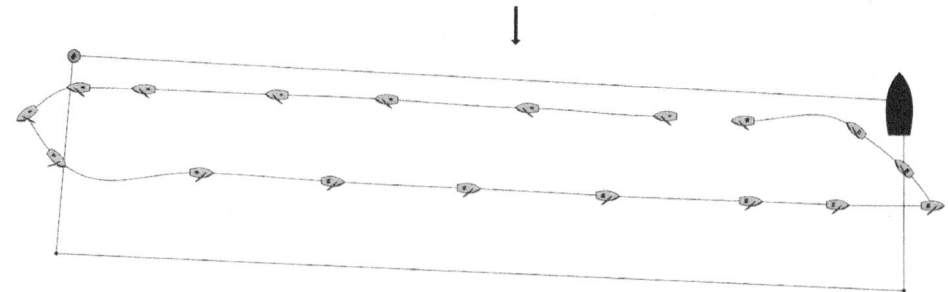

utes then again 2 1/2 minutes out from the start, to see which way the wind may may be shifting. Bearings taken too early, and you may have decided too soon which end is favored. Done too late, within one minute before the start, and there may not be time enough to get to the favored end; all spots have been reserved.

Should neither side seem heavily favored, plan to start on the same end of the line where you think the best pressure is, not only on the line, but on the course. In other words, if all is even, and you see more wind on the line toward the RC boat, start near the RC boat. If you strongly believe the left side of the course is favored, start near the pin. If you've sailed the beat before the race and observe carefully, you can increase those odds a lot.

Once you're in sequence, it's important to stay in what is called "The Box." The box is an imaginary box running from the start line to the pin, extending about four boat lengths to leeward of the line. The lighter the wind, the more you need to stay within that box.

All race committee PRO's think differently, but I like the ones who will set the line just slightly favored to port. When the line is set as such, there is better spacing within the fleet. It's good for them to mix it up, but a heavily favored starboard line will result in many general recalls as it's harder to see the boats as they are blanketing each other. Perhaps varying which end is favored is good way to test all skills

STARBOARD FAVORED START

Kerfuffle happens at the boat end on a starboard favored line. Everyone who didn't read this book wants to be there, thinking they are being clever? Luck of the cards will come into play; you'll draw an Ace of Diamonds or be some joker who is OCS, tacks into the fleet, and all pandemonium breaks loose. More swear words! With a bit of good luck, you draw the Ace, hit the line running in clean air and you'll be winning right off the bat. But there's only one guy who gets that perfect start, and in a top-level fleet, the odds are against you.

Depending on the size and skill level of the fleet, part of your pre-race strategy is deciding how much risk you want to take on. Two's company, three's a crowd, ten is a pack of disaster waiting to unfold. Pull it off? Chapeaux!

Photo: Deb Fewell Durbec

Many sailors don't know that it is illegal to luff another boat, forcing them into the RC boat. The RC boat is an obstruction. At the same time, you can't come barreling in there from windward and try to squeeze out the boat that has prime position next to the RC boat. It's called BARGING. Don't be Bully or Betty Barger. If the line is even the least bit starboard favored, you'll be blocked by the Larry Allen's of your fleet (great guard for 49ers!), and probably a pack of other boats risking the RC boat end. The resulting log jam won't end well for anyone if you try to bull your way in.

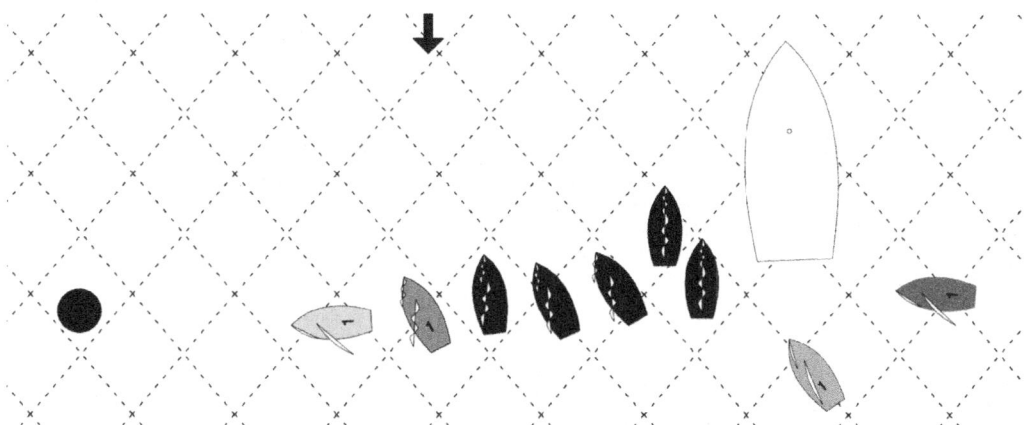

When I decide to mix it up for a starboard favored start, I use a variation of what Dick Lamb informed me is the classic Vanderbilt Start (named after Harold Vanderbilt who was the first to use this strategy in J-Boat racing). Starting from the RC boat, I head off on a port broad reach, having previously timed how long I should go before tacking or jibing and coming in on the layline with speed. It's more of an approach for smaller fleet starts, and the timing takes practice, but if you can hit the line already at full speed, why not? Right, kerfuffles.

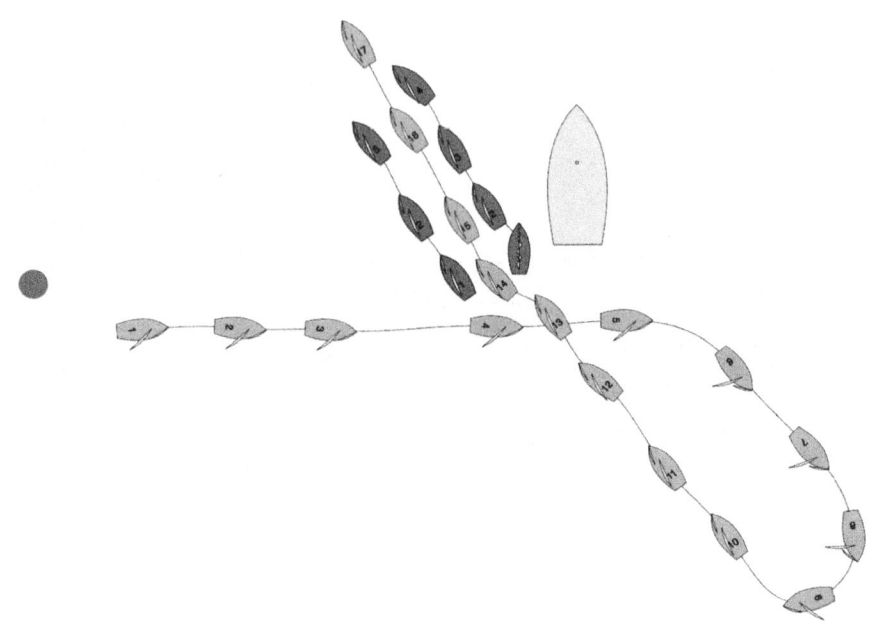

This approach won't work if there is are a ton of boats crowding the RC boat end. However, if you're strategy is to get to the right side of the course as soon as possible, it's not the worst approach, particularly in large fleets. If you know you have good speed, it's a good plan. The first row of boats will have to wait for you to tack. If you know you are slow, it's also a good plan, as you will otherwise get buried within ten seconds after the start. At least you can tack out, clear your air, and begin observing what others are doing to be so darn fast.

Photo: John Cole

PORT FAVORED START

First, take a look at how favored to port the line has been set. From which direction you approach the line on a port favored start depends upon the degree favored to port. To me, the perfect line is not one evenly set, but slightly port favored. This configuration prevents pile ups, yet is still quite challenging.

If you've placed your boat to windward of a big gap, you have the opportunity before the gun goes off to "rev up" by running down the line on starboard. However, in larger fleet starts where gaps are small, and if in particular, racers have distance-to-line electronics onboard, there will be no line sag. Boats to leeward might push whatever momentum you've gained up and over the line. Squeeze plays at the pin never work.

If slightly port favored, I typically approach the line on port, then look for a gap to tack into next to notoriously slow sailors. If the fleet is late, I'll try to jump into a position that will place me at speed as close to pin as possible. If the fleet is early, I find a gap at a distance to the pin I figure will place me just making it with speed at the gun. Practice makes perfect.

Port tacking the fleet is risky, but if you can spank the fleet, good for you. The bigger the fleet and the better the sailors, the chance of success drops very fast. Port tacking the fleet takes a lot of guts, skill, and great timing. Done well, you should be firing off the line. The race is yours to win.

With the line more heavily favored to port, the fleet tends to get a running head start. If you've chosen to start within that parade, you will not find an easy way out of it. Your timing has to be impeccable. It's much easier to utilize my typical approach on port, find a gap, tack close to a starboard tacker and jealously guard your space to leeward, If anyone looks like they want to tack beneath you, aim right at them and yell, "No way, Pirate!"

Photo: Marcy Sherman

Larry Bird was asked about being overly competitive with opponents like Magic Johnson. When asked how he could be feisty with such a nice fellow, Larry replied, "With that big smile always on his face, I'd make sure to take home a few teeth." While sailing is nothing like that on the lower levels, you can bet in the bigger events that nobody on the line's handing out party invitations.

The danger to being on the pin end, if you're not known for your boat speed, is that you risk getting buried soon after the start. Then you'll have to tack and start ducking boats. It's not that ducky of an approach. But when the line is heavily port favored, you will see almost the entire fleet quickly flip onto port to get onto the long tack. The longer you are pinned to port, the worse your VMG.

As the line becomes more heavily favored to port, you will now be concerned with being too far downwind from the line, unable to lay the pin. As long as the I flag is not flying, which prohibits you from being OCS within a minute of the start, you can approach the line from on the course side (above it). This enables you to stay high on the line, then duck down below it just in the nick of time.

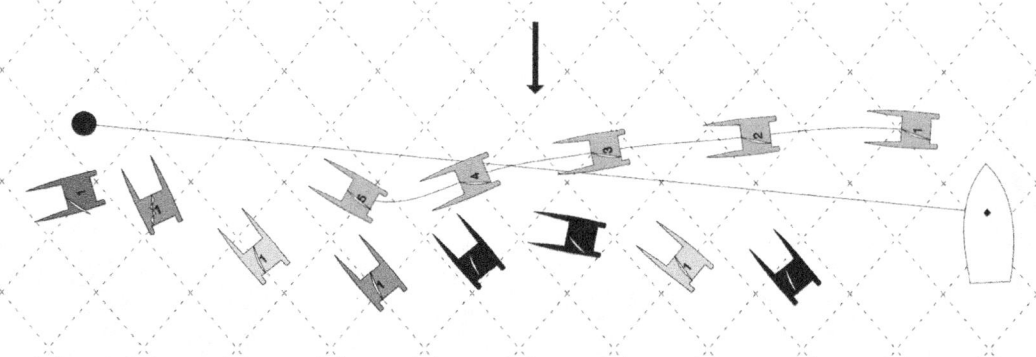

As long as the I flag is not flying, which prohibits you from being OCS within a minute of the start, you can approach the line from on the course side (above it). This enables you to stay high on the line, then duck down below it just in the nick of time. If the wind shifts heavily to port favored, you should find your position up on the line and to weather of the fleet, clear to tack onto port.

The danger to being on the pin end, if you're not known for your boat speed, is that you risk getting buried soon after the start. Then you'll have to tack and start ducking boats. It's not that ducky of an approach. But when the line is heavily port favored, you will see almost the entire fleet quickly flip onto port to get onto the long tack. The longer you are pinned to port, the worse your VMG.

EVEN STEVEN

If there is an even set to the line, neither side is favored, a middle of the line start is going to work best. On a long line, when I write middle, I really mean middle left if the line is slightly pin favored, or middle right if the committee boat end is slightly favored. In a smaller fleet, if the favored side is not yet determined, best to hit the line running in the middle. Next to what?

Next to the slowest people as possible:

"*Hunt down a Turkey and baste them.*" *Evil Racer*

Photo: Will Keyworth

Paul Elvstrom: *When you come to a regatta, look down the list of entrants, review the strengths and weaknesses of the ones you know and find out about the ones you don't. Because when you come to the start you know what they are used to doing, and if they're used to being wrong you know it. And you can calculate that they can be a little stupid sometimes, like falling down into you at the start, or they don't respect the rules. And I never try to fight against people who break the rules; I try to get away from them.*

I might add that with the modern invention of the World Wide Web, you can now research the strengths and weaknesses of the fleet on Regatta softwares. Who are Concords, who the Turkeys? The guy holding the beer, is he bluffing?

Photo: Deb Fewell Durbec

With as much speed as possible:

If you've been sitting in your parking spot for a minute, luffing your sail(s), hitting the line with speed is an art form. That's why people do clinics. You will learn by doing how to quickly put on the gas and accelerate. It also depends on your boat. Are you on a Ferrari or an AMC Gremlin? If on the Gremlin, you will need to place more emphasis on accelerating up to the line from further back.

Those heavy Gremlins have momentum, so toeing the line is more difficult. With just a slight catch of the sail, that momentum will send you OCS or down the line with a hope and prayer. You have to ramp it up at least a couple of boat lengths off the line, then sheet in with ten seconds to go. That way, you are at full speed at the start. Hard to do with a packed line of parkers, but watch those gaps open up by people who have not attended clinics.

If on a Ferrari, you still want to preload your acceleration. The best racers who park at the line will maintain their position, luff their sail on a reach with boom fully extended to ward off the leeward boat. They sheet in just

moments before the start and are off to the races. It takes practice.

I'm of such habit from sailing Ferrari's that when I race a Gremlin, I often get to the line too early and park. It's a bad practice meaning I'm out of practice. In smaller fleets, parking on the line is a big mistake. The better starters will come roaring up at full speed, hitting the gap left below or above me if I've drifted down from the RC boat. Drifting happens.

In as clear air as possible:

You really want to position yourself to windward of a footer and leeward of a pointer. If both are slow off the line, you've got instant clear air and freedom to play the course as you choose.

Yacht Club SanRemo Int'l 420 Class Association Photo: Andrea Lelli

Some sailors carry on far longer than they should in disturbed air. While your goals are heading toward the pressure, being on the long tack, and getting to the favored side of the course, a quick tack to clear your air is often essential to maintaining boat speed.

If you're not the fastest sailor in the fleet, moments after the start, you are going to have to face the music. Clear your air. I typically try to keep away from the fastest guys (unless that's me, hah), and I certainly don't want to jam into a gap just to windward of Paul the Pointer. Paul doesn't get it yet, that you need to get the boat moving and driving, the water rushing over the center/daggerboard to provide lift. He (or she, Pauline), just points right off the bat, and you will have to wait for all starboard boats to clear before you can tack away and gain speed.

You have a couple of choices here. You can try to blast through his lee if there's room for it, or tack and duck a bunch of boats. I find that unless I'm trying to get out of current, or there's obviously a favored side with more pressure to head toward, going around a boat through their wind shadow doesn't work. But sometimes, you have to just slow up, then find room to tack and start ducking boats. Whatever you do, you've got to get out of the epic dearth, cut your losses and cut them quick! Clear your air. Get that boat moving again!

Melges MC Scow Midwinters   Photo: Morgan Kinney

If you have no turkey's in your fleet, it's better to start to windward of Fred the Footer. Fred the footer will bear away at the start, and you can, too. If you really think one side is more favored than the other due to current (or past events!), keep your sails full and driving toward that side. Don't pinch to death! If you're dog slow and you know it, it's best to start second row near the committee boat with speed, then tack out as soon as you can to clear your air. This doesn't mean banging the right corner. Just get out on the course so you can see how the race is developing. Don't start playing shifts unless they're big and will place you on the long tack. Your top priority is getting the boat up to speed and in position to win. You've got nothing to lose but a sailboat race!

Most newbies tack on a 3 degree wind shift, then tack again and again and again, dodging boats right and left until they look around... and wonder what just happened. If I have too many cups of coffee, I do the same! Or, Nelson Newbie gets a bad start then eats dog wind from the faster cats. Tack out!

Clear your air! Hard to do on the port end. That all said, if the line is heavily port favored, try to time your tack over to port, not right in someone's shadow.

DIRTY AIR DOUG

Occasionally, you get invited to come along on someone else's boat to coach them up a bit. In one case, the skipper of a U20, Dirty Air Doug, didn't really invite me on board, his crew did. They were growing tired of winning the Wooden Spoon, eager to change their skipper's losing ways. Simply put, they thought I could offer Doug a bit of tactical advice.

I would normally recommend taking a good look at the fleets starting ahead of us. They will often be the best sign not only of pressure, but seeing which side of the course is working best. Where on the course are boats heeling the most, or lifting the highest? There you will probably find the pressure. However, being the first fleet to start and being the last to leave the dock, we had little to go by.

I told Dougie, stand up in the boat. What do you see? The darker water on the left looked like Ringwraiths flying across the sea from Mordor. We had enough time to do our line check, running back and forth, and it seemed even enough. I didn't expect Doug to fight for the pin. Like in surfing, only the best fight for the crest; but starting somewhere not too far from the pin with clear air seemed like a good enough plan.

My suggestion of sailing the line on port with a minute to go and finding a gap in the fleet was completely ignored. We approached on starboard, fifteen seconds late, which put us third row, and then tacked right into a boat on the second row's shadow. At this point, Dougie would need a big shovel to dig himself out of this hole. Maybe that wooden spoon would come in handy. I recommended that a quick tack clear our air.

"Tim told me I tack too much."

He was speaking of Tim Porter, top U20 gun, National Champion. Avoiding tacking too much was sound advice. You, or should I say I, tend to do it too much when I'm behind after a bad start, attempting to force my way to through the fleet by taking advantage of every little shift. "Yeah, but I doubt he would have advised you to stay right here in Rock Lobster's shadow. You might want to tack again to at least clear your air. We're headed to the wrong side of the course as well." We sat in bad air for a record amount of time.

Tim was on the favored left side, on the long tack, with speed. After finally taking another tack, I discovered why Tim recommended Doug not tack very often. He overtacked, then he undertacked, and by that time we were DFL.

I wondered why Doug invited me along, until we broached going downwind. "Get the kite down! Bail!" That ends my story of Doug the bad air digger.

PREVENTING LINE SAG

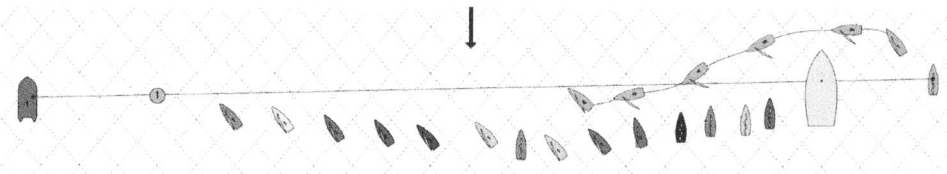

If the starting line is long, and the fleet is sailing sans starting instruments, they will generally toe the line at the ends, but sag way off in the middle. Randy Smyth's trick is to line sight an object from above the RC boat, in this illustration, the anchored RIB. Another method to make sure that you are up on the line in a big fleet is to not let the boat above you edge up and over your wind. By staying just a nose to leeward in the windward boat's shadow, you are also hiding your number from the view of the RC boat. Using a predetermined reference point really helps, as the boat above you may also be way off the line.

If you and the boat blanketing you are over early, and your number is called, you are most likely being spotted OCS by that secondary RC boat. If that boat is not anchored, you can protest the Race Committee. Good luck with that!

While this is great knowledge of the rules, restarting is much easier than protesting the Race Committee, as you would never know who called your number (unless the hail comes specifically from that direction). However, it's always good to check and see if there is any boat on the leeward pin,

During this Fleet 6 Lido 14 start in Alamitos Bay, it appears that the guy on the blue RIB is calling someone over early. If that's the case, you could protest the RC, as he is not anchored. More likely, he's calling for a sandwich.

anchored or not. If there is, you can also use that boat as your reference point.

Get on the long tack as quickly as possible.

What is the long tack? That is the tack that you will be on the longest to reach the weather mark. Get on it as quickly as you can in a lane of clear air. You might have figured which tack is the long tack before the start (few RC's set the weather mark perfectly), but if there is a major shift of wind during the start, that's a good clue of which is going to be the long tack.

For example, if the wind shifts to a heavily favored port tack, port tack is in most cases going to be your long tack, and vice versa. You will probably be only one short tack away from laying the mark. Make that short tack when you've run the long tack for the majority of the leg, in which case the short tack will become the long tack. The object is to take the shortest path to the weather mark, and that is done by the way of the long tack.

Typically, if the line is set Even Steven, and then becomes favored to starboard, starboard is going to be your long tack right from the get go. If port favored, a quick tack to port will put you on the long favored tack (port). Don't hesitate or it'll be too late!

On the long tack, if you get lifted, you're golden, just like these vintage Stars! We'll cover this more in the First Weather Leg chapter, as it's a biggie.

Paul Elvstrom: *The most important thing on starting tactics is to know which way you want to go after the start. If you want to continue on the starboard tack, do all you can to have free water to leeward. If you want to go onto port, you may have to start one boat length late so that you can be sure to get onto port immediately. Because what is expensive at the start is to go the wrong way. Now, if the line favors the port end, or its even, I will start near the port end, because soon after, starboard tack is usually headed. But if the line favors the starboard end, I can be sure most of the boats will try to start there. Then, I position myself to leeward of the group because even though I'm behind at the start, I quickly get free wind, and if it turns back a little, I get more free wind, and finally it goes back more and I can tack and cross ahead of the group. Trying for the best start risks getting forced into a very bad start or being forced to tack immediately.*

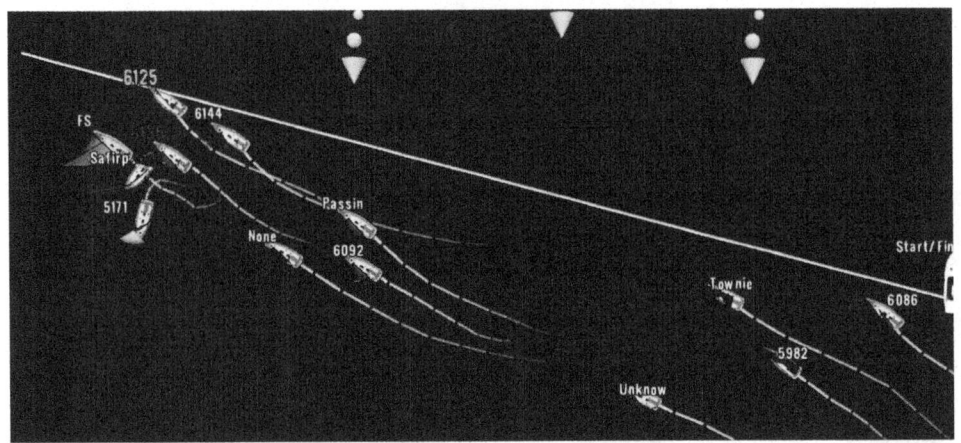

Race tracking software like RaceQs is great for debriefs. 6125 is Dave Rink, showing how a port favored start is done, son.

Heading toward the most pressure...

Sailing toward and getting into greater pressure trumps being on the long tack. Even if you've had a clear air start, there might be somebody equally fast on your hip to weather, keeping you from going toward the pressure. I paid the price once in a Highlander regatta. My pre-race strategy was to get to the left side of the course, where I had determined there was more

Paul Abdullah & Company heading toward fleet murdering felonious pressure on their way to killing yet another Thistle Nationals.

pressure. But I was so proud of myself, nailing the start with speed, quickly tacking onto the long tack, I kept going to the right. Boy was I wrong! We led the fleet a long way to the wrong side of the course, only to look over over our shoulders halfway up the course to see Dave Rink, who had briefly taken the short tack, now on the long tack lifting ten degrees higher and in breeze. Time to put:

As much beer in your hand as possible.

Hey, however you make it fun! If you are a minor, this is only to hand the beer to Mom and Dad.

STARTING LIKE A HOT DONUT

The first thing to do before starting is to make sure your lines are in order, the board down, and vang loose. You don't want to start with a tight vang, as it will make it tough to luff for slowing the boat or parking on the line, especially when backing up (beep beep beep!).

Stand up in the boat to determine which side of the course might have more pressure. If fleets have started before yours, note which end of the line was favored, and as their race proceeds, who is making out better; those on the right or those on the left? Which way did the local sailors go?

Photo: Josh Jones

Dave Rink & Joel Blade checking whatever is out there to check. Looks like not much!

The next thing to do is run the starting line back and forth, staying within the box, gaining a feel for not only which end is favored, but which end has more pressure. This also helps to "learn the line." Each time you tack, pause head to wind for a quick line check.

Although I've talked about staying in the box, my final approach to the line is rarely on starboard. Unless I'm getting tired, lazy, or avoiding becoming too predictable, my preferred approach is on a port reach. Why? From this position, I'm not locked in. I get a complete picture of whether the fleet is going to be late or early, of how spaced out they are. I'm looking for a good hole to duck into; as well for where the top competitors in the fleet are lined up. Steer clear!

This approach is easier when the line is even or favored to port, more difficult when heavily favored to starboard. When the line is favored to starboard, I

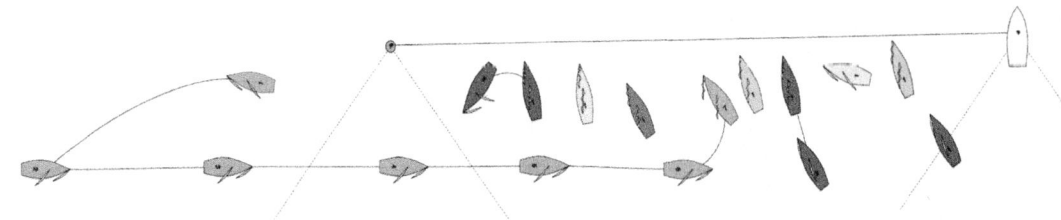

still tend to use this approach, but I start coming up the line on port a lot earlier. Then I either tack in front of the fleet if they're edging up late, or find a gap between two boats if the fleet is early. Whatever flock of the feather they are, try to stay a couple of feet ahead of the windward boat's bow. Otherwise, you're going to get smoked when then gun goes off.

If the line is heavily favored to starboard, I abandon this approach, and try to start with speed not right at the committee boat (unless I've eaten an Alpha dog sandwich for lunch), but not too far from it, either. Start with speed, in clear air, and you can give up the optimum dog position right by the RC boat.

BIG FLEET STARTS

Melges15 #583 started far down the line with speed in clear air. As the wind veered to port, they had a solid lead over the fleet of 130 boats. Like Abdullah says, "Speed kills."

Starting on a shortened 40 boat line can be challenging, yet, starting in fleets bigger than 100 boats is a whole 'nother kettle of fish. You can throw timed approaches to the line out the window. Boats toe the line early, particularly in highly competitive fleets, Olympic caliber fleets. But let's face it, if you're in a regatta with that many boats competing, you're in a competitive fleet.

It's akin to surfing at Sunset Beach on Oahu. If you want that peak position, you're going to have to battle for it. If fearful, hesitant, you're going to be sitting on the shoulder, yeah, like a kook. You don't just show up with your shiny new board and Birdwell Beach Britches and have a go at the peak. It takes a lot of sitting on the shoulder and observation – a bit of respect gained – a courage worked up – to get in there and jostle for position.

Similarly, it's probably not in anyone's interest to get on a big start line and duke it out if you're not able to control your boat in these pressure-cooker situations. Work up to it in smaller regattas. But at some point, you have to come out swinging like Jimmy Spithill! Or, you'll never take home any trophies.

Up to a minute before the start, boats are hustling to the line for front row seats, nervously waiting for that gun to go off. As boats drift away from the boat end or fall off the pin, they try tacking back to gain way lost from even a wind current. There's a lot of chatter going on – gaps defended, rails rubbed (rubbing is racing!), Sailor's words shouted – while others remain cool, calm and collected.

Seconds before the start gun fires, sails are sheeted in and they're off. It's incredible to watch! It's not so incredible to be watching from the second or third row.

Melges A Scows in a tightly contested start. The Inland Lakes racing on Lake Geneva provide some of the most competitive scow racing in the Midwest.

There's a reason that some sailors sweep the trophies off the table at regional regattas where fleets are typically 40 boats or under, and then others shine in big fleets, or pretty much at both. Just like immersion in big winds is the key to winning in heavy air, it's a matter of experience on big fleet start lines to keep cool in pressure cooker situations. Andy Burdick is one of those cool cats in big fleets. He offers some great advice on how to best start in them.

WINNING WAYS

Andy Burdick: Some of my major wins have come in fleets with over 100 boats on the starting line. Over 100 boats may sound overwhelming, but there are some simple points to apply to navigate the chaos and achieve your best results.

1. During your pre-start routine, keep your boat on the starting line or even slightly above the line. Do not let your boat get below the line and into the mass of other boats. Stay above the line so that you have a sense of where the actual start line is; this also allows you to see upwind.

2. You want to start in the best wind pressure off the start. Look up the body of water and figure out where the best wind is. Be above the line and then dip down 90 seconds before the actual start. Start in wind!

3. Start in the front row and get clear air - it is mandatory! Position your boat in clear air right away.

4. If you are new to starting in big fleets, start at the windward end of the start line and tack out right away. Instant clear air. If you have great boat handling, duck and weave through traffic to achieve clear air. Focus on speed and clear air will come

5. There may be 107 boats on the line, but only two boats are close to you off the starting line–the boat above you and the boat below! You must beat these boats off the line.

DEFENDING THE GAP

This bit is more for advanced sailors and is a highly useful tactic in bigger fleet starts. It can be used in small fleets as well, and good to know if someone is slamming a gap shut on you. When I speak of gaps, it's the space left between two boats on the start line. Even when a single row of boats are parked on the line, gaps develop.

In smaller fleet starts, which are 99% of my starts, I find myself getting to the line too early. It's an old Laser big fleet habit. I like to park early, and if in a boat like a Flying Scot with momentum, I'm a bit of a sitting duck. The bigger the fleet, the earlier I'm getting to the line.

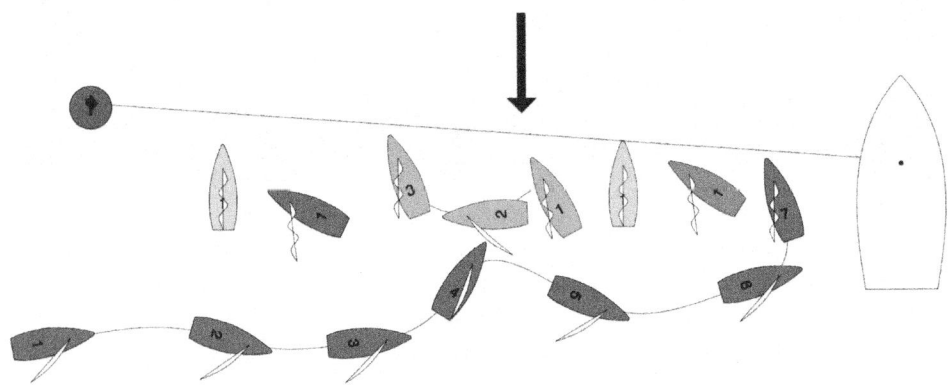

I usually try to keep the boat to windward of me forced high, to create a nice lane to foot off into and gain that speed before trying to point. That's when people who are crafty come shooting into the gap I've created to my lee. They're either running down the line behind and shooting in, or approaching on port, tacking from behind, and shooting into that last minute hole in the line.

At this point, you've got to defend that gap. You've got to give them stink eye, shout, "No way!" and bear off just enough to close the gap without creating a bigger one to weather. The guy coming in on port or late and close hauled, is not easily going to pinch into your gap left to weather. But they can do it. The gap you're defending is to leeward.

There was a humorous moment of someone trying to test my rules knowledge, sailing into my leeward gap. As I bore off to shut the gap, the sailor shouted at me, "Hold your course!" I replied, "A horse is a horse!" There is no proper course before the start, but rule 16 still applies; that means you have to protect the gap quickly.

TAKING DINNER OFF A PRO'S TABLE

by Peter Commette

The key for a good start is to control the person to windward of you. Stop your boat dead, as near to him as possible, with your bow at least a few feet in front of his. Don't be afraid to push your boom out to stop your boat, but never forget that you have to work with an acceleration buffer. Each boat's is different, but on average for small, one-design, high performance centerboard boats, it's about 10 seconds. I always tell my crew to trim in at 10 seconds, unless I say the rule is off.

"How do you protect your gap?" First of all, you want to take someone else's. That means coming in late and setting up no earlier than one minute before the start (one and a half to two minutes in good international competition). Second, you must be alert. Watch for port tackers and boats going behind you that might want to take YOUR spot. Let them see early on that you will protect it. Look them off. Make eye contact and let them know that you are watching them. When someone makes a movement for your hole, before he gets an overlap, bear off at right angles and place your boat across the gap. By placing your boat across the gap, you will force the other skipper to set up further to leeward of you or, more likely, to look somewhere else for another gap.

If the better gap is to leeward of the person whom you are faster than, then take the gap, stuff yourself up as near as possible to him, be careful of your mast coming to windward and hitting the windward boat as you glide through his lee, stop your boat bow out on him, and stuff him. Then, concentrate on trimming in before the boat to leeward of you. The key to trimming before them is to listen for the sound of ratchets and watch body and eye movements. (For that reason, I turn my ratchets off in light to medium air at the start.) If the better hole is to windward of the person whom you are faster than (I prefer this), work your gap so that you have something to bear off into and concentrate on trimming before he does.

I usually avoid starting near a pro. Sometimes, that is where the gap is, and for good reason, because he's fast and no one wants to be blown off at the start by him. However, every once in a while, when I find myself there, I just say to myself that I'm going to trim before he does. There is nothing like stuffing a pro on the starting line and taking dinner off a pro family's table. (I got that phrase from Carl Buchan.)

Duckboats! What's for dinner?!

ALTERNATIVE STARTS

Though the windward start with a line set between the pin and RC boat is most used, there are other start lines you might encounter. While it is doubtful you will ever see a downwind start, or a reaching start as seen in SailGP, the Rabbit Start is more common. The 505 fleet also uses it for their big regattas. The biggest event in windsurfing, Defi Wind, uses it to control the start of 1500 participants. Penalty? Getting run over by the RIB.

Photo: Weston

WINNING WAYS

Pulling a Rabbit Start out of the Hat

by Ed Baird

In our early days of Laser racing, some events were so large it could be impossible for Race Committees to set up fair starts. You can imagine that with over 100 boats on the line, picking out OCS boats was challenging. And once a few boats start pushing over, there were quickly too many to fairly identify and recall.

Event organizers learned that rather than having multiple recalls and resorting to a day of black flags, it was possible to get a fair start using a rabbit. A lottery-chosen competitor would sail upwind on port tack with a chase boat behind it. At the start time the fleet would cross behind the power boat and start racing. At an appointed time, the rabbit was freed and the line would close. If you started early, you were disqualified. If you started after the rabbit was freed, the power boat would have stopped, and you were behind the fleet. By starting in the time window, everyone was more or less even off the line and there were no recalls.

At one such Rabbit start in the Netherlands, I wanted to get to the left side of the course. I fought to be first to duck the rabbit when the start time opened. But as the rabbit got closer, I realized I was early and had to bail out. I turned down, reached off to gain space and then tacked. During the tack my mainsheet hooked on the transom, and I capsized. I quickly righted the boat, but the fleet was already several lengths ahead of me.

I started sailing on port tack to find a hole to tack into. With 130 boats it was a long way to the other end of the starting area, but as I sailed, I noticed I was gaining on the fleet. By the time I was halfway up the line I was only a length behind the front-row boats that were starting on starboard. Before reaching the starboard end of the start area I was starting to ease my main and reach behind the starboard boats. I finally found a nice hole and tacked into it. From there, the shifts were kind to me, and I finished 2nd in the race.

While I appreciated the result, the lesson learned was especially significant. The fleet, all sailing on starboard as they normally do off the line, was twisting the wind. As the only boat on port tack, I was experiencing a left shit that allowed me to gain up the ladder rungs of the course. With enough time and boats, the gain brought me several lengths closer to the front line and I could once again play the game.

This happens at the start and any time there are several boats crossing you on the opposite tack, like at the windward mark. As the wind flows onto and between the upwind boats their sails twist it a little, making it exit the sails as short-term shifts. Boats that cross close behind feel a small lift. If there are multiple boats crossing, that lift can be felt for as long as there are boats crossing ahead.

This lesson has stuck with me through all my racing. Even when match racing, when you're behind you can gain a little on your opponent by crossing close behind them. Enough so that smart opponents won't wait to cross you when they are ahead. They will tack where they are straight ahead of you to keep you from gaining in the lift you give them.

Check it out the next time you cross behind someone. You'll feel the boat want to point a little higher just before you reach their wake. And if there are several boats, you feel it for a longer time. The fleet is actually making wind shifts!

Ed has a truck follow him around to cart all his trophies. This one, for winning the America's Cup for the Swiss. I don't believe he got to keep it in his trophy room.

WINNING WAYS

KNOWING THE RULES

Without rules, there is no game. Whatever fleet you sail in, even social club races, play be the rules, and do your turns. It's good practice, makes friends.

As Bryan McDonald College Sailing HOFer and member of the College Sailing Rules Committee suggests, "If you really want to master the racing rules of sailing, it's easy—simply read 'The Case Book' by World Sailing (online), 'The Appeals Book' by US Sailing and 'Case Book' by the Royal Yachting Association. These are authoritative interpretations of the racing rules of sailing covering almost every aspect of the rule book. The actual rule book is an extremely dry read. These case and appeals books fill in the blanks, flesh out the nuances of the rules, give context and are amazing aids to any racer preparing to race, preparing for a protest or any scholar of the rules interested in learning more."

Even these guys have to play by the rules to win.
Photo: Bryan McDonald

As well, if you ever get the chance to attend a Dave Perry talk on the rules, count yourself lucky. Otherwise, you can find his seminar with online options.

Tom Pace: *At the leeward mark there is the greatest amount of conflict between boats. To make it safely around, I ALWAYS speak to the skippers around me. if nothing else, to make perfectly clear what I'M going to do just so that we can avoid those worst-scenarios of contact, protest, and penalty turns. Nobody wants that! Don't try to sneak in silently for mark room when you don't have it. It's a risky proposition.*

Paul Elvstrom: *Here is an important idea: If you are fair and a nice man to everybody, they will accept that you are first; if you're not, then nobody will accept you are first. So it's much easier to be first if you are nice. Let us say for instance, starboard/port. If the port is a little close to you, let him sail past you, because you shall pass him if you are better or you are faster. If there's doubt, let him go, because this man, he will always accept that you will beat him, because he felt you were so fair.*

KIDS SAY THE DARNDEST THINGS

by Stephanie Taylor

In many cases what is supposed to be a FUN youth regatta, can be turned into a pressure cooker for some. Not only is there the excitement of competition, but the weight of expectations from parents, coaches, and sometimes even the sailors themselves can be overwhelming. Managing all those dynamics while helping young sailors sharpen their skills can be a delicate balancing act.

Since our sport is self-policing, as Chief Judge at youth regattas, I always emphasize the importance of sportsmanship. C.S. Lewis wrote, "Integrity is doing the right thing even when no one is watching."

In the first race of a youth regatta, with super light air of 2-3kts, the incident occurred about halfway down the downwind leg. Joey and Susie were overlapped, approximately three boat lengths apart. Joey jibed twice and gained a lead of two boat lengths. A minute later, Joey performed three quick rocks and extended his lead to three boat lengths ahead of Susie.

Photo: Will Keyworth

Susie: "Hey Joey! Stop the rocking or I'm going to Protest!"

Joey: "No one protests for kinetics."

Susie: "I'm not no one and if you don't knock it off now, I'm going to yell, Protest for rocking."

The conversation continued as they sailed down the course toward the gate. Down that leg, Joey rocked a few more times for good measure.

Susie: "Okay, you asked for it. Protest, Sail 1934. Rocking."

Joey: "Shut up, *@#%!"

In the protest room, Joey got disqualified for using body movement to propel his boat forward. Additionally, due to his unsportsmanlike behavior, including cursing at a fellow competitor, his DSQ "disqualification" was changed to a DNE "do not exclude".

Susie did not have to hail the offending sailor's sail number, but if there are other boats around, it's a good idea to do so that it's made clear who is being protested. She is required to say, "Protest" loud enough for the sailor being protested to hear. Joey acknowledged, though not in a sportsmanlike manner.

Note: A protest by another sailor for Rule 42 cannot be exonerated by doing penalty turn(s). As seen in the Paris (Marseilles) Olympics in the ILCA classes, sailors being protested for kinetics by the Judges boat *could* exonerate themselves by doing turns.

If Appendix P was in place at the Paris Olympics, Judges would be on the water with yellow flags. Judges blow a whistle, hail the sail number and state the RRS42 infraction. Sailor is then required to do 2 penalty turns to exonerate themselves if so stated in the Race documents. To be clear, Appendix P enforcement is different than a sailor protesting another sailor for illegal "propulsion".

Lessons learned:

- Kudos to Susie for enforcing the rules and holding Joey accountable.

- Understanding and applying the rules can make a difference between winning and losing, not just on the water but in the protest room as well.

- For youth sailors especially, knowing when and how to protest is a critical skill. It's about protecting your rights, promoting fairness, and learning how to handle conflict constructively.

- Losing your cool and cursing at your competitors on the racecourse not only can you get tossed from the race, you could have harsher penalties imposed such as removal from the regatta or even future suspensions.

- Sportsmanship and the idea that a reputation built on honesty and fairness is a win in and of itself.

- Winning at all costs, especially through intimidation or unsportsmanlike conduct, disrespects the sport and undermines the spirit of fun competition.

AVOIDING COLLISIONS

by Annie Nelson Gardner

Typically, Annie only sails with two on the wire, but the conditions on this day called for a little extra pink and kneepads. Photo Sharon Green, Ultimate Sailing

When I was just getting back into catamaran racing, I chartered a Prindle 16 to race in the Women's National Championship. It was a beloved P16 owned by a fellow competitor. Fresh off retiring from professional windsurfing, I wanted to stick closer to home and start a family. High-performance catamaran sailing was the answer for my need for speed. The one design racing put my head in the game.

With a good friend as crew, Shirley was someone I knew and trusted. So, there we were, the last race of the day, blasting downwind. We jibed onto port. At first there were no boats to contend with on starboard. We thought for sure we were in the lead, but the discussion was lively as it was difficult to see with all the spray. Were we clear ahead or not? With speed comes deeper angles. Both of us concentrated hard on going fast and Shirley had her head swiveled watching for other boats. But with more wind benefiting those behind, it started looking like it would be closer than we originally thought. The top sailors in the fleet were closing in on us on starboard, at speeds of about 20+ knots. We hoped we might make it, but being out of practice, there was some serious hesitation.

There were two ways to get out of this predicament. One was to head up hard and go behind. This posed a risk of capsizing. Another choice was to crash jibe in front of the other boat, but it was already too late, and we risked collision. We should have jibed sooner, but by hesitating, it was already too late to make either decision. We held our course, hoping we might make it across.

Yet, the wind and ensuing shift were in her favor. She was screaming at us, "Starboard!" Our opponent would only have to alter her course slightly and yell protest. We would acknowledge the protest, do our penalty turns, and she would most likely win the race.

Being in a borrowed boat, I silently pleaded with her not to hit us. She chose to prove her point, hold her course, and crash into our hull. Well, not our hull, my friend's hull! We had a time of it separating the two boats. Then we started to sink. She yelled, "Protest." I yelled, "Protest!" "Protest! Rule 14! Avoiding contact!

At the protest meeting we were both found guilty. This result was the best I could have hoped for. I was guilty of Rule 10, port/starboard, and she for Rule 14, avoiding contact. That meant we split the cost for repairs.

RULE 14: AVOIDING CONTACT

14 Avoiding Contact If reasonably possible, a boat shall
   (a) avoid contact with another boat,
   (b) not cause contact between boats, and
   (c) not cause contact between a boat and an object that should be avoided.

However, a right-of-way boat, or one sailing within the room or mark-room to which she is entitled, need not act to avoid contact until it is clear that the other boat is not keeping clear or giving room or mark-room.

Author's note: In 2025, This rule became more strict. Not only do you need to avoid hitting other boats, but you also can't cause **contact between other boats** or between a boat and objects like RC boats. On with Annie's story:

While she went on to finish the race, we jumped onto the starboard side trying keep water out, limped over to an anchored boat. We eventually got towed in.

> Lessons learned: #1 Be familiar with the type of boat you're racing (and the rules). I was new to this class and was out of cat practice. Knowing the rate of turn, how the cat cradles in different conditions, all attributed to my misjudgment.
>
> #2 Always avoid a collision regardless of who has the right of way. If someone else causes the collision, even if you were the give-way boat, go ahead and say the word: "Protest." You have to say it. You need to inform the other party, or the protest won't be valid. The umpires or jury will then listen and decide if the other boat indeed tried to avoid a collision. In this case, there were witnesses. She didn't. We wound up 2nd overall, and I have no idea what place she ended up, but it wasn't first.
>
> #3 If you borrow or charter a boat, treat it like it's yours.

I was devastated having never been in a collision, much less causing it. I called my husband crying. I felt terrible for the hole in my friend's cat that I helped cause and was shaken by my own mistake of judgment, as I considered myself a good judge of time and distance. Thankfully, my husband put it all in perspective. "Well, at least it wasn't a 50-footer!"

RULE 17: SAME TACK, PROPER COURSE

Rule 17 has to be the most misunderstood rule in the book. Even top amateurs get this one wrong, and yell at other boats to sail their proper course at all points of sail, all stages of the race. It's as if luffing another boat has gone out of style. What fun would that be?! They would eliminate college sailing and one of my favorite moves – carrying a boat past the mark – altogether. Of course, you do this at the peril of losing other boats. Sometimes, that matters not a lick.

Rule 17 was only written to protect a boat being overtaken to leeward. When that happens, the now leeward boat, even though they have leeward/windward boat rights, must sail their proper course. In other words, you can't come

screaming up from behind, blanket another boat, take their lee, and luff them up. As long as that overlap exists, the windward boat can *yo ho ro ho* go about their way.

However, if the leeward boat separates themselves by two boat lengths (get out your measuring tape) to leeward, they can then come in for the Jimmy Spithill hook. They now have luffing rights, and the windward boat, perhaps holding a jar of Grey Poupon, can yell "Proper Course" till they're blue in the face. It won't cut mustard.

Rule 17: If a boat *clear astern* becomes *overlapped* within two of her hull lengths to *leeward* of a boat on the same *tack*, she shall not sail above her *proper course* while they remain on the same *tack* and *overlapped* within that distance, unless in doing so she promptly sails astern of the other boat.

In proper terms, Proper Course is the direction a boat would head toward the next mark, taking only into account an area of increased pressure, shift of wind (with a bit of insurance taken for good measure), or play of wave. You'd really have to make your case to alter it to head to the bar.

Secrets to Success in One Design Racing

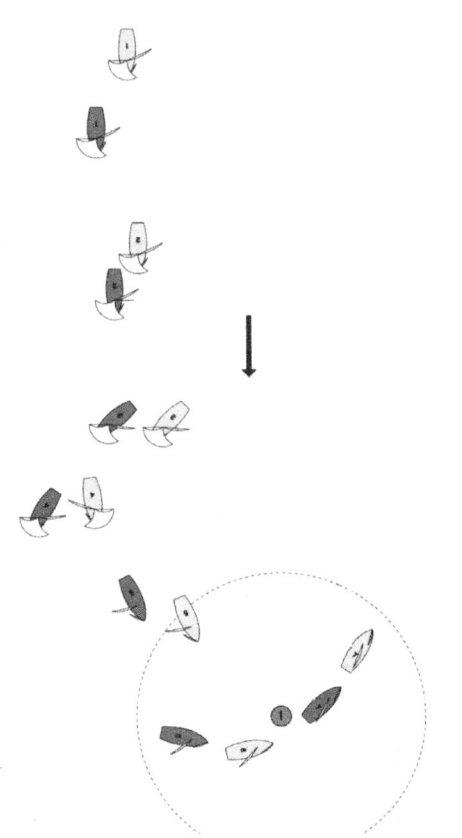
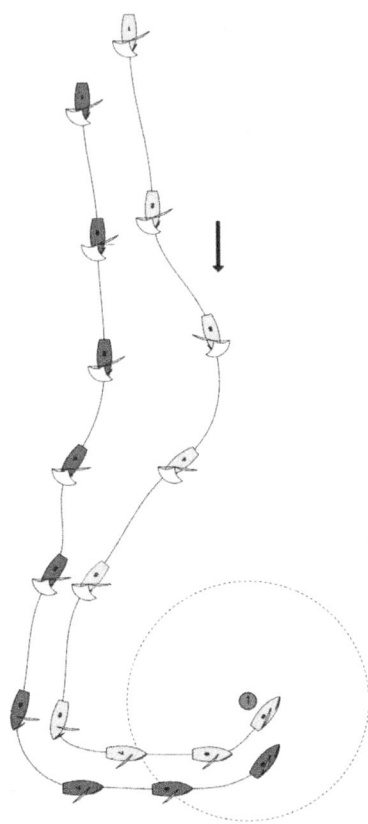

In the illustration left, yellow boat has overtaken blue boat. Blue boat can maintain their proper course. Yellow boat doesn't know the rule, so tries to head them off their proper course. Yellow boat is in the wrong. Foul!

In the illustration right, yellow boat has overtaken blue boat, however, they then separated by two boat lengths. Now yellow boat, as leeward boat, can take blue boat up and grab room at the mark. Smart move, yellow boat!

Int'l 420 Class Association Photo: Andrea Lelli

WINNING WAYS

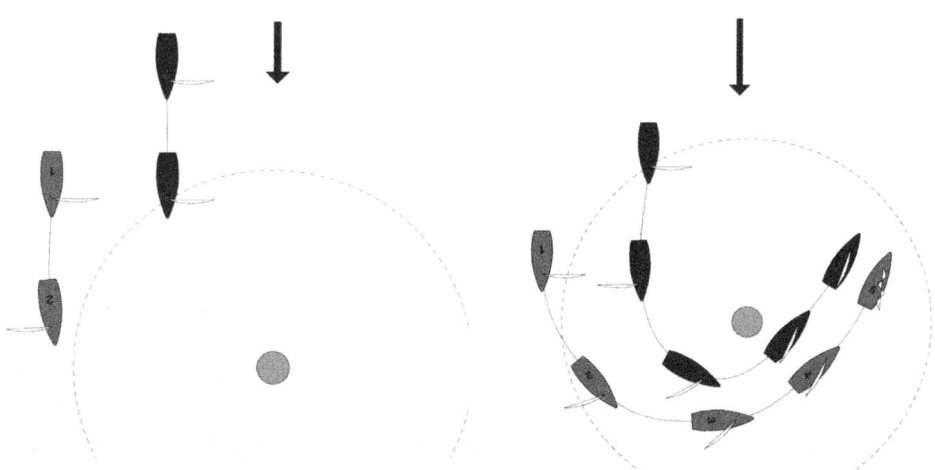

In the illustration left, red boat is clear ahead, but is not within the 3 boat length mark rounding zone. Black boat has entered the zone first, so black boat has room to round.

As much as red boat can shout for room, black boat has read the rules and can throw the book at them.

New Rule 18: You should always keep up with rule changes, and in 2025, Rule 18 was also slightly revised. Rule 18 has for the past few years at least, defined a three boat length "zone," around a mark. The boat clear ahead or with an inside overlap has within the old rules, room to round the mark. The alteration in 2025 basically states that whatever boat reaches the zone first gets inside room. There can be a case where an outside boat is clear ahead but sailing wide of the zone, allowing the boat behind to enter the zone first. It might rarely happen, but if it does, there you have it. No room for the clear ahead boat.

HOW TO LOSE A PROTEST

by Dick Lamb

Back in the day before one could take penalty turns, there were a lot more protests. If you fouled someone, even if you thought you'd probably lose your counter protest, for some sailors the attitude was you might as well roll the dice with the jury and see what happens. This was particularly true during the Windsurfer Team Sailing Championships held in the late '70's and early '80's. Some sailors who migrated from dinghy racing to windsurfing knew the rules cold, while the majority of Windsurfers knew the basics and then there were those who appeared to know nothing.

I was one of those unfortunates who was tasked with being on the jury for four Windsurfer Worlds and three Team Sailing Worlds. It seemed like every other protest (one Worlds had 70 protests in one day of racing) was between a Frenchman and a German; particularly in team sailing, as the rivalry between teams from those two nations was fierce.

While exonerating yourself on the course is a good idea if you know or think you fouled another boat, there are times when you think or know you're right and the other boat does too. Then the only alternative is a protest, and it is obligatory if there was contact between the boats and no one does turns. Often, it's a good idea to take a penalty turn to avoid getting DQ'd and then protest the other boat. You might lose a few boats, but it's better than the getting thrown out by the Jury. And, juries get it wrong. I was thrown out by a club pickup jury who didn't know rule 18 well; their decision was overturned on appeal.

Here's some sure ways to lose a protest:

Don't know and thoroughly understand the rule or rules you think your opponent broke. I remember many occasions when a sailor told the Jury "I didn't have to give him mark room, I was on starboard".

Don't make sure your witnesses agree with your story, keeping it truthful of course. I can still hear the Italian judge, speaking in French, during a hearing between two Frenchmen and their witness who had teamed up and fouled the leading German at the start line in the final race, but had given quite different accounts. We concluded the foul was intentional to boost their compatriot who stood second. The witness thrust a dagger through his countryman's protest. We also threw out the beneficiary of the collusion for unfair sailing, being quite sure he was in on it, thanks to implicating statements by the witness.

Don't explain the incident and which rule(s) apply and why. If the jury suspects you don't know the rules, then the odds against you go up tremendously, especially if the other party does know them.

Don't make sure to ask questions of the other party about the incident. If you can uncover inconsistencies and get them to be defensive or elusive, your story will be more credible. If their story is different, the jury will have to decide which is the most believable. Most juries can see through BS and attempts to tailor the incident to the rules, rather than the other way around. Telling the truth is the best way to win your case, as most people are terrible liars.

Don't show up when called. Most juries, especially if it's 1:00 am as it was for many of the team sailing protests, won't wait. You're unlikely to win a protest if your opponent is the only one who shows up. That happened a surprising number of times. If you're not willing to wait around the protest room while everyone else is partying, then don't protest. Or better yet, avoid fouls as best you can or do your turns.

GOOD SPORTSMANSHIP

Harold Gilreath Sr. was one of the top two competitors on the lakes of Atlanta. The other top dog was Ted Turner. Being a junior in Harold's employment at his rigging shop, I had the good fortune of crewing for him on all types of boats. After a race, Ted would commonly attack Harold with verbal warfare that would shock not just a kid, but the ears of George Carlin. Ted wasn't called The Mouth of the South for no reason. While Harold would win Snipe Nationals, Ted would not only win the America's Cup, but the Flying Dutchman Worlds as well. Talk about bragging rights. But I'd much rather have dinner with Harold.

"If in the process of winning, you have lost the respect of your competitors, you have won nothing." Paul Elvstrom

LtoR: Ted Turner/Jim Markley, Harold Gilreath/Lindsey Walthers, Warner Guedry/Brad Foss, Atlanta YC Open (Lake Alatoona) 1966!

Being a good sport is one of the trademarks of a sailor. World Champion Snipe Sailor, Kim Couranz, says in one of her many great Spinsheet magazine articles: *"Just because you can do something doesn't always mean you should. That "just one more" rum and coke, just because there's an already opened can of soda? Maybe not a good idea. Polishing off the tray of lasagna, because you're "just helping to clean up"? Not if you're trying to be healthy. Tacking on a random competitor halfway up the first beat, just because they're there? Nope, not okay."*

My last word for this chapter is that after you cross the finish line, if you win, don't gloat. Congratulate your competitors.

STRATEGY AND TACTICS

Mike Martin, 505 Worlds — Photo: Bryan McDonald

FIRST BEAT

The gun has sounded, your engine started. Time to put your foot on the gas. Are *you* ready to rumble? Winning the start will certainly give you a leg up on the fleet, but the first weather leg defines the outcome more than any other. The first leg typically determines, if not the winner of the race, at least the top five. You can make a lot of mistakes on the following legs and still have a good result but screw up that first weather leg and without superior boat speed, you're toast.

The first weather leg is the most complex and advantageous leg of the race-course, and the second/third weather leg is played completely different than the first. Therefore, it's necessary to break the weather legs down into several segments, to chunk it out, to fully understand how to navigate the course and execute winning tactics. Let's take a fine comb to how you can either fall apart like schist stone or shine like a diamond.

GET THE BOAT MOVING

There's a saying: boat speed trumps tactics. Boat speed certainly enables your choice of tactics, and there is no better time for boat speed than right off the bat. The boat that gets off the line with speed will have the opportunity to keep going or to tack. The boat that does not will have to either start on the RC boat end and tack right away, or if anywhere else on the line, wait for others to tack. Or duck boats. Or bang the left corner. Get the boat moving fast, and you won't have to do any of the above.

Mike Martin: *The biggest difference between a mid fleet sailor and people at the front is speed. You can be the greatest tactician on the racecourse but if you don't have top of the fleet speed, you will not be able to execute those tactics. So whatever it takes, tuning, gear, practice, get up to speed and then the tactics get easier.*

The closer you sit to the start line before the gun goes off, the longer it's going to take you to get up to speed after the start, particularly if you've parked on the line, luffing at a higher point of sail than close hauled. The good guys can sit on the line with their sail(s) luffing at a reaching angle dead stop. As the gun goes off, they sheet in and go. They get the boat moving. Don't forget to vang on in breeze but get the boat moving first if moving off the rail is required to do this. Not all boats have controls conveniently located where you hike.

In highly kinetic boats like the ILCA, you might see sailors give it a few body pumps off the line (sharp hikes to weather) for good measure. To what degree you can legally pump is a fleet by fleet, regatta by regatta judgement. I now see Olympic 470 crew out on the trapeze pumping the crap out of the boat. Who knew? Don't do it, and you quickly fall into bad air. The action effectively fans the leech and the boat forward. (In the Windsurfer LT Class, for better or worse, sail pumping is legal for 30 seconds after the start). In larger, less kinetic boats, a heeled roll back to weather combined with a quick sheet in at the start can be effective.

Whatever you do within the rules, get the boat trimmed and moving. That means loosely trimmed sails (in most classes) and a properly heeled (or not heeled) boat. As soon as the boat is up to speed, then you can trim the sails tighter; not before.

The common mistakes I see a lot of people make are to, a) bear off from a head to wind position as the gun goes off, placing a lot of pressure on the blades, and b) trying to point from the get-go. They look at other competitors, who thirty seconds after the start, are pointing five to ten degrees higher. They tighten their sails even more, choking the main leech and the jib slot. Now they are really wondering what the heck just happened. They go home and sand their blades some more, perhaps order some new sails. Or sell the

Photo: Will Keyworth

boat and find another one that points better.

It's like taking up golfing, shanking a few in the woods, then buying some new Nike clubs. They might shank it into the woods further, but they're still going to repeat the same behavior. Good for the ball companies and the sailmakers I suppose but to get the boat pointing and moving (you knew I'd get around to it), you have to first get the water rushing over the centerboard. That big blade down there (unless you forgot to put it down after the last race... another matter... obtw, your glasses are on top of your head). Let's start over. That big blade down there, it's your lifting tool. If the water is not rushing over it, you're not going to point worth a blip.

Get the water moving over the blade. Get the boat moving. Then you can point, tack, choose your side of the course, or play the middle.

Dave Rink: *The most common ailment of going slow is an overly trimmed mainsail. As a result, the sailor appears to be pointing high – the boat is pointed at a higher angle to the wind – so this builds their confidence and makes them think they're doing the right thing. However, they're going slow and their VMG is terrible. Where I see this most often is at the start. They're trying to force the windward boat away but going slow at the start is the absolute worst time to be slow. You want to be come off the line at full speed, go fast, and separate from the fleet. If you go fast, that will give your boat lift, resulting in true pointing VMG. This speed plus height will equal VMG, naturally taking care of that windward boat.*

For the first weather leg, you should go in having a plan, developed from your pre-race reconnaissance, line checking and past regatta experience. That plan should include which side of the course you will aim to get to, and at what point on the weather leg you will make your way over there.

You should also be constantly aware of where the weather mark is in relation to the start line. Was the mark set perfectly, the wind not veering one way or the other since the mark was dropped? I'd wager it is no longer centered, at start time favoring one long tack over the other.

Following golden rule in sailboat racing, what are you trying to find? You guessed it! The pressure.

FIND THE PRESSURE

Let's say you had a good start with clear air. Now you need to get your head out of the boat – or use your crew's eyes if not – to start scanning again for pressure. You planned to go left, but then you see some darker water over where that pontoon boat is fishing. Winds will shift and pressure will change. It doesn't just sit there like slalom sticks in the snow. The best way to determine how much the wind has shifted from those readings you recorded before the start. That's why it's good to get out on the racecourse an hour early, to see what wind or current patterns (if applicable) might be developing.

DARK WATER

Andy Burdick

Growing up sailing on Inland Lakes and having early success one theme would always ring true. Get in the dark water (the wind) and sail the lifted tack. Meaning, get in the wind, if you are headed, tack and sail the lift. Pretty easy right? As we all know it is never that easy.

My MC racing started back in 1987. I am still racing these great boats. One moment in time really stands out in my MC sailing career. It was at White Lake, Michigan. The National Championship. Over 100 boats on the starting line. I had a string of consecutive National Wins and this event was marked on my calendar for a year in advance. It was the big event.

You sort through all the "musts" as you prepare for the championship. One "must" was to make sure you sail clean. No fouls, don't over commit to one side or the other, don't be over the starting line. Sail Smart, Sail Clean.

We line up with over 100 boats on the line. The line is pin end favored so I set up near the pin. Thinking to myself the entire time, "stay clean, don't be anxious don't be over the line". As I watch the starting time countdown on my compass, I feel myself pressing the line. The starting gun goes off and I know that I was close to the line. I could see the race committee's eyes sighting down the line from the flag and I could tell that I was close. Sure enough, they call my number. Race one of the event!

My boat heads down and I dodge a few late starters at the pin end and I round the leeward pin boat on port. Trimming up could sense the massive port lift with good pressure even though I am in bad air from the other competitors. 100 boats! I am ducking all of them! As I am ducking though I can notice that the port end leaders are not tacking. Everyone is pinching and going slow.

Finally, I duck the final starboard boat, all the way from the other end of the line. I sail the entire distance on port and pop out into clear air. Still being lifted all I can think about is dark water, lifted tack. As I look up the lake in an attempt to view the wind and get into phase I see a new line of breeze rolling down the lake. Dark water!

The majority of the fleet is now on my hip, on port tack but headed. As I approach the new wind on port tack I get headed. Over 20 degrees! In the dark water and now tacking to starboard only to view the entire fleet tacking under me. I can view it through my mainsail window!

Ducking over 100 boats after being over the line was not the way I wanted to start off my national championship run. But, after getting clear air, the basics of sailboat racing kicked in. Dark water lifted tack. This propelled me to win the first race and the regatta.

The basics in sailboat racing will get you ahead every time.

STRAIGHT UP THROUGH COMPTON

While I'm all for choosing a side of the course to gain advantage, if there is no current or shoreline lift or an unopened can of IPA sitting on a dock,

2025 Flying Scot Midwinters John Cole Photography

Sean O'Donnell (5171) leading a pack of boats up the middle of Lake Eustis. Sean's one of those guys who seems to always get it right... right up the middle, until he decides that one side of the course has more pressure lifting toward the mark. Always on the long tack, thinking one step ahead, he's not the guy you want on your lee bow and certainly not blocking your wind. 6090, time to tack out! 5787, you're about to get outpointed (cunningham more slack on Sean's main, weight forward).

I'm playing the middle. The further to one corner of the course you sail, the further you will have to travel if the other side of the course rears its beautiful dark water patchy head. Unless it's crystal clear – I'm like a beer importer – a middleman.

Only in light air and fleet traffic do you want to avoid the middle. There is a great deal of backwash when boats are crossing back and forth, particularly in a multi-class fleet. It's most often better to favor one side or the other.

Of course, a boat can't physically head up the middle, so what do I mean by that? The general middle. By playing the shifts strategically to keep your boat sailing on the long tack, you will keep to the general middle of the racecourse. You're taking the shortest path to the mark. Only if there is much greater pressure on the extended path will it make sense to do otherwise.

Things at the start may go according to plan or they may not. I'd place the gravy on my biscuits they will not. Once that gun has fired, or horn sounded,

everything is in flux, and that's what makes one racer better than another: the ability to flex your flux muscles, to change the plan on a dime. To not flux it up.

SITUATION: Lucy Luffed You Up

But suppose you just did flux it up; you didn't time your port tack approach and find a nice gap next to a turkey though not complete turkey as planned. You did just what that author said not to, and picked a spot on the line too early, just to weather of Lucy Luffyupp. The gun sounds, and Lucy has started with more speed, a running start. She has her boat going upwind like dynomite. In effect, she is pinching you up and the fleet is charging away on all sides. What do you do?

    a) Pray for a General Recall.

b) Stall, drop back, bear off with speed, and sail through Lucy's lee.

c) Tack away and start ducking boats.

d) Stay your course and hope to out-pinch and out-speed Lucy.

Solutions:

a) At least jot down in your Playbook, "Never start to windward of Lucy Luffyupp." You're going down in flames.

b) Unless there is a small fleet and you are by far the fastest in it, this is like walking in the shadow of death. Don't yield to temptation.

c) Tack away. If you chose, C, you are the ducky winner. Tack quick and quack quack, just do it. Even if you have to stall and bear off to get room to tack and duck, suck it up and like a stinky old Nike shoe, just do it.

d) Sit there, get gassed. Wonder what the heck just happened.

Even with the best laid plans, you're probably aware of the challenges you face. For example, if you've had a bad start in a big fleet, you have a big hole to climb out of. You must use your observational powers to analyze the situation you've put yourself into and figure out how to get out of it. The quicker you can react to adversity, the sooner you'll be on your way to correcting course. It's time to put all your preconceived strategy of going left on that first leg and focus on getting out of that bad situation. Otherwise, it will be your throw-out.

SITUATION: Port Shift

When you checked the line at the Preparatory signal (4 minutes to go), the weather mark and line were set square. Good job, RC! Thirty-seconds before the start, the wind has clocked left a good twenty degrees. As you were following a pre-start plan of approaching on port, you were only halfway down the line toward the RC boat end when the shift occurred. You tacked and made your way toward the pin, barely making the line. You've got good speed, close hauled and only two boats between you and the pin. One boat port tacked the fleet, while the two boats ahead clear her stern and bang, they've tacked over as well. You'd like to do the same, but now you've hesitated. There are a couple of boats right on your hip to windward. What do you do?

a) Kick yourself for not tacking right away onto the long tack.

b) Continue on and enjoy the header.

c) Bear off to give yourself room to tack and then duck the two boats.

d) Yell at the two boats on your hip. "Let's go, Bob! Tack! We're overstanding!"

e) Pinch up to entice the two boats to tack.

Solutions:

a) Kick yourself hard. You should have tacked as soon as you cleared the shadow of the two boats ahead. This would put you on the long tack and making the best VMG.

b) You're most certainly out of phase with the wind shifts. You'll probably bang the corner and overstand the mark for good measure.

c) Bearing off and ducking is the second-best option, since you didn't take the first. Just make sure you follow the ducking directions, or Bob will tack on top of you.

d) Actually, sometimes this works. It will at least plant a seed in their head that they need to tack.

e) This is a good tactic but can take too long to pull off. Yet, anytime you have a boat on your hip and want to tack, pinching up will do the trick. If you loosen your Cunningham, having the draft back in your sail will help you pinch, as well as trimming the main of course.

If there is no real indication of which side of the course is favored, quick efforts should be made to get onto the long tack as quickly as possible. That way, when you hit the next header, you can make shorter work of the short tack. Eventually, as you travel toward the weather mark, the long tack becomes the short tack, in which case you need to get on the new long tack.

DONT LOOK BACK

If you have the luxury of a crew who can call tactics, search out the pressure, tell you whether your up or down on the wind and report relativity to the fleet, as skipper and helm, you should focus on making the boat go fast.

WINNING WAYS

Monty Spindler: *Singlehanding is different from double handed and more crew... when alone, the helmsman has to do it all. When helming with crew, the skipper should be laser focused on boat speed both upwind and downwind. Looking upwind*

for wind- shifts and strengths- and position relative to the fleet, is best left to the crew so that the skipper can concentrate on boat speed... with an occasional gaze upwind.

Dave Perry: *When I am driving, I try to look at my jib telltales and the water in front of the bow. I am in "speed mode." But I always have a trusted tactician sitting next to me whose head is 100% out of the boat watching the fleet, looking for tendencies in the wind, and for clear air lanes going the way we want to go. When you are sailing singlehanded, you have to have a great feel for the boat so you can spend time with your head out of the boat while still going fast through the water.*

Peter Commette: *I'd agree that looking back when going upwind or on a reach is probably not going to help you much, except for those times you might get to gloat. When I'm racing, a large majority of my focus is placed on my system. I have rules for everything. For upwind and reaching, the rule says, in progression, look over your shoulder for wind and boat angles, forward at 45 degrees for waves and wind, the leading edge telltales, the upper jib leach telltales, upper mainsail telltales, and then progress back the other direction. It's my standard rotation of the head one way and then back to the other. Each stop does not get the same amount of time, but no stop is left out.*

Keep your head inside the boat and you're going to miss out on all that outside information; where's the pressure, on which side is the fleet lifting, (and if a multi-fleet regatta) what are other fleets experiencing? Of course, you have to be locked in on speed when blasting off the line but focus too much on small incremental details within the boat and you may miss out on a big shift. Big shift, big gains.

Notice you didn't hear me say anything about the compass. I try not to be a slave to the compass. If I have a good crew, they'll feed me that information; but singlehanded, I've got my head outside the boat. On a boat like the E Scow, where I might have three excellent crew feeding me information, I feel that as skipper, you still have to be the one to make the call.

SAILING BY THE NUMBERS (USING A COMPASS)

I'm not a sail by the numbers guy. Being the creative type I was never good with math. And here's that math I'm not good at: $450 bucks for a Tacktick. That's a lot of Tictacs. I'd rather buy new sails with my lunch money.

I prefer to sail intuitively, to go by long developed seat of shorts skills, using objects on the shoreline and my position relative to the fleet. You don't need a compass to know when half the fleet is lifting ten or more degrees higher than you are. I also believe that new racers should forgo the compass. It's better to keep your head out of the boat, to spend your time in regatta developing intuitive skills, as opposed to staring at a compass. That said, if you have a crew to take that focus, let them feed you with the information in a way that takes little brain space: "We're up five." or, "We're down ten." Not, "195, 196, 198, back to 197." I'd rather hear, "Joey just tacked!" There are a lot of other things to occupy my mind.

The Laser Class legalized digital compasses after the Rio Olympics. Upon legalization winning out, there were three legal options, the Nautalytics Simple, the Velocitek, and the Ticktack. I couldn't tell you which is best. I rarely look at them even when they're placed on a charter boat. I'd go through the entire regatta, then when unrigging, go, "Oh yeah! A compass! Speedpuck!" Call me a Luddite, but I know when I'm going slow or fast in the wrong direction, and when I'm going in the right. I'm winning the race! The answer my friends is not blowing in the wind. It's right up there on the score sheet.

But... but... but, Sir. You just wrote to get out on the course an hour early to check the compass readings. How do you do that without a compass? If the line is set early, or at least the committee boat, I will get on starboard tack and see what land object I'm pointing at. If a half hour later, I'm looking at a house to the left or right of that reference point, I'll have a good clue which direction the wind is veering. Or maybe the wind is just oscillating back and forth. Either way, it helps to calm the nerves.

It's a lot easier to know when you're being headed than when you're being lifted. A header worth tacking on is going to ragdoll the sail(s). Bright sunlight with white sails can disguise the leeward telltale, so you have to feel that lift in the tiller. What am I keeping an eye on? It's not a compass. It's the fleet. It's the telltales. Dead telltales do not tell a lie.

Ed Baird will tell you just the opposite, and with an America's Cup, Laser Worlds, and a ton of other trophies that could fill a shipping container, it's hard to say he's going about things the wrong way. However, a lot of his latter experience was winning the round the world Whitbread Cup, and the high stakes TP52 Worlds multiple times. There is certainly a time and place for a compass, even on a Laser.

Paul Elvstrom: *To calculate where the wind is moving before the start, I begin sailing upwind once I am near the course area and notice my compass headings. I might notice that I was pointing one way for two minutes, then I was pointing lower, etc. So I know what are the high compass direction, and the low. Then I say the highest we had three-quarters of the time, the low for one-quarter of the time, and from that I calculate an approximate median. Whenever the wind changes, there is a good possibility that it will come back, unless there's an obvious reason why it won't. For instance, the starboard is very high, so I stay on starboard because there is a very good chance it will go back.*

As the race progresses, and I'm behind, I will use the other boats to tell me when I will get the wind shifts, and take the benefit of them, because sometimes people bear away in headers and wait a little to see if they will stay.

Dave Perry: *When I am sailing very near land, I do not use a compass. But when I am in open water, I rely pretty heavily on the compass.*

Maru Urban Clinics Photo: Hannah Lee Noll

Annie Gardner: *Using instruments is great, but only if you don't depend solely on them. Too many compasses are not swung and aren't even consistent tack to tack. Instruments need to be calibrated often, and most aren't. Getting my head out the boat is a priority, and it's a constant cross check (like an instrument pilot) to grasp everything quickly and make quick decisions and good judgment calls.*

Tom Pace: *No compass... grew up racing windsurfers, and for me it has always been the feel of highest upwind angle without choking speed, and deepest angle downhill for shortest distance to the mark.*

Monty Spindler: *I like a compass especially when starting an upwind leg- to reference the wind based on the previous beat. A compass is always handy!*

Let's hear from Ed Baird about how a compass helped him when he hadn't the foggiest:

FINDING MY WAY

By Ed Baird

When I was 20, I had never raced dinghies with a compass. Digital compasses didn't exist and the weight and size of compasses big enough to see easily and be reliable was too much for small boats. On keel boats they were worth having, but for smaller boats most of us got used to "feeling" shifts or seeing them in relation to the fleet.

That summer I met a Swedish guy who had found a way to attach a removable mount with an easily readable compass on the Laser and asked me to try his invention out. In a national Laser event, I brought the compass along for the first time and tried to use it to monitor shifts. It was helpful—more as a confirmation tool—but not invaluable, until the day the cold front arrived.

I was in 6th place at the last mark and headed for an upwind finish line. There was a squall line to the right that was ahead of an approaching cold front. I worked out towards the right side of the course looking for more wind and a right shift with the rain that was approaching the course.

The shift came and the wind veered from SW to W, building from 12-25 as it hit. The fleet was suddenly all on starboard tack, fetching the finish line. The rain closed in fast and I could see it was going to obscure visibility. I reached into my big boat experience and sighted a heading for the finish line on my new compass. The rain hit and I couldn't see anything. I kept hiking and tried to stay on the compass course.

After a few minutes I felt like I should be approaching the finish line and started to look around. Through the blinding, stinging rain, it was barely visible to windward about 100 yards (about 91.44 m) away. I tacked away from my closest competitor and headed for the line. As I crossed it there was a gun, which I wasn't expecting. It seemed like they thought I had won the race! Boats just behind me crossed the line and got horns, acknowledging their finishes.

A couple of minutes later the rain dissipated and you could start to see the whole course. The boats that had been ahead of me had all missed the line and sailed into the shallows beyond the finish area. Skippers were standing on the sandbar holding their boats and as soon as they could see they jumped back aboard and headed for the line. Some sailors had capsized. Others had sailed past the line on the upwind side. Chaos!

Some sailors complained that the race was unfair. But with the right tool, it was not hard to find the way to the finish line. Needless to say, I never left my compass behind again. Lesson learned!

Ed Baird enjoying a bit of weather. I'd wager that even if he was without a compass, he would have sensed the finish line. But getting used to sailing with a compass did not hurt his future years as a big-time big boat skipper.

Mike Martin: *We use the Tacktick compass anytime that we are sailing upwind. We always get headings before the start of the race and are always aware if we are lifted or headed.*

In the 505 class it is not allowed to have any data correlation while racing. We do however sometimes track our practice sessions and look at the data. In other classes where it is allowed, I think there is a huge amount to be gained by collecting and sharing data of the races.

BY THE TELLTALES

What am I looking at the most? When not looking around for pressure and checking my position relative to the fleet, it's the tell tales. In flat water, it's easy to know when you've been knocked by a header: the sail is luffing. The challenge comes when knowing you've been lifted, particularly in light wind or a sea state. The tell tales tell the best tale. I'll get more into this in the sail trim chapter and tell the tale about which tell tales I'm looking at the most. Pardon the interjection but felt the need to explain where I'm placing the majority of my concentration. For it is the power of concentration that will bring you to the top of the fleet.

TACKING ON THE FIRST SHIFT

Thinking Jordi Zammar, winner of Sail GP 2004, knows when to tack on the first shift, though his crew, Nora Brugman, may have called it. Also to note, the incredible boat handling skills, including the backwinding of the jib to speed the rotation.
Int'l 470 Class European Championships, AleN Photography: Nikos Alevromytis

Going to weather, the rich often get richer. What does that mean? A new boat? A new car? No, it just means that you not only sail into greater pressure first, but are the first to get to into phase playing the shifts. To do that, you most often will tack on the first solid shift *with pressure* that comes your way, placing you on the *long tack*. This will place you on a shorter trajectory toward the weather mark while sailing at higher speeds. You're also sailing free and clear of disturbed air. Hitting that first shift, if it's a solid one, will place you on that shortened path to success.

Yet, grabbing the lead is not always about tacking on the first shift that comes your way, and certainly not about tacking on every shift that comes your way.

You still have the goal of sailing toward more pressure. If you're headed toward dark horses and a sucker shift lures you on a path away from it, do not heed! Charge forth on the header toward the higher pressure.

More often on a lake than by the sea or on the sea, you will encounter these sucker shifts. They often arrive with sucker puffs. There is no magic dragon involved. You get a small header and tack, which quickly turns into another header, and you tack. Essentially, you've slowed your boat to a dead stop and made zero VMG. You grab a beer, chug it down, and hope for a better outcome. This is called...

OVER TACKING

Do you have shifty eyes, or an eye for shifts? If you keep calling tacks more than is beneficial, your crew if you have one, might roll their eyes and think, *Gee Skipper, you're so over tacking.* Even as a single hander, you will most likely be kicking yourself in the cockpit as you lose boats for over tacking. Unless you have a significant wind shift, it's wise to get on and stay on the long tack. On lakes in particular, wind shifts can last as little as ten seconds and shift right back. It could just be a wind disturbance, so it's important that if you're going to tack on a shift, dig into it for a few seconds. There are multiple reasons for this, making racing up the windward leg so challenging and exciting.

Paul Elvstrom: *Once you have started and are sailing upwind, and the boats begin to tack away, it is most important for you to sail your own tactics. If you see that you won't gain by tacking, don't tack. If you tack just because others are, then you are only following, waiting for them to pass you. You must not be weak and say, 'I think its better to follow the fleet.' Because you are not the winning type, you are the careful type. And the careful type is never the winner because of this.*

Here is another important rule: When you are sailing upwind and you feel you cannot point as well as you'd like to do, then keep the speed. If you get a header, bear off and keep the speed -speed, speed, and speed. And then if you see the advantage by tacking, tack, and always keep the speed. And when you have bad luck, or when you are on your own, don't try and point the boat too high or force the wind. Bear off and think, speed, speed, speed. And if you stay calm and work hard, you will go fast and point well, and soon you will have good luck, too.

Tom Pace: *Lakes can be fantastic, and also fantastically shifty. If your boat handling is pretty good, tack on almost every shift on the lake, but in tradewinds or more steady ocean conditions, I keep tacks to a minimum to get the race done in the shortest distance sailed as you can while playing the major shifts. If the breeze is coming off the ocean as opposed to being disturbed by land, it will often clock in one direction, rather than rapidly shift. This is why it's important to travel to regattas to get a handle on it all.*

Below, Tom Pace on his way to winning the venerable Fish Championships (in a bay, actually), proving that sailing fast boards in fact does translate to winning on old restored and classic boats. He's a big fish on land, too, as Commodore of Pensacola Yacht Club, where they host not only major world championships, but American Magic as well.

LIFTING FLEET TO WEATHER

Aside from a poor start, the toughest hole to dig out of is when the fleet is lifting to weather, hence on a trajectory taking them closer to the mark than you. This typically happens with a wind sheer, just as you're feeling great about nailing the pin end with speed, counting your chickens to cross the fleet on the next header. The header doesn't come; the fleet is lifting and lifting hard. You're sheerly not on it. But don't give up yet, not if you're *Betty Boatspeed* or smartly, *Charley Cutyourlosses*.

CUTTING YOUR LOSSES

Aside from a poor start, the toughest hole to dig out of is when the fleet is doing just that, lifting to weather. If I only had a nickel for when I did not cut my losses. But how do you cut your losses? And what the heck do I mean by this? I was once traveling through Nevada and stopped at a gas station with a slot machine inside. Just as I walked in the door, an old codger put a coin in, pulled on the lever and out came a fountain of coins. I'd guess there was over 5 grand spilling into his bucket. When that bucket was half full, not one ounce of emotion was written on that man's face. It was half empty. He just grabbed one of the coins, pulled the handle, and fed the machine again.

What was the point of that story? The man did not know when to cut his losses. I asked him why he wasn't elated at the windfall. He simply stated, "Took me 30 grand to get just that." How this relates to sailing, I'm sure you've guessed by now. Let's go back. The fleet is lifting on you. You have two choices: a) keep going and hope for windfall. b) cut your losses. What does B involve? A gut check, for one. You've got to get over to the side of the course that's winning. And that means one thing:

THE ART OF DUCKING

Just like there is a science to rounding a mark, there is an art to ducking a boat. Most importantly, you need to crack the sails off and not wait until the last second to duck. The earlier you start ducking, the less arc you will make, the less speed you will kill. You'll actually gain some, so that when you come up on the stern of a starboard boat, you are sheeting in with good speed, using the lift from their backwash to gain a bit to weather, and pull back even with that boat.

It's just like Ed said. Nine times out of ten, when you meet those boats you just ducked again, you will be on starboard, often so far ahead it won't even matter. Why? If the wind is phasing in the direction your heading, once you tack, you will be lifting over those who were lifting over you. Amen.

Ducking is not just about ducking starboard boats when on port tack. It also works the other way around. Be loud! Let them know to keep going.

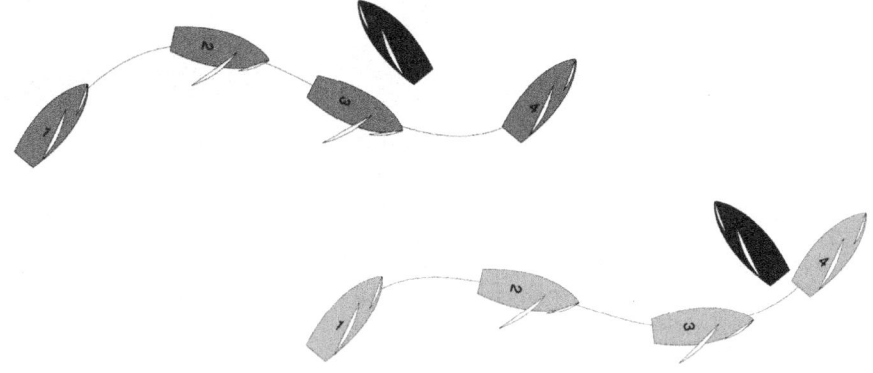

Dave Rink: *When 2 boats meet going upwind somebody is going the wrong way. If you're on starboard and want to keep going on starboard, just wave that port tack boat across. If you yell "starboard", that boat is going to tack to starboard and lee bow you. Now you're in bad air and have to tack off the favored tack. Instead, just dip that port tack boat and keep going the way you want to go. As well, if perfectly on or above the layline to the weather mark, and a boat approaching on port is even steven to just slightly ahead, wave them on. Every yard (or meter) they carry on will see them that much further behind when they tack. They've overshot the mark.*

CUT YOUR LOSSES RANDY

Any regatta held in his backyard, Choctawhatchee Bay, FL... US Sailing HOF'er Randy Smyth usually won. Any regatta not held there; he won as well. At the 2018 US Multihull Nationals... being held there, Dave Berntsen

won a couple of the windy races to kick off that regatta, and I placed second. This worked out well as we both gave a talk that night titled, "Heavy Weta." But then came the light air days, the drifters. If I must write so myself, I played it smart. I followed Randy. We took 1,2. Berntsen did not follow Randy and a few other big names finished in the 30's out of 50 boats.

I had never spoken much to Randy before, he's an absolute legend. My tongue would tie in three bowlines. But he sat at my table that night. I thought he might be a little ticked off by our free clinic, as he often puts on clinics and rightly charges for them (I know, the book should be free, right? Bezos gets the lion's share anyway). Perhaps our little speech about sailing in heavy air might have rubbed him the wrong way. But he said, "I heard your talk last night. Not bad. I agree with most of it. But what impressed me wasn't your heavy air sailing. It was your light air sailing." That was like Steph Curry telling you your slam dunks are pretty good, but what he's really impressed with is your passing. So, on the next day, I followed Randy again so I could do a lot more passing.

We both didn't need to do much passing as we hit the middle of the line running. He's much lighter and thus, going faster than me, so I was hoping to hang onto his heels by some magnetic vortex. It was working. We were enjoying our lead over the fleet, playing the middle-left side. All of sudden, the right started to lift bigtime. More pressure, the whole ball of wax. I was hoping

that by continuing left, those on the right would run out of luck and the left would pay off. How quickly the tide turned. We were both now a good twenty boats now upwind of us. *Gooshfavah!* (It's English... *Anger Management* movie reference).

Randy cut his losses. He tacked and headed to the right; even he could take a few lumps to the chin. Dummy me, I kept going for what would be about twenty seconds too long, completely falling out of phase. Randy dug a little further right than the pack that was ahead, and with his boat speed, nearly led the fleet to the mark. Only Cam Farrah was in front of him. Fortunately, the wind crapped out and the race was canceled, but I'll remember his tactic of cutting his losses. And Cam remembered that she could lead the fleet, winning the following Wetafest regatta. Below is Miranda Powrie. She was intimidating the fleet the previous year (her sister, Polly Powrie, NZ Gold Medalist in 2012 Olympics.

TAKING YOUR GAINS

Just as you should sometimes cut your losses, even if it means going onto the short tack, you should take your gains. Tack. Cross the fleet. Don't get greedy.

However, you need to be confident in doing so. Are there boats so close to you that they will be the ones making gains on you if you tack away out of more pressure? Something to consider when rolling that dice, but if you're out there with a decent lead and the pressure is on, go for it, mate.

LEE BOW SQUEEZE PLAY

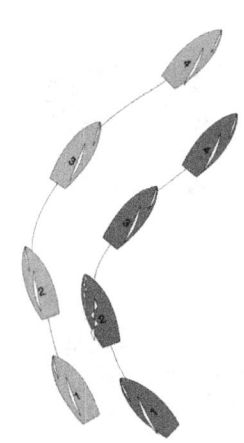

If you feel like you'll give up too much of your gains by ducking sterns, think about tacking into a lee bow situation. Most people do this as they don't want to give up valuable distance gained. It makes perfect sense when you were planning to tack anyway to get onto the long tack. Depending on how close you cut it, lee bowing is an aggressive maneuver that requires great tacking skill and acceleration. The risk is blowing the tack, slow acceleration, or a combination of both? You'll simply get mowed over.

Just be careful not to tack too closely. If the other boat is forced to alter course, they're likely to call the foul; it's not worth it. A squeeze play is always a good idea if you know you are the faster boat. Bad idea if you're not.

Maru Urban Clinics   Photo: Hannah Lee Noll

DON'T BANG THE CORNERS

"Banging the corners" is rarely a good strategy. What do I mean by the corners? Banging the corners means heading all the way over to one side of the course. You have probably gone on the short tack to get there, on a gamble to escape a bad start, or have some wild idea an app gave you about the wind swinging hard in one direction. One in twenty times you might get lucky. Don't Harvey Cornerbang.

If you draw the laylines from the start line to the weather mark, and keep to either one of those laylines, you are banging the corners. Whichever way the wind shifts, you lose. More often than not, you will overstand the mark, as you will be riding the layline to the weather mark far too long, vulnerable to anyone and everyone who tacks on top of you. The only way to clear your air is to tack and overstand the mark. Simply put, don't bang the corners unless there is really good reason.

Only in rare instances does corner banging work. When you're traveling far along what you think is the layline, you will lose no matter which way the wind shifts. If it doesn't shift and you're in more pressure, you're going to make the biggest gains. If it does shift, you'll suffer the biggest losses. That's why playing more to the middle in the first part of the race is part and parcel my strategy. I can cut my losses without paying a big price, and often seal gains at a small one. Less risk taking. In truth, I've corner banged way too much in my sailing life, but looking back on it, I sailed with a half-baked strategy, getting away with a lot on boat speed. But through this exercise of writing a book about it, can reflect on many instances of diminished gains, and few of hitting the jackpot.

The rare instance where corner banging pays off is when there is current, and you are heading to get out of it (SF Bay).

Don't bang the mark, either. Notta pinata. Mike "Picklefork" Mead.

But in this case, you're not alone. The entire fleet is heading to the shore, and the first to get there and call for water to tack will often win the race. Another instance is a place like Huntington Lake, where it's imperative to get to the shore and hit that big thermal lift or kiss the fleet goodbye. Or on a lake where the cows rotate with the wind. You need to move on over there and milk the lifting shoreline pressure. Cowshifts happen, I cowshift you not.

CURRENT PLAY

When sailing on a river or the ocean, currents play a larger factor in choosing where to point your boat. On a river, you need to know the strength of flow on both sides of the course. Writing with a marker – a note on your boat – of the tidal changes occurring throughout the day will give you a great advantage over those who don't. Noting the currents changing strength and direction applies to all points of sail.

Playing the current is not rocket science. You take whatever measures to get out of the current when running against you, and into it when running with. In typical conditions on San Francisco Bay, we call the current flowing into the bay, typically in the direction of the wind, the *flood* tide. When the current

Laser North Americans, SF Bay — Photo: Weston

is flowing against the wind, it is called an *ebb* tide.

If, when getting out of the current, you are also heading into lighter wind, there is a trade off. You may have seen it during the America's Cup. One boat heads for the City Front wharf, while the other stayed out in better wind. That's a roll of the dice in dicey conditions. However, in most dinghy races taking place between StFYC and the GG Bridge, during a flood tide, there's a parade to shore. The wind typically strong and water flatter there as well.

Photo: Weston

Not everywhere is as predictable as the SF City Front. When racing Wetas and 505's, they StFYC starts us by Alcatraz, right in the middle of the bay. Down the bay at Richmond YC, where much dinghy racing takes place, there are more variables in play. I can remember one particular race in Lasers, where the entire fleet headed to shore and I had started late, fixing my outhaul strap. Gambling, I stayed out in the stronger

Aero North Americans (windy!) getting out of river current — Photo: Weston

breezes. I won that race by such a margin that the RC approached me to ask if I'd skipped a leg.

More often, I've also lost big by not playing the current. That's why knowing the tidal changes, ocean topography, and pre-race reconnaissance are so important.

Photo: Weston

THE PHASING BREEZE

You often hear someone at the YC bar either talking about having been in phase or out of phase with the shifts. If they're talking about having been out of phase, they may be pounding a few beers. It's similar to getting into the groove or in a rut. Everyone has those days when they look upwind after

Local knowledge comes heavily into play not only on lakes, but in coastal areas as well. In Alamitos Bay, the sea breeze can gradually clock to the right at a certain time off day. If you know what time of day that is, big advantage to play the right.

a pin end start and see the fleet lifting. You're out of phase. Or you woke up on the wrong side of the bed and every time you tack, you get headed again.

Another way to get out of phase is to be incognizant of local wind patterns. A blind mind to wind oscillations can nail your coffin. In some places like Alamitos Bay, the wind will come in like clockwork and clock to the right. At that time, you need to be on the right to be in the right. Otherwise, you'll be sailing in circles. Been there, worn that t-shirt.

CHOOSING THE FAVORED SIDE

At some point on the weather leg, you want to gain an advantage. You want to choose the favored side of the course. There will be no graphic that will tell you where that pressure is, where that big beefy lifting long tack awaits to be milked.

If you're in the lead or near it, the only indication of the favored side will be dark patches of water. When the water is flat, that's pretty easy to see, but when it's a lumpy sea state, your seat of the pants sixth sense wind whispering will come heavily into play. If leading, at least you will have a clearer view of where the patches of dark water lie, or whatever indicators are pointing to them. If trailing behind, you need to look at the leading boats. Their heading and heel will serve as solid indicators of which side is working well.

Paul Elvstrom: *If all you had to do was to sail with your eyes, anyone could do it. You must also use all your feelings; the wind on your face, the palm of the hand, the sensation of the boat. I cannot sit to leeward. Then, you can only see the sail. You must always steer to the waves, not follow the sail.*

Choosing the favored side is a win or lose proposition. Even if you're batting .500 on seat of the pants wind whispering wizardry, you're going to come out ahead of where you would be if you just stuck your finger up in the air. To play it safe, you need to sail conservatively – in the middle – and stick to the law of averages. I'd say it will most likely be your safest bet, but by playing the middle, all bets are off. There will be no gains. Then again, there will be fewer losses. We're back to gambling, aren't we? Call 1-800-LAY-LINE.

Once you've established your side of the course, at this point, you've got to stick to your guns. You win some, you lose some, but you won't win that much nor lose much if you've chosen right or wrong. Where you will lose, if you get on the long tack layline too far away from the mark.

OVERSTANDING THE WEATHER MARK

The layline: that ever-moving, most poorly judged imaginary line that indicates what should be the final tack of the windward leg. Quite often, the biggest gains and losses involve the layline. It's not advisable to stay on the layline too long, as it is an imaginary line that often shifts with the wind's fickle finger. Hit the layline too early and you'll risk getting lifted and overstanding.

WINNING WAYS

You're giving away valuable hard-won boat length's.

Yes, if the wind does not shift, you will be saving two tacks. On a lake, the wind usually shifts, and if headed, you'll be doing those tacks late and in traffic.

That's why being Harvey Cornerbanger rarely works out, particularly if you are lifted and overstand by a mile. If you are too far out from the weather mark and think you've judged the layline perfectly, you risk getting lifted. You also risk a boat tacking on your wind. That leaves you the only options of taking two tacks to clear your air, overstanding the mark, or bearing off and losing yardage.

It's okay to nail the layline ten boat lengths away. If you get lifted, just take a bit of insurance to weather before you, then Colonel Krackoff... crack the sails off onto a close reach. I wish I had a nickel for every time I've been lifted once on the layline, allowing those who tacked short of it to make up significant ground. If I did, I'd have a bucket full of nickels.

Dave Ullman still enjoying sailing Lido 14's in his young age. Lido's are a very popular fleet in Southern California, often with enough numbers to run A and B level fleets. A fleet sailors have included Dave Ullman and Dennis Conner. Slow little boats mean the emphasis is placed on strategy, tactics and incremental sail adjustments. This is what most sailors need to focus on before stepping up to higher performance craft.

Being on the starboard layline too long is better than being too long on port. When lifted, overstanding on port is much worse, as you will be dealing with boats rounding the mark. Pick your poison or avoid being long on the laylines altogether. Don't hit the layline too early.

Robby Wilkins, a very fast sailor who grew up crewing for Dave Ullman, wrote that Dave takes one tack to the layline and then to the mark. While I questioned the tactic as it goes against everything written in this book, if the

event is on the ocean where the wind is less shifty, and you are as fast as Dave Ullman, it might make sense. Otherwise, as my Russian father-in-law used to say, "*Ерунда. Научная фантастика!*" (Nonsense! Science fiction!)

UNDER STANDING THE WEATHER MARK

Dave Rink: *Skippers tack onto the starboard tack layline a little short, so they're pinching all the way into the mark. In some cases, this is warranted, but I've seen boats that are 20 boat lengths from the mark trying to pinch their way around. If you have the space, just go fast and put the 2 extra tacks in.*

WEATHER MARK ROUNDING

In this book, we'll cover weather mark rounding from three different perspectives: Tactical rounding, boat handling, and sail trim. Before getting to what is needed for optimizing boat and sail trim, let's focus specifically on mark rounding tactics.

Penguins! Photo: Will Keyworth

The act of rounding the weather mark is actually not that difficult, the leeward mark being far more challenging. You're not gathering in heaps of rope; you're just letting it out. Unlike the leeward mark rounding, there is no real danger of ending up in a bad position, getting toasted by the boat to windward. Just the opposite; if you have a bad weather mark rounding and a boat takes advantage, you are now the one blocking air. Like quenching a fire, it's an easy loss to gain back.

Photo: Will Keyworth

As well, if there is an offset mark set, it is hardly a rounding. You're just bearing off a bit. Let's interject here and lay down an offset mark:

THE OFFSET MARK

Wetafest 2014, heading for the offset mark. I'm 622, Cliff Farrah 875, Keith Rice 437.

Hopefully, the RC has set an offset mark. The offset mark's purpose is to prevent casualties from happening. Because heading straight into oncoming traffic can be counterproductive!

Should you be unfamiliar with an offset mark, it's typically a small round (hard to see) buoy set about 6-10 boat lengths away from the weather mark, at a close reach. If set, it needs to be rounded right after rounding the weather mark, or you'll be sorry. A RC mark boat will be watching out for those who miss it. Most that miss it never realize it, and those that realize and correct their course will lose at least a football field on the fleet if not more.

Tip number 976, use an erasable marker to draw the course on your boat somewhere you can see it. Include the offset mark in your drawing and write on the boat, OFFSET MARK! Yes, that means you, Bob Hodges, who after driving x-country, missed it Race 1, but the good guy he is DSQ'd himself after realizing it. He had won that race. Throwout!

WINNING WAYS

This photo is very special to me, not only because I'm remembering that there is an offset mark, not only because it's blowing dogs out of kennels, and not only because I'm winning Nationals at Cascade Locks (Columbia River Gorge) at age 60, but Dick Hitchcock, who drove the class and the laughter around the dinner table has passed on.

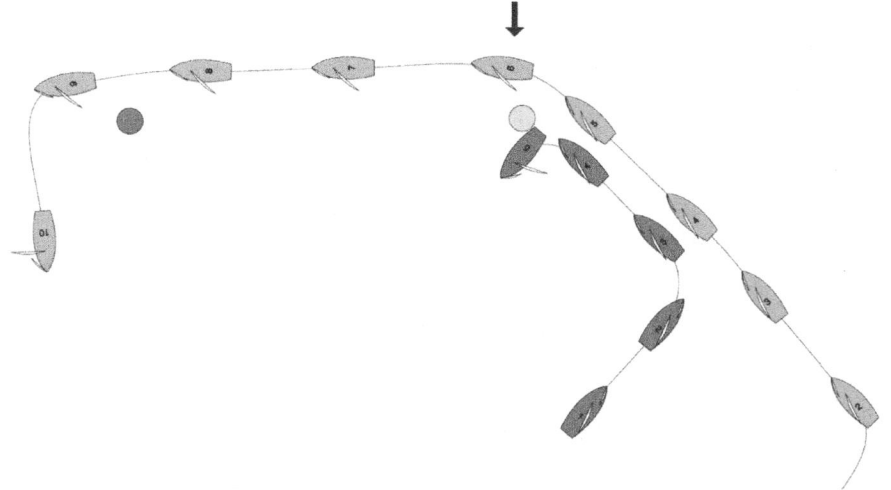

FINAL APPROACH TO THE MARK

While rounding the weather mark is a piece of cake, the approach to the mark can be an unfolding nightmare. There are two approaches to the weather mark and I'm not just talking starboard or port Are you a risk taker or a conservative sailor?

Bjorn Dunkerbeck, who won 44 World Championship events in professional windsurfing, says,

"Taking risks is not risky if you're good at managing risks."

Photo: Weston

I think what he's trying to say (and he can say it in 7 languages) is that if you're going to take risks, you need to have a solid escape plan. Or don't take the risks that are going to ruin your day, tank your race, sink your ship. Most likely, those risks are taken around the corners. The weather mark is one of those corners. Yet, it's coming into the corner, not pulling away from it that big gains and losses are made, which is again, just opposite of the leeward mark.

Let's say you are of equal speed, where tactics and taking risks wins races. The slower the class of boat, the more likely you will be in this predicament, particularly in highly competitive and large fleets. Risk-takers come into the weather mark on port and in droves.

It's worth repeating: the conservative approach to the weather mark is to come sailing in on starboard above the layline, giving yourself plenty of "insurance" in the event you get headed. The downside? Like a good neighbor, you'll give

away yards (or meters, take your pick) to not only the "risk-takers" coming in at the last second on port, but to the boats that tacked to starboard below you and made the mark. It can be a big deductible. Okay, I'll stop. You get the points. The main thing is, know those rules before you take them risks.

If there's current flowing with the wind (flood tide in SF Bay), the conser-

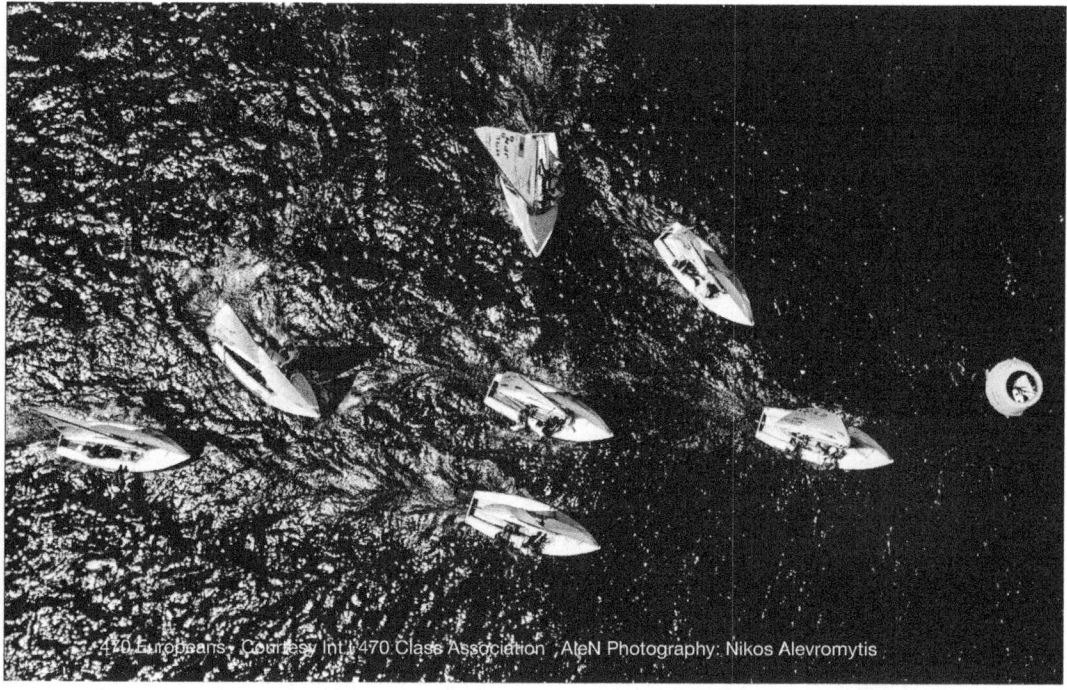
470 Europeans, Courtesy Int'l 470 Class Association, AleN Photography: Nikos Alevromytis

vative approach might save you from hitting the weather mark. Being on starboard, you'll also be safe from being fouled by anyone. Let the jackals be jackals. Don't get into shackles with them and get all tangled up in blues. That doesn't mean you won't get fouled, but if you overstand, your chances are quite slim. And if boat speed is your game, the conservative approach is definitely the way to play the game.

You're probably familiar with driving in traffic, when some necktie in a Beamer comes sliding into a slim space ahead of you like you don't even exist. Taking risks can get you home earlier, but it can also get you into a five-car pileup. The bigger the fleet, however, the more I tend to take risks. You can advance up to 10 boats at a time by doing so. You can lose 20. On a scale of 1-5, what kind of risk taker are you? Complete marshmallow, somewhat risky... risky business!

Dave Rink: *The next most common error I see sailors make when approaching the weather mark, is tacking onto the starboard layline a little short. This results in pinching all the way into the mark. In some cases, this is warranted, but I've seen boats that are 20 boat lengths from the mark trying to pinch their way around. If you have the space, just go fast and put the 2 extra tacks in.*

SITUATION: Weather Mark Risk-taker

You've hiked your tail off and want to finish the leg strong. The left side of the course was favored, and you want to hold onto your advantage. You've been lifted coming into the mark, charging in on a close reach with speed. Lucky for you, there is an offset mark, so no need to cause panic and mayhem. There is a solid line of starboard tackers, all working for Allstate. Yet, there are a few slight gaps. What do you do?

a) Wave your BMW flag. Shout, "Incoming!"

b) Find a gap to shoot through, perfectly ducking the sterns, then tacking immediately when clear.

c) Yell, "Covid's back!"

d) Look for a boat taking out too much of an insurance policy and tack, squeezing in below them.

Solutions:

a) Get your Jack@ss merit badge, wear it proudly.

b) This would be the safest bet.

c) Might not work against the Vaxxers.

d) This would be risk-taking. Is it worth it?

Andy Burdick: *When approaching the windward mark, position your boat for ultimate speed. So many boats will make the mistake of tacking too close to other boats, pinching to make the mark. In this scenario, fouls happen; you go slow and get rolled by windward boats, people hit marks, or even get hung up on marks. You cannot do this—it's too big of a risk. You are better off sailing clean, a bit beyond the layline, coming in fast, and then hoisting your spinnaker in the "Passing Lane" – a higher lane than the boats below. Approach with speed.*

2025 Lake Eustis MC Train Wreck John Cole Photography

I asked Morgan Larsen and Trevor Baylis what their secret was to winning the 505 Worlds. "We're good in traffic," Morgan said. "We take risks," Trevor added, "We're not the biggest guys so not the fastest upwind, but we get around the marks pretty well in traffic." It also helped that they were light and fast downwind.

The question is, when approaching the weather mark late on port, how big of a risk do you take? How solid of a line of starboard tackers are on the layline, i.e., are there gaps to duck and squeeze through, or is everyone coming in high above the layline, giving you ample opportunity to squeeze in there.

The other question is, how Tom Cruise thick is your spine? (*Risky Business*). For sure there will be people yelling "Starboard" and "No way!" A lot depends

on how quickly you can tack and get back up to speed. If the boat you're trying to squeeze tack in front of has to alter their course, you may hear them yelling, "Protest!" It's not advisable to tack directly in front of someone, but it is a marginal call if the incoming boat has taken that insurance, leaving you room to effectively lee bow and squeeze in there without hitting the mark. It's a risky move. It won't make you popular at the bar, but might at the trophy ceremony.

The boat that comes in super conservatively is akin to the surfer who sits on the shoulder and never catches a wave. You've got to be aggressive. But if you think you're going to foul someone by squeezing in there, just don't, particularly if it's me you're tacking in front of. It all depends on where you're sitting on the leaderboard. If it doesn't make sense to take the risk, if coming into the weather mark on port, it's time to pull the plug on risk taking and find a gap to shoot through. Ducking a couple of boats won't kill you. Fouling a couple of boats will.

THINK AHEAD

Before you get to the weather mark, and thanks to Sean O'Donnell for this one… you need to be thinking about which jibe you're going to be on after rounding. If on a spinnaker boat, particularly an old school spinnaker boat where they actually call them spinnakers, this is highly important. Is it a set then jibe? Or a jibe set? Either way, you should have it all figured out before you round, as the same golden rule applies here as it did to weather. You want to be on the long jibe. Gybe. However you spell it, you want to be on it.

The way to determine this is to think about which tack was the longest tack on the weather leg. If it was starboard, you will want to jibe set, or simply jibe around the mark. If port was the long tack, then you just round the mark and carry on the long starboard tack. In this case, you can ready whatever bloopy sail you have to power downwind.

If there is a reach involved, which there unfortunately rarely is these days, you don't need to think about any of that. But if you are planning to jibe right after rounding the weather mark, take a look behind you to see if you're about to cream a bunch of your best buddies. In that case you need

Melges 15 Winter Series   Photo: Morgan Kinney

real insurance, boat insurance, low deductible. I'm sure someone in the fleet can sell you a policy.

One of the many advantages of getting out on the racecourse early is to see how the marks are set. In an attempt to defend my club championship in the Flying Scot, I gained a sizable lead at the weather mark. There was no one within ten boat lengths besides my crew. I cut the corner as I normally would, giving about a boat length's empty water. However, the water being shallow and mark's anchor line too long, I caught the weather mark with the centerboard.

On a Flying Scot, it's not like you just grab the board and raise. It's a process. I effectively took the windward mark downwind, so that other boats following had less distance upwind to sail. There is nothing fast about dragging a mark around. A little mark rounding reconnaissance before the race would have avoided this error.

THINK AHEAD

by Scott Steele

My years sailing a variety of different boats and boards have given me a perspective that is unique in our sport. Whether you're racing dinghies, keelboats, or windsurfers, preparations for decisions made around the windward mark are all similar. While campaigning the Melges 15 with fleets of 90 boats on the starting line, we often arrive at the windward mark surrounded by a significant number of boats.

My crew, Eliot Caple, is a recent grad from the College of Charleston Sailing Team. Together, we've realized how important it is to always think ahead. Quick decisions have to be made. As we are in the final third of the weather leg, we discuss and prepare for the rounding and for strategic positioning on the following leg, whether it be reaching or downwind. Sailing with asymmetrical kites (referred to as A Sails in this book) emphasizes focus on clear air and optimum wind pressure, resulting in top speeds and low sailing angles.

WINNING WAYS

There are two mistakes you must avoid in a big fleet:

Melges 15 Midwinters — Photo: Morgan Kinney

1. Avoid being immediately too low on the Starboard reach leg. This could result in being passed by boats as they are heated up to windward of you, using that extra speed to bend the apparent wind and roll over the top of you.

2. Avoid jibing too early onto Port when there's a large fleet behind, even with an offset mark. If you do, there is a fair chance you will enter a dead zone (a zone blanketed by starboard tackers approaching the windward mark and across to the offset).

Here's our experience:

The good: As we approached the windward mark on starboard tack, we got lifted in big pressure. The following leg was downwind, so this told us that the long tack downwind would be slightly favored to port. We would need to first focus on a perfect kite set and then jibe at the first opportunity while being sure to stay out of that dead zone. After the set, we focused on defending boats behind us going high, while maintaining a clear position to jibe. With such a big fleet right behind us, patience proved to be virtuous.

We sailed a comfortable distance while being ok with a few boats beating us to the jibe inside, allowing us to use them as a reference. The first boat that jibed suffered miserably then another and another so we kept going until we saw the wind was filled in past the dead zone before we made our jibe. The result was while we lost one boat that picked a slightly better time to jibe, we picked up over 25 boats on our way to the leeward gates.

The bad: In a second race, we again foresaw that a jibe-set at the offset would be advantageous. However, this time we took our eye off of the high lane and mistakenly didn't defend the train of boats to windward. We suffered to get going while boats got under and over us. We were pinned to the unfavored tack by boats just below us, preventing us to jibe.

The ugly: Above us, boats rolled over the top of us. By the time we were free and clear to do so, boats had passed us on both sides resulting in a net loss of 40 boats. You win some, you lose some! But you always learn from your mistakes.

Lessons learned: Plan ahead, and stick to the plan when you can. If not, improvise, but don't wait too long to correct your course. Stay out of the dead zone, and never fall to leeward of a big train coming behind you. If one boat rolls you from behind, aggressively come up and defend the train, or jibe to the favored long tack (only if clear to do so and the wind pressure is there)! Think ahead and focus on maintaining fleet positioning until the opportunity presents itself for gains. While quick decisions can be crucial, patience can be your friend as well. Good luck and sail fast!

REACHING LEGS

Most courses set these days for One Design small boat racing are simply Windward Leeward. The only variance is whether they are one lap or two, finish upwind or down, and where those lines are set. You also have to be aware by reading the SI's about whether that line is restricted or not restricted to cross during the course of the race – when not starting or finishing.

Mike Martin/Adam Lowry Photo: Bryan McDonald

In the good ole' days of the Olympic Triangle, the first lap of all races involved just that; a triangle – enabling two reaches – followed by a windward leeward on the second lap. The course served iconic Olympic boats such as Finns, Solings, Stars, Flying Dutchmen, and other boats hapless fools have since excluded from the games. Kite foiling, right up there with break dancing. Either way, the Aussies dominate!

Today, the only classes where the RC is often deploying reaching legs are for windsurfers, catamarans, and trimarans, as this is their fastest point of sail. Once in a great while the course is used for skiffs. The reason often given for removing these reaching legs is there are fewer opportunities to pass; that it's a less tactical game. Bollocks! I high wind disagree. Bring back the reaching legs!

There are still some regattas where permanent buoys are utilized, which often require reaching at some point. Huntington Lake in California comes quickly to mind, but one of the most iconic reaching legs I've come across involves the One Mile Buoy, a permanent mark lying a mile offshore from the Santa Cruz Wharf. Of lead changes, there are many, with lots of capsized boats!

The High Sierra Regatta is a highlight event of the year, where all types of fleets (Lido being the biggest) converge for a camping, racing extravaganza. Courses run on permanent marks for miles up and down the lake. I suppose the cats and tri's took up too much beach space, so they now run them separately in the Commodore's Cup. Told my daughter not to take the picture if Bruce caught me downwind. Bound to happen! I took her on one race and she sat on my hiking stick as we spun donuts. "Chill, Dad!"

REACHING MADE GOOD

What I really miss about reaching legs is the tactical game of bearing off in the gusts and heading up in the lulls. Just like the fastest path to success is not a straight line, the quickest path to the next mark is wiggly as well. Not squiggly wiggly like the path to success, but you really want to soak up some downwind good on those gusts, so that you can head up in the lulls, thus ensuring that you are coming into the next mark with good speed. It's important to close the leg out well and gain inside room at the mark, for that is when and where you can really put a nail in your closest competitor's coffin.

Peter Commette: *The once in a while fun gloat: When my oldest daughter was 14 and crewing for me at a Snipe Nationals on Buzzards Bay, one race it blew a pretty good 18-20. The race was a double triangle, finishing windward. We'd gone from about 10th at the first mark to pretty much smoking the fleet as we approached*

WINNING WAYS

the first jibe mark. We were gone, and we had more reaches to go!

On my boom, my wife had written in big letters the most important part of team communication, "What's the Plan?" This was the first time at such a big event that we were so far out in front, so my daughter, always serious as hell, asked me when we were about 50-75 yards from the jibe mark, "Dad, what's the plan?" I said, "Take

your palm like this." showing her an open palm. She thought I was going to show her how to do something jibe-related.

I continued, "Face your palm facing the back of the boat. Now wave goodbye!" Then, I got what I planned for, "Daaaaaaaaaaaaaad!" Quality time with the family and a well-executed plan. Beats the heck out of a trip to Disneyworld.

BEARING AWAY

As you bear away onto a reach, maintain your speed so that you're "bending" the apparent wind. The faster your class of boat, the more bent the wind will become. Check the data on SailGP boats, and you'll see that the highest speeds come when rounding the weather mark. Yet, even on a Flying Scot, you can bend the wind… just not nearly to the degree of those all out One Design speed machines.

INITIAL ANGLE OF ATTACK

The first thing you should be concerned about is the angle of attack. Find the reaching mark. If in multi-class regatta and you were keen enough while sailing the weather leg to note what angle the fleets ahead were on when reaching, or unfortunate enough to notice what angle boats ahead of you in your own fleet are demonstrating, you'll know in advance whether you need

Inland Lakes   Photo: Morgan Kinney

to stay tight on the wind or to use that initial burst of speed to soak it (make downwind VMG good).

By trying to soak it downwind too early, you're not going to be taking advantage of that burst of speed. You won't be bending the wind.

If you're carrying a spinnaker, screecher, or a bloopy sail by any other odd name, try not to soak it too far downwind so that you have to have to douse early, particularly if there is another kite carrying leg to complete. My approach has always been to get the kite up quickly, often on the short leg between the weather mark and offset, or at least ready to set quickly if the offset is set too high.

WINNING WAYS

PLAY THE WAVES

You can't win in One Design's unless you optimally surf the swells. If the breeze is producing a surfable wave state, your gains will come in playing the surf at accelerated angles. Every off-wind leg will present a different lake or seascape, but you want to try to angle your boat so that you're constantly running downhill; so that you're carving a line along the face to go faster than you possibly could on flat water (unless so fast you are climbing over the hill to the next. As soon as you run into the back of a wave, you're going to lose ground, and fill the boat with water. Water filled boat, slow.

Int'l 505 Class Association   Photo: Christophe Favreau

If pumping is legal, pump. But once you catch the wave, you may find it better to just stay sheeted in a bit until it's time to angle the boat further off the wind. In this case and in marginal breeze, you may have to ease the sheet back out a bit, soak it, and then as you're approaching a speed bump, head up. Stay on that wave! Again, a straight line is not the fastest way around the course. Piggly wiggly does the job.

Don't get too carried away trying to pass a competitor to windward. If you can surf a wave and blow through their lee or soak it far enough downwind to avoid their shadow altogether, this will avoid being luffed, giving away distance won to all other racers not in the scuffle. This is when sailing a "proper course" comes into play, and all the misinterpretations of what sailing a proper course means.

Okay, now let's assume there are no reaching legs.

DOWNWIND LEG

This is where you get to kick back, pop open a beer, and relax, right? That's what other people picture when you tell them you race boats. *In your tub, right?* As you may be well aware, it's no Splish splash taking a bath (unless death rolling a Laser. There is a whole lot happening on the downwind leg; the reason most racecourses stick with the Windward Leeward design is due to the large gains that come from mastering this leg of the course.

FULL SPEED AHEAD

It's best to begin the downwind leg by getting up to maximum speed, hopefully surfing on a wave if there is one. Unless there has been a major wind shift or the RC was drinking when they set the weather mark, you should always be spending some time on starboard, so you might as well do it now and get clear of disturbed air. The idea of gybing around the weather mark,

Photo: Will Keyworth

even with an offset mark – particularly if you are flying any kind of spinnaker – is rarely the best idea. Unless there is very good reason for it, you're just diving back into disturbed air and delaying the flight of kite. Jibe set is a hectic maneuver. Better to get set and planing, then jibe.

It's important to get your boat tracking onto the optimal path. We'll be talking about downwind boat and sail trim in another chapter, but futzing around with sail controls and adjusting your pants should not be your first order of business. Getting the board up, loosening your outhaul and Cunningham should with good practice become second nature, but if it's not, everything you do with sail controls will be for infinitesimal gains. The wind is now pushing on sails nearly perpendicular to the wind, so sail shape is not as important as boat trim and angle. *Alors*, getting your boat pointed downslope, up to max speed, and aligned well against your key opponents should be your premier order of business.

On the first downwind leg of the first race, you probably don't have any particular opponent to track and target. Don't waste your brainpower thinking about that. Don't waste worry about where's Waldo who whooped you in the last five regattas. Take Trevor's advice and think about sail trim, optimal downwind angles, clear air, positioning your boat inline with the next puff, and then start optimizing the boat for ultimate speed.

Once you get up to full speed, you should pull that board up quickly, enough to clear any weeds on it, then drop it into optimal position. If you're in a boat that sails optimally dead downwind, you will probably be dropping just enough board to keep the boat tracking. In breeze, again depending on the boat, you may want to drop it halfway, so that your death rolls aren't so deadly, and you have something to right with if you do flip the boat.

UNDER PRESSURE

While the Boston song recommends, "Don't Look Back," once you're good and going fast, somebody on your boat needs to. You have to put eyeballs on where the pressure lanes are flowing, right? Glad you agree. I always tell people when I'm onboard coaching, "The rich get richer upwind. The rich get poorer downwind. How do you make a million dollars in sailboat racing? Start with two million. All Dad jokes aside, there's a good chance that the fleet

© 2023 420 World Championship | International 420 Class Association | Andrea Lelli

is going make gains and come running up on your stern if you're not paying attention to those pressure lanes; it's that fleet that will be the best indicators of where those lanes are ripping. That's why you take every puff to the bank, staying in that lane of breeze as long as you can without getting blanketed.

BLANKET, NOT BLANKETED

It's advantageous to put the blanket on other boats. A common tactic is to

Photo: Deb Fewell Durbec

blanket and then use the speed of a wave to soak it low to lee of a boat, gaining eventual inside overlap if a port rounding. That's some real tomfoolery! Sailboat racing at its finest. To head up above them is just inviting a fight. It might be worth it if the wind is light, but if the breeze is on and your boat is surfing, avoid battles at all costs. They only benefit the fleet. The result of soaking low and heading to their lee, if played right, is going to overtake them or at least give you room at the mark.

If you're in a spinnaker boat, the need to keep boats from riding up on *your* tail becomes paramount. Throwing in a gybe before it gets too late is a splendid idea, to put you out of their way. Too late for what? Too late to gybe because a boat has soaked it lower than yours and would now be square in your trajectory if you gybed. They would then probably be taking room at the mark if not completely overtaking you.

However, boats like Lasers and Finns sail well and often faster by the lee, so a gybe may not be called for.

THE LONG GYBE

Tactically speaking, aside from sailing in good clean pressure, your next job is to stay on the long tack. Call it the long tack or the long gybe, spell it however you want. Live to ride, ride to live, it's the same thing. And the same as when you are sailing upwind. The long tack will have you sailing the least distance. In short, VMG.

I write this lastly, as I'm not of the school that being on the long tack going downwind is as important as going upwind. Why? You can sail straight downwind, but you can't upwind, so you aren't factoring in that exclusion zone. The one time it becomes critical to get on the long tack going downwind, is if the wind has shifted so radically that if you gybed at the weather mark, you would be on a reach to the downwind mark. Effectively, there would be no downwind leg.

Therefore, I feel it's more important to stay in that good clean pressure, to sail at optimal angles, and I'll go out of my way on the short tack to get there. You may sail some extra yards but particularly in light air, to get to that puff before anyone else is going to send you ahead of a chunk of boats.

OPTIMAL ANGLES

Photo: Lexi Pline

Some boats such as Hobies and 49ers sail much faster downwind at angles. It took me awhile to master those angles, as it does any sailor. It's just a matter of VMG. How low can you soak it... how far downwind can you point the boat... without sacrificing speed. While this is probably something that can be compass and speedpuck calculated according to windspeed, I've always chalked it up to experience.

Sailing optimal angles is not like riding a bike. It takes practice and time in regatta. Your speed and relativity to other boats is very much more indicative than when sailing on your own. "Hmm, feels pretty fast! Great angle!" And then you get in a regatta and get smoked. In Cats and skiffs, the difference between someone who sails a ton of regattas and those who do it once in a while is football fields. You can't just jump back in the game after a few months off and be successful at it unless you're sailing similar types of boats that sail similar types of angles.

Using a compass to try to dial in your optimal angles might work for some, adjusting as necessary to varying wind speeds. The greater the wind, the higher the boat speed, the lower the angle. I'd rather be looking at the swells I'm riding, or about to ram into and flood the cockpit. Not a good idea to ram into any boats coming at you on the opposite gybe either. With spray flying everywhere, they may not see you, particularly boats coming through from a faster fleet.

Unless you're foiling of course, on a Birdyfish, the main thing is to look at the swells and your relation to the fleet. Try to keep to similar angles that your nearest competitors are sailing, unless you're finding yourself at the back of the pack. Then it's a horrible idea! But most sailors coming into a new class find that they do very well on the upwind leg. It's playing the angles and riding the swells where they fall apart. And as the great Aussie legend says, "Make sure you don't overcook it!" (Don't sail past the optimal layline).

I always say, *Time in regatta beats Time in the water.* This really depends upon who you are spending time in the water with, your lonesome or a bunch of training buds. By yourself is going to help your boat handling sans pressure. Find some good fast sailors to measure up against.

SITUATION: Blankety Blanketed

You've rounded the weather offset mark, easing the main quickly and heeling

Flying Scot 2025 Midwinters, Lake Eustis, FL — John Cole Photography

the boat sharply to windward to assist the turn while not braking the rudder. Good job! You're surfing downwind at whatever is the optimal angle for your class of boat. If you have a kite to pull out or spinnaker to hoist, you're calmly instructing your crew, "Don't shrimp the kite!" You feel the wind kind of waffling, so you look back, and there he is, Clem Cadiddlehopper, hopping on your wind. In the last race, you took the advice from this book, and burned Clem downwind, taking room at the mark. Clem thinks it's payback time. What do you do?

    a) Gybe into disturbed air.

    b) Take Clem up to the cleaners and lose three other boats.

    c) Throw some gas barrels behind the boat and explode with shotgun.

    d) Sail by the lee and let Clem go to weather of you.

Solutions:

a) Probably not a good idea unless there was a clearing of boats.

b) Never good to lose three boats and probably Clem as well.

c) Only if a shark is about to devour your boat, but not Clem. Clem is your friend.

d) Let Clem go. He'll probably get into a scuffle with the next boat, particularly if neither have read this book.

SAILING BY THE LEE

On a spinnaker free dinghy (monohull, e.i., Laser, MC Scow, Lido), sailing by the lee is faster than sailing dead downwind. To stay on a wave, or even in light air with no waves, you will see the best sailors alternately sail by the lee and then on a broad reach, throwing in some roll gybes to boot. It's a learned technique, and that's where clinics and practice with other boats (better than you) will improve your sleep at night. Nothing will egg you regarding why you keep getting smoked downwind.

There are even times when sailing by the lee on a spinnaker boat come in handy, particularly when grabbing an overlap approaching the mark (well before reaching the zone). You've blanketed Fred Farleystone, then dip to leeward by sailing by the lee. It's not as simply done as in a Laser, as you won't have the ability to let your sail out anywhere near 90 degrees. Easing the vang will allow the main to twist off, which effectively is giving it enough of an angle so that it won't gybe over. If on a Laser or similar, it's essential to have a long mainsheet to allow by the lee sailing.

The most confusing rule about by the lee sailing comes when two boats converge. The wind may be coming over the port side of the boat, but it is the side the boom rests on that really matters.

KEEP INSIDE THE LAYLINES

On a boat where you play the angles downwind, the final gybe on the downwind leg can also be done to your advantage. If following in the tracks of another boat, it's advantageous to keep watch on when they are preparing to make their final gybe. Gybe just before they do, and you will most often come into the mark/gate ahead, or at least with an overlap (unless coming in on port with a gate set).

Gybe too soon, and you will have to slow to dead downwind or throw in two more gybes. In this case, you make no gains and lose any boat that traveled further to the layline.

18 Footers in San Francisco

My take is that it's best to play it short than long, particularly if you have surfing conditions. Heading dead down in this case can easily be done without losing what you have gained. Sailing past the layline will place you on a tight reach where you may even have to drop the kite, as well as reduce your surfing ability. Keep within the laylines, and you will stay up on the leaderboard. I guess that's why John Bertrand calls his blog, "*Inside the Laylines.*"

BASIC INGREDIENTS (GRITS & GRAVY)

by Robby Wilkins

Growing up on Lake Murray in Columbia, South Carolina, there were not a lot of opportunities to be exposed to great sailors and winning teams. I was lucky enough to win the Y Flyer Junior Nationals and a Lightning Junior Nationals, but racing against the nation's best Laser sailors, I would only have my moments of glory winning the light air races.

I won a lot of regional events, but I was missing all the ingredients to win consistently and on the national/world stage. After a short, successful collegiate career, and a quick Olympic effort in the 470's, I moved to Annapolis and quickly learned what it took to win.

I was lucky to sail with Olympic Medal winners Scott Allan and Dave Ullman. This is where I got to learn my basics to win:

Boat Prep

Time in the Boat

Having the best team/crew

Having a game plan on the racecourse

The first year that the J-24 came out, I had the pleasure to race in the MORC Nationals with Bob Johnstone, Dave Ullman and Major Hall. As I walked down to the boat to meet everybody for the very first time, Dave greeted me with a question: "Are you putting that gear bag on the boat?" There came my first lesson in boat prep: Light boats are faster than heavy ones, and I was only taking what I was wearing.

I suppose I did well enough on that team to crew on a Thistle for Dave Ullman. He was just faster than everybody else, knows well the top end of the tiller stick. We would pick a favored side and start at the boat or the pin. Sailing with Dave, I did not learn much ado about how to recover from a poor start. He was like Alpha dog, nobody fought him for top spot. If the right was favored, we would start at the boat and tack as soon as possible, using our superior speed to get out right in the clear, then tack, seal our gains and cross the fleet. Same deal if we started at the pin, we'd get ahead and consolidate with the fleet. Because we were faster, this always worked. At a Thistle Midwinter regatta in St. Pete, we used this game plan and won every race. It didn't hurt that our team with Paul Murphy on the bow could droop hike up all the weather legs. You don't see that much from other Thistle crew. We were droop hiking FAST.

Later in my career, I began racing with Bob Johnstone on a J-105. I would sail on the boat at Key West Race Week, Block Island and events around Newport. We had all the ingredients. In a very competitive fleet of 40-50 boats at Key West, we won three years in a row. One of our keys to winning was having Bob 100% focused on driving the boat and giving the crew feedback. It was all about teamwork.

I took my dinghy racing experiences to bigger boats, and my big boat experience back to smaller ones. Though few would consider the E Scow a small dinghy, it's still a dinghy that requires balance, boat trim, and hiking leverage. With four crew, it also requires great teamwork.

In the E-scow class, boat prep is easy. Melges Boatworks is the only manufacturer, and the class rules keep modifications to a minimum. No fairing of the hull is allowed. A tip that we always use that works for all boats is to put a dehumidifier in the boat at the end of the day. Dry boats are both lighter and faster.

At the 2023 100th Annual E-Scow Nationals, all the ingredients necessary to win came together. 127 E-scows on one starting line is an amazing experience, like eating Pound Cake. In such a large fleet, the race committee has to set the starting line almost one mile long. Clear air was paramount.

In race two, we knew the left side of the course was going to be favored, making the port end a traffic jam. Deciding to start mid-line area with clear air, we gave up a few boats, but didn't get tanked by the fleet in the light breeze, either. We rounded the top mark in the top ten, then turned on our superior southern lakes downwind speed to start picking off boats. On the next leg, we played the shifts up the middle. Boats were gambling hard left and right as well, but we stuck to our game. As predicted, six boats from the left side of the course rounded ahead of us and we went around in seventh. Those that went right lost big.

Downwind in an E-scow typically requires the skipper to sit on the low side to get the proper heel angle. You are basically steering blind. My spinnaker trimmer, Shawn Burke (Lake Lanier SC legend), is constantly talking to me, calling pressure in the spinnaker, making sure we are always at maximum speed. My son, Reese Wilkins, calls downwind tactics and puffs. A third of the way down the leg, we start getting lifted. Reese pulled the weather board down, which is code for time to jibe. You never want the boat next to you to know what you're up to, which in this case, was all good.

As we get closer to the lay line, we get a heading puff and jibe to the gates. We round the port gate with a 100-yard lead, and 126 E-scows behind us! What a sight! Using loose cover, we extend our lead and win the race using our basic ingredients of winning sailboat races.

With only two races completed, we didn't win those Nationals, placing third.

However, we took that experience to the next big regatta, etching in our minds the bullet; as well remembering the lesson of not banging a corner to the layline, unable to erase the 13th. But now the slate was clear, so onward and upward!

This was the 91st annual Westerns E Scow Championships, in White Lakes, Michigan, and we were chomping at the bit, southern boys and grits! With light winds for the first few races, we kept the crew light with just me, Sean and Reese. Taking a page out of Buddy Melges's playbook – win the start and extend your lead – we scored bullets for the first three races. Burnt Church Whiskey (South Carolina's finest), we were on fire!

But then the wind kicked up its heels to 15-18 (spicy!), which if you've ever seen the size of those E Scow sails, you'd be looking for a fourth like pirates for treasure. Luckily, we found a crew of perfect weight, Zoe McNeil. Once on board, we learned she was a professional dancer based out of Paris. For Southern boys, we had really upped our game! We  also learned that Zoe had skipped dancing in the Closing ceremonies of the Paris Olympics. As we stood atop the podium, we were looking good as Gold, and more importantly, had made a sailor out of Zoe.

I've raced Lasers, J24s, J105s and many other boats in my time, but I enjoy the hell out of being on an E Scow, screaming downwind on a full plane at nearly 20 knots. With the water gushing off the hull, it feels like you're going fifty, especially now at this time of writing I'm pushing 70! On a scow, full planing with a team of your best buds is what it's all about, unless you're taking someone new along and opening their eyes wide to the enjoyment of racing boats. We all race sailboats for the love of sailing, but deep down, we want to win.

My friends ask me why at this ripe age, I'm still racing sailboats all over the world. Well, that's easy. If you were a golfer, would you go play golf with Tiger Woods, and all the other world's greatest golfers? Yes, but you can't. In sailing, I get to race against Olympic medal winners, America's Cup sailors, and all the pros, and when I put together all my ingredients of winning, this good ole Southern crew can tiller sticks dang well beat them.

THE LEEWARD MARK

The apex of the racecourse where most gains and losses are made, is the downwind mark. As you approach the downwind mark, it's time to put on your race car driver's helmet and Ricky Bobby light up your *Talladega Nights*.

If a single mark is set, you will typically round it to port. If two marks are set, known as a Gate, you will have a few more tactical decisions to make, but sometimes half the boats to deal with (the other half being dummies because they rounded the wrong gate).

Depending on how many boats are going to be stacked wide, you must decide whether it's going to be to your advantage to fight for the inside lane, take it wide with speed, or stall and wait for the inside lane to open again.

Aside from drawing the perfect arc around the mark, the key to a successful rounding comes partly with sheeting in the sails. We'll cover all of that in the Boat Handling chapter, but suffice to say, the sailors who can sheet most efficiently will make juicy, secret sauce dripping gains.

Either you're going to come out of those marks smothered like a down blanket or fresh as a clover bud. With kite, a bad douse or furl and you'll unfurl your regatta standings. Who knows, maybe in the excitement of it all, you forget to put your board down. Let's first cover typical situations you will certainly encounter during a single mark rounding.

Clear of all boats... no overlap

You're coming into the mark clear of all other boats. All boats behind you have no overlap. With a fluid mark rounding, you can either gain advantage or blow it. If you're an experience mark rounder, you know the drill: approach wide, making your turn so that you come around the mark as close as possible on the lee side without touching the mark. You're close hauled and hauling away. You've left no gap for any boats to come tighter to the mark and take your windward advantage. Provided your boat handling skills match your mark rounding skills, You will have the advantage of being the most windward boat, free to tack at will.

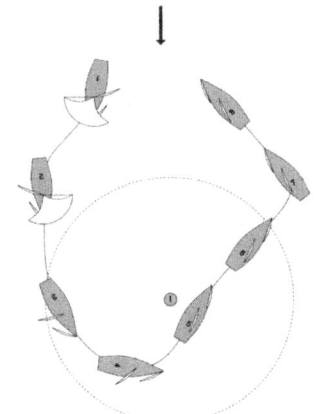

Overlap with one competitor

In this scenario, you're battling for inside room at the mark. You need to establish a solid overlap on Sam Regattaham well in advance of those 3 boat lengths, leaving no argument as to when you've reached it.

Once you have established that overlap, make sure that you stay well overlapped, keeping Sam midships. This way, when you make your turn, he has no way of slipping inside of you on the other side of the mark. You'll

WINNING WAYS

be well ahead on your way back upwind in clear air and Sam will be in your dirty air and have to slow to tack. You'll already be in a good position to cover if he does.

Situation: Overlap

You're both approaching the mark on starboard about ten boat lengths out. You have a slight lead over Sam, but he's gaining on you, starting to blanket your wind, with a good possibility of grabbing the overlap on the inside. What do you do?

a) Take a quick jibe to port, gybe again, and approach the mark on starboard hoping you have the right of way.

b) Offer Sam a beer.

Photo: Christophe Favreau

c) Sail by the lee to prevent Sam from turning you into Rice Krispy Treats.

d) Drop your centerboard to slow the boat.

Solutions:

a) If you are with just a main or additionally an A-sail, this is a good tactic. But if taking those two gybes with a spinnaker pole to set, you'll lose ground and risk a foul up. You may be coming into the mark with greater speed, but those two gybes will have cost you. Sam is clear ahead but slow when entering that imaginary zone. Inside the circle, you gain an overlap, yelling "Starboard" till you are blue in the face. Sam is wise. There was no overlap entering the zone. You'll have to bow to Sam and smell the barbecue sauce, most likely until you can tack onto the short tack and the wrong side of the course to boot. You've booted it.

b) This might work, as long as Sam is of age and you put a beer opener on the side of your boat to place him outside of the overlap.

c) Sailing by the lee, defending inside position is the best defense against an overtaking boat. If a gybe happens, you might get in trouble. Don't let the gybe happen. And don't be the fleet marshmallow. Turkey's are not always sure which way to fly, but they will put up a fight. Don't let Sam push you around. Keep him to your outside. Rounding the leeward mark is where the battle worth fighting. Win the war!

d) Well, it's always a good idea to drop your centerboard before rounding.

Log Jam!

Lots of boats are converging on the mark at once! Oh nooo! Mr. Bill!

If you're in a larger fleet, or another fleet has converged on the same mark (this situation will occur quite often on that first downwind mark rounding). You see a lot of boats ahead of you, and a few to your side. Looking behind you, you see a gap, so nothing to worry about boats sneaking in there to grab inside advantage while chaos ensues. What to do?

Stall. Sheet in your sail. Let the boats ahead get locked in that logjam, with Bob Buttermark fouling Fred Muttermouse fouling Cheeky Rodriques who's got his brand new Helly Hansen jacket wrapped around Nancy Boatfancy's boom. I don't know. I'm running out of names, but there's a log jam alright, and you're best tactic is to stall to avoid getting fouled up or trapped on the outside. Instead, you will be Bilbo Baggins, put the ring on and sneak inside of it all. One mark to rule them all, one mark to bind them!

Photo: Deb Fewell Durbec

Keeping your nose clean means avoiding log jams completely. Should the other gate be not sorely unfavored, head for that gate. There's a chance with that you're going to be ineffective at stalling, or the logjam is so tight that you're forced at the last second to dive behind a bunch of people whose names do not even exist. If you've got superior boat speed, and the course is rife with shifts, you've got a better chance at speeding around the apex by not interacting with any boats at all. Remember, if you can't grab the inside, don't try to force the inside boat into the mark, or grab their boom and knock yourself in the head with it. Give space, keep speed, live long and prosper.

If you've got Risky Bobby let's mix it up see what comes out of the blender... you might come out of the mark full speed ahead. Alpha dog! Or you might not. Marshmallow cat. If it's super windy, keep your nose clean at all costs, and this means rounding marks wider than you normally would. Then let your boat speed do the talking.

If someone else tries to be a Risky Bobby and come screaming in there after the 3 boat lengths, like Tom Pace says, shout it out! Let the other boat know they don't have. Let them know when they're taking too much room. Because if it is a port rounding, and you are both on starboard, room is needed to gybe and clear your boom. That's nearly 3 boat length wide! Regardless, whatever happens, don't just ram into the other boat to make a point.

Cutting the corners close will give you an advantage, but one time out of ten, you're going to bleed out your throwout nose.

While the RC may or may not attempt to set the gate marks at equal distance from the windward mark, 9 times out of 10, one of those marks is going to be closer, requiring less distance to sail the course.

You can usually tell by the boats in front of you which gate is favored. It's a bit harder to guess when you're in the lead, particularly in a one class dedicated regatta. Let's assume you can decipher which gate is the favored gate. Why would you want to round the less favored gate?

One situation would be if you are trailing another boat and trying to split tacks, preventing your opponent from closely covering; at least for the first chunk of the leg. Or you may want to explore greater pressure occurring around that gate and take that side for the gain.

The number one reason to head for the disfavored gate is to avoid a gate clusterfuffle. While losing a bit of ground to the boats that get around cleanly, you are going to make significant gains on the boats that don't. You're sailing at speed in clear air. You've done your clean air clearing tack. Just make sure that the gate is not tragically off kilter, or off with your Kilt. (Scottish heritage from way back Bruce Fleming joke). I don't make too many jokes about Bruce, as he sails with a cooler full of beer and a bottle opener attached to his rail.

You will find many situations similar to the left gate rounding as you would a singular mark. Rounding the right gate is easier, as you are able to come in on starboard, douse the spinnaker to port, and round without the usual panic. Someone can still call room on you coming in on port if they have an overlap or are first to zone.

All things being equal, I always choose the gate that gives me clear air coming out of it, heading toward the favored side of the course.

ANDY BURDICK: *Eeenie meenie minie moe.*

Photo: Lexi Pline

1) Which side of the racecourse has more wind? Start the decision process halfway down your downwind run. Wind is a major factor in your decision, so stand up, look around, and begin to decide well before the leeward mark.

2) Which mark will have less traffic? Not only should you look for less traffic as you enter the leeward gates, but you should also determine which mark will have less traffic as you exit the gate. In a big fleet, the downwind boats will create a lot of bad air – enter the marks clean and exit on the side with less downwind traffic so that you can sail full speed.

3) Which mark is closer? If there is a large discrepancy between the gates pick the mark that is closer and prepare for the rounding well in advance. Board down, outhaul on, Cunningham set, sitting on the high-side ready to trim your sail fast and smooth. Exit the gate, focus on angle of heel, mainsheet trim, and speed. Focus is key after you exit the mark.

Andy: While simple in theory, none of these are that simple. Determining wind strength often comes quickest based on the experience on the upwind leg, plus how the fleet is shifting downwind. Assessing traffic requires a crystal ball, particularly as the approach to the mark is done in the final third of the leg. And then there's deciding which of the bobbing marks looks closer. However, ask the questions early, involve the whole crew, and commit to your decision.

SECOND BEAT

Hog Island Race, hiking whole hog!

The second beat or third, if there is one, will require different tactics that the first. By this time, the fleet is far more spread out. Your key opponents become identified. Or perhaps you just have it in for someone who always tacks on top of your wind. You want to give them good hell.

Conditioning also comes into play on the second beat. That's when it's time to Joe Duplin "open up the bailers and let the blood flow out!"

Like identifying the long tack on the first weather leg, before rounding the mark or gate, you'll want to pre-load this information into your strategy. Typically, you can tell right away which it will be. If the wind has shifted and the course has not been reset, if you're coming into the mark on a reach instead of downwind, you'll want to round and tack very soon, if not a rounding tack.

The second leg is all about BOAT SPEED. If you have it, you'll make big gains. If you don't, the only way to keep a good boat down is to smother and cover.

COVERING

Situation 1: You're leading the race, thinking that the right side is heavily favored, but your key opponent, Carly Comeinfirst, is going left. However, you're hesitant to cover her as you are quite sure that the right is right. Many other boats feel the same way. What do you do? Well, it depends on the point spread. If you can let the other boats go, and your "I love the sound of the horn blasting as I cross in first" ego, you've got to cover Carly, Charley.

Situation 2: Same situation, only the point spread is tighter between you Carly, and the next three or four boats. You know Carly is just swinging for the fences. What to do? Keep your boat between the mark and the other boats. Stay on the long tack, keeping as much to the middle as you fiddling can, and sail fast! Hot tin roof it! Upwind, the rich always get richer, unless they're not paying attention and sail into a big fat hole, no pun coming on that one.

Situation 3: You're Carly. You're trying to get out from somebody's cover, without losing a bunch of boats behind you. You also know the right is favored, but Jackal up there with his Hot Donuts sign lit, has already hit the pressure line and on the long tack. He's nailed you at the leeward mark. You're in his bad air. Take a short tack, clear your air, and hope he covers.

After all, you're Carly, and you have some wicked tacking skills. Every single time the Donut tacks, you tack. He's bound to make a mistake. Hopefully, you out-tack him and when he comes across next time on starboard, he's too close to cover. You're on your way to victory. If not, you tip your hat. It's very hard to come back on the second and third legs.

Paul Abdullah: *In one championship determining race at the 2024 Thistle Nationals, things were going sideways mid-race, but we knew our speed would give us opportunities later in the race. At the last leeward gate, we were just behind Dave Dellenbaugh and victory was in sight. We never panicked whenever things weren't going our way. Our saying in our boat is "boat speed kills" and each race we found our way back in the top 10 by focusing solely on our boat speed and technique. I'd gather "Boat speed kills" refers to competitors. Hence the boat name, "Crime Scene."*

SECOND DOWNWIND LEG

The second run is pretty much a parade, unless you've got Bruce Fleming dynamite downwind boat speed. Again, at this point in the race, it's all about boat speed. This is the time to try to shut Brucespeed speed down. You need to cover him jibe for jibe, so you can throw a hot doughy smothery blanket on that boat speed. If your boat handling is up to par, get into a jibing duel. Just don't let them get 50 paces away, or they'll be gone. Sometimes, you just have to tip your hat. Lots of hat tipping going on here, which is why I like sailboat racing. Up your game or it's *Chapeaux!*

The one thing you don't want to do, is go off on flyer to try to take the win. Don't get greedy unless you've got the point spread. Going for Gold at the 2018 U.S. Multihull Nationals, I fell completely off the podium by gybing

Me and Davo down by the school yard.   Photo: Tracy Berntsen

in the opposite direction of the fleet. I was in second place on the final leg. All I had to do was follow and finish. I knew I wasn't going to catch Randy Smyth by following in medium air, so instead I gybed, taking a flyer to the left, getting passed by 11 boats. That's okay to do if it's the last race and you have a good throwout, but I had two breakdowns already, so had to eat the points along with some crow for falling off the podium, finishing the regatta in 4th. But if you're going for Gold, you're going for Gold. Nobody remembers who finished second.

GET UP, STAND UP

Here's a common situation: you're in the lead and everything's going great. Much to Boston's chagrin, you look back. What do you see? A bunch of white caps and the whole fleet up on a plane. *Barnacles!* They're coming up fast and soon riding your tail. Now you're up on a plane. What actions do you take?

Peter C: *Well, first I try to determine which gybe I should be on when that wind finally reaches my boat. I want to follow one of the oldest rules of sailing, to bear off in the puffs and head up in the lulls. In this situation, I'm in a lull, so I want to begin sailing high on whatever gybe I've determined will get me to the edge of the puff first. I'm not going to complicate things by talking about the angle of the waves. So how do I do that? One of the things that I learned many years ago sailing E Scows, was watching Buddy Melges go off the wind. He was always standing up and looking around. Standing, rather than sitting, helps you see a little further, see a little bit better. It gives you a wider view of what's going on, so when something bad like that is happening, you will always see me stand up before making any decision.*

Dave Perry: *I always try to sail above the line of the boats behind me, so they realize I will not let them sail above me and take my air. If you stay below their line, you are asking for them to sail high and try to attack your air, in which case you are forced to sail high to defend...and everyone loses. I try to be proactive in my defensive positioning.*

THE FINISH TO WEATHER

Whether the finish is to weather or a downwind finish, this is the most exciting moment of the race. It's the point where all of your fun work to get here can either pay off with a strong finish, or wither. Finishing strong relies on good fitness, keen tactics, and nerves of steel. The bigger the moment, the stronger the steel needed.

TOO MANY CHAMPIONS TO COVER

by Hal Gilreath Jr.

Sailing the final beat of the second race of the 2003 Snipe World Championship, we were battling an adverse current in the Baltic Sea off the coast of Borstahusen, Sweden. My crew was James Liebl. In this high level of competition, we were in uncharted territory: out in front, leading world champion competitors from Spain, Brazil, and the U.S., all pushing us in a tense and close race. One mistake, bad tack, poor decision or drop in boat speed and our lead would evaporate instantaneously. When James wasn't alerting me of our keen competitor's moves, he remained silent while he balanced the boat between puffs and lulls. Our confidence from practicing countless hours was the only thing calming our nerves.

As we were nearing the starboard tack layline on port, the former world champion from Brazil started to gain on us. The Spanish boat was on our hip and lifting slightly. We tried to remain calm and relaxed, yet the moment was intense. Who to cover? One mistake and one of ten boats could win the race. There were prior world and national champions nipping at our heels.

There was no thinking about anything else. This was the moment. We had practiced countless hours for this. If we could only make it to the finish line before those storied sailors caught us.

A strong current slowed our upwind progress. The layline seemed infinitely further away. As an integral unit, we communicated silently, maintaining focus and concentration on not only speed, but nailing the layline to the finish. With a little ease of both sheets, we pointed the bow down to avoid stalling. The Snipe picked up speed, which did magic to calm our nerves. It was time to go and we rolled onto starboard with a perfectly executed tack, coming out with good speed.

The Brazilian was also on starboard about five boat lengths behind. The Spanish boat tacked to weather on our hip. Though the finish boat was in sight, the current pulled us downwind. No! A slight lift came in and the Spanish boat gained a touch. As long as we didn't have to tack to cross the finish line. As long as we just remained calm and focused on sailing the boat, "fast forward," our motto.

The finish line could not come too soon. As the wind lifted us up and over the finish line, we realized we'd done it. We won the second race of the Snipe Worlds. It was a memorable achievement. We sailed well the rest of the regatta to finish in the top ten of the highly competitive fleet of sixty. It took years of practice through ups and downs, disciplined planning, and overcoming sailing plateaus of our own to achieve this result. All well worth it, as these skills both enrich and translate well into life. – Hal Gilreath

Most anyone who has led even a regional regatta can relate to the nervousness of that moment. The more moments like this you experience, the less jittery the knees, the quicker that line will seem to come.

RC's can set the finish line wherever they please. Generally, it's set a third of the way up, and only at the top on the last race of the day or a shortened course. This is where you really need to be cognizant of where the finish line has been set (or reset... there's a flag for that. Flag C, and they must give an audible signal and display a white board with the new compass heading).

Wherever it's set, as you approach, make sure you identify which side of the finish line is favored. Nail the favored end on starboard so that no oncoming port tack boats can lee bow you and squeeze in to steal the point.

Typically, at this point in the game, you're duking it out with one or two people. That point you gain or lose often makes the difference in the final results. If I'm behind, I'm splitting tacks. If I'm ahead, I'm covering closely. There's no rocket science there, yet sometimes a fast sailor can slip your cover. That's why the best tactic is to plan your final approach to the finish on starboard, with the layline being dead reckoned to the short end of the finish line. Nail the final layline, and you leave no room for the leeward boat to finish.

Speaking of strong finishes, Violette Dorange got her start in the Int'l 420 Class, before progressing to the IMOCA Class under the tutelage of Jean Le Cam. She is the youngest at this time to finish the solo round the world Vendee Globe Race.

THE DOWNWIND FINISH

Downwind finishes are often the most exciting, where you can have multiple boats vying for the line at once. Big gains and losses can result. If someone is skilled, they will blanket you at the last second and cross ahead. Like a Formula One race, pass too soon and they will be passed right back.

Just as you would determine which mark gate to round, you need to determine which side of the finish line is favored well *before* arriving. You can win many places by choosing the closest side (with the most pressure if a factor). I remember both losing a long fought downwind battle by choosing the wrong side in less pressure (20 knots instead of 25!), and winning one when Berntsen went for the favored end, only to be shut off the line by a fleet of starting Hobies! That one point won Santa Cruz YC Multihull Invitational.

COVERING DOWNWIND

Photo: Christophe Favreau

Just as you would cover an opponent upwind, you also need to cover them going downwind, particularly when heading toward a downwind finish. It's a more difficult proposition, as going downwind, any pressure coming from the top of the course is going to make the poor richer. The last thing you want to have happen, is to be blanketed a few boat lengths from the finish and have some boats fly in right before the line with room to finish. But there's more to it...

Monty Spindler: *Stay between the next mark and your competitors, trying to keep an inside position at the leeward mark.*

Let's hear from guru Windmill sailor, Alan Taylor, on how he used this tactic to keep Hummingbird from becoming the word.

HURRICANE HUMMINGBIRD

by Alan Taylor

It was the third race of the 2016 Windmill Nationals at Oriental, NC. In the fleet of 25 boats there were eight past national champions and at least 15 sailors who have finished in the top 10 at past Nationals. This was my crew's first time in my boat, "Hurricane". We had been improving our position over the first two races, getting to know each other and adjusting to the conditions. The wind was building to the 18-22 knot range with a steep 2-3 foot chop.

Photo: Marcy Sherman

At the weather mark we were about two boat lengths ahead of "Hummingbird". "Hurricane" (that's us) had good boat speed and we were slowly increasing our lead. There was less current to the left side of the course, but "Hummingbird" was going right, looking for more wind. No choice but to go to that side of the course as well. I didn't want Hummingbird to fly off to one side and gybe back ahead of me. I was focusing on surfing waves and keeping us moving fast. With this heavy wind, we were broad reaching, optimizing speed, rather than sailing dead down.

"Watch them and tell me when they gybe" I told my crew. "And let's focus on a clean gybe. Did you see those monster jellyfish? Let's keep the slimy side down. NO SWIMMING!"

We had extended our lead to 5 or 6 boat lengths, but I wasn't taking any chances. In those conditions, I can get too focused on surfing waves and going fast, forgetful of what's going on behind me.

When "Hummingbird" gybed, "Hurricane" gybed, maintaining clear air and our position between our competition and the finish line. We crossed the finish line ahead, knowing we had sailed a good race. Good communication, staying between our competition and the downwind finish made the difference that day.

Protect your lead! Cover downwind!   – Alan Taylor

ROOM TO FINISH

There's an important rule (Rule 18) that comes into play here. Many sailors still haven't wrapped their head around it. I was once one of those, as I was quite pleasantly surprised when I was passing at the last second to windward of Texas John. Texas John was famous for falling off his Weta, catching a ride on a motorboat, and jumping back on it before it hit the shore. Weta's like to think they sail better no handed. Okay, let's finish the story.

Drone footage: CJ Lacour YT @tallflyer

Texas John and I were heading to the finish line on a broad reach. Both on starboard, I was the windward boat, and we were overlapped, with my boat slightly ahead. I thought for certain John was going to luff me up, forcing me off the finish line to windward of the pin. That's how it was in the 'dog old days.' Read the new rulebook, Dummy! To my surprise, John bore off and hailed in his slow Texas drawl, *"Geau Ahayid."* What? Go ahead? Why certainly! John gave me room to finish.

Rule 18, Room at the Mark, applies at the finish line as well. You must treat the finish line marks just as you would a downwind mark. I don't feel too bad, after seeing the USA boat luff one boat off the finish line in NZ Sail GP

This photo was taken from the RC boat at the finish of Wetafest. Cliff Farrah (Cam's Dad. green boat) is in the money position. By the quite old rules, yellow boat to leeward could have luffed both boats off the line, but under revised, all have to be given room to finish.

2025. They wound up with a penalty, allowing another boat to finish ahead of them below, and in last place. Disaster! It's one thing to bone the finish in a club race, quite another in front of a grandstand and TV audience. Let's hear it for armchair quarterbacks! Even the Opti kids were posting face palms.

Lose the battle. **Win the War.**

WINNING WAYS

NOT OVER TILL IT'S OVER
by Cam Farrah

One of the most valuable lessons I've learned in sailing is that the race isn't over until you cross the finish line. As an avid foiling catamaran sailor, I have seen (and been) the boat leading the race that suddenly falls off the foils and drops into nearly last place. On the far more fun flip side, I have also been the boat in last place who catches a miracle puff and foils through the fleet into first place.

Cam Farrah sending it at A-Class North Americans.   Photos: Tim Ludvigsen

My favorite memory of this was at the 2022 A-Class Catamaran North American Championship in Burlington, Ontario. In one particular race, I pushed the start line a bit too hard. As I grimaced at the sound of my sail number being called over the VHF, my fellow competitor to leeward, Bruce Mahoney, confirmed my fears—I was over the line early. After a few mumbled expletives, I bailed out of the fleet sailing upwind and foiled down to dip the line.

At this point in the A-Class Catamaran fleet history, upwind foiling was not very widespread in the USA. We were all just figuring out how to foil upwind while keeping our VMG halfway decent without reaching off into la-la-land. This process of learning how to upwind foil led to some pretty spectacular wipeouts throughout the fleet (many of which I proudly claim). Our European and Australian counterparts had upwind foiling pretty much dialed in at this point. In the USA, we were all resorting to short Facebook videos to try and learn as much as we could about this new element of sailing.

As I looked back upwind, the race leader was rounding the top mark. Part of me said to write the race off as a throwout, but another part of me said screw it, let's see how many boats I can grind back. Few things are quite as fun as the challenge of slowly passing boats one by one and really working for it. I started to sail upwind in a skim mode, somewhere in between displacement and foiling. Finally, I committed to experimenting and upwind foiling the whole race. I started upwind foiling and slowly started to pick boats off one by one.

As I finally got to the top mark, I remember seeing my good friend and sailing mentor, Mike Krantz, cheer for me from a support boat. That downwind, I pushed as hard as I could and caught a few more boats. I foiled the next upwind and again saw Mike cheering as I passed a few more boats. At this point, I was so out of breath and so fatigued with the added stress of upwind foiling that I didn't think I had another max effort downwind left in me. On the last downwind I looked and saw that the breeze had died and the top pack of 5 boats had swapped to displacement mode. I did everything I could to stay on the foil and remembered a few sketchy moments just praying the foil would hold on.

One by one, the leaders turned, saw me closing the gap, yanked their travelers up, and scrambled to rebuild their apparent wind to hop back on the foil. In the end, I think I finished the race in the top 5 and I remember it being one of the hardest fought races I have ever had.

Don't give up and keep pushing hard until you cross the finish line. It is important to be open-minded and recognize opportunity on the racecourse when it presents itself. Whichever boat I'm racing, I've learned that every race presents opportunities for comebacks. You will have races where you catch a miracle puff or a lucky shift and pass the majority of the fleet. Or you will have races where you realize the guys behind you are in the biggest puff in the world and this will give you time to defend. It all counts, and it isn't over until it's over. – Cam Farrah

THERE ARE NO DNF's

David Troup, a successful sailor in Green Bay, gives great advice to his kids. It's not only a sailing lesson, but a life lesson. There are no DNF's. I tried to tell this to the Race Committee at the Laser Worlds in Brazil:

There were three boats vying for the lead, and I was one of them. Stu Neff and I got into a battle, which let the third boat escape. The line was favored on the pin end, so I headed for it and caught back the yards lost. I think he may have had me by a hair, but as we both crossed, a big gust hit, and the Dutch sailor capsized right on top of the RC boat! That meant I just won my first race at the Worlds!

I was ecstatic, telling my American friends all about it, maybe boasting just a bit, when John Geyer came into my room to tell me the news. "Dude, they scored you as DNF."

"DNF? What? No! I never DNF!" Indeed, I had thrown up all over the boat and taken 100 points for race one. "Well, you'd better get to the RC and file a protest. You'll need a witness." "Did you see it?" "Hell no, I was way far back."

Stu. I went to see him. "Hey Stu, you saw me finish just ahead of you, right? I mean, we had a tacking duel. You had to have." "Oh yeah. Sure. I saw you. A good duel." "Great! Can you be my witness? I'm protesting my result right now." "Um, sure. I guess so."

When we got to the protest room, Stu had either downed a strong Brazilian beer or came down with amnesia. Most likely, he realized that by claiming what I said was true, he'd lose a valuable point. The RC decided to give me whatever my average score was up until that race, which when adding up the 100 points, was middle of the pack.

Lesson learned? Don't rely on competitors to vouch for you. Pass by the RC boat after you finish to make sure your score has been recorded. But the real lesson here is, unless you're so broken down you can't, to finish the race, no matter bad it's gone. And if you do bail, try to let the RC know however possible (if on shore if you've busted up something).

Paris Olympics (Marseille)   ALeN Photography   Photo: Nikos Alevromytis

"If you're going through hell, keep going." Winston Churchill

Photo: Will Keyworth

JOHN KOSTECKI INTERVIEW

By John Bertrand

John Bertrand is author of Inside The Laylines, a sailing blog found online that explores the minds of champions and what it takes for them to be successful.

Adding to an already stellar career, John Kostecki claimed the 2024 Star World Championships, an accomplishment that is the sailing equivalent of winning the Masters in golf. The rich history, prestige, and level of competition associated with these events place a sailor's name alongside many of the sport's greatest champions.

Kostecki is now the only sailor to have won an Olympic medal, the America's Cup, the Volvo Ocean Race, and, most recently, the prestigious Star World Championship. His name is now engraved alongside other legends of the sport on the Star World Championship trophy, cementing his place as one of the great sailors of all time.

However, you would never know his celebrity and notoriety by how he acts, as he rarely seeks the limelight. He is a purist, an athlete who loves sailing and enjoys winning, embracing the ethos that "you are only as good as your next race."

I've enjoyed watching John develop during his early days as a St. Francis Junior Program beneficiary. Although I never competed against him in dinghies, I have raced against him in keelboats, sailed together, and even coached him at the Farr 40 World Championships.

Interviewing him was an opportunity to catch up and learn firsthand about his last-minute preparations, key moments, and the journey to his 2024 Star Worlds victory.

Secrets to Success in One Design Racing

John Bertrand: Take us into your boat two minutes after the start of the final race of the 2024 Star World Championship. Six boats could win it, and you were tied on points, being chased by five other teams. The pressure was high, and the Championship was on the line. Take us into your head: Where were you positioned? Where were your competitors? Were you on the front foot? What was the game plan?

John Kostecki: We actually had a great start, positioned about a third of the way down from the committee boat on a super-long line. We weren't focused on any specific boats; we were just trying to get the best result possible since six boats could win. We liked the middle-right side upwind, and a few minutes after the start, with a left shift, we were able to tack and cross the boats that started to the right of us.

The moment we tacked, I looked through the window, and we were looking really good compared to the boats on the right. But, looking back now, I think most of our competitors were actually to the left of us (laughs). We were focused on speed, avoiding mistakes, and staying precise, as the legs were long, and it took time to figure out the shifts. About three to four minutes after the start, on port, we were in a strong position. Austin kept looking back and updating me on how we were doing. The boats to our left tacked onto port and fell behind us, so we gained on them. That's how it played out, and we rounded just ahead of the five boats we needed to beat.

Photo: A. Lelli

John Bertrand: Growing up in San Francisco during your time, how did that shape you as a sailor? What impact did it have on your pursuit of the Olympics and your professional career? Could you share more about the mentors, yacht clubs, and racing on the bay? I know the Richmond Yacht Club and the St. Francis Yacht Club played a big part in your development.

John Kostecki: Yeah, I went through Richmond's junior program. I started when I was seven or eight and finished the program when I was 17 or 18. In the meantime, I joined the St. Francis Yacht Club when I was 15. Kimball Livingston got me connected after I attended the Tinsley Island Symposium. I guess he liked me and thought I should become a member, so he pushed hard for me to join. That was a nice boost to my career.

We weren't a wealthy family growing up, so St. Francis really helped me. They provided me with a Laser for campaigning and even helped with expenses. They gave me a credit card for gas and provided the club van and trailer. We'd load four to six Lasers on the trailer and travel to regattas, which was really helpful in getting my career started.

San Francisco Bay is an incredible place to grow up sailing. The conditions are diverse, with strong winds and current, which helped me develop as an all-around sailor.

In terms of mentors, I was fortunate to have people like you, Paul Cayard, Steve Jeppsen, Craig Healy, and others, including Tom Blackaller. Guys like you, who were three to ten years older, had such successful careers, whether it was winning Laser Worlds or competing in the Olympics. Watching your success showed me that it was possible for me too, and that was pretty cool.

John Bertrand: How did your partnership with Austin Sperry develop, and what made you two so successful at the Worlds?

John Kostecki: Austin and I sailed Stars together about 20 years ago for roughly a year and a half. We were sponsored by Duraflame and spent most of our time sailing in Florida and Miami. We were aiming for the 2004 Olympics, but about a year before the Games, I got recruited by an America's Cup team. I took the job, leaving Austin without a skipper. He teamed up with his father-in-law, John Dane, and they went on to have great success, even winning the 2008 Olympic Trials and competing in the Olympics.

We stayed in touch over the years, and he recently got into the Etchells class. Last year, he invited me to sail the Etchells winter circuit in Miami with him, and we did three to five regattas. We had a lot of fun.

When he set his sights on the 2024 Star Worlds, he needed to find a new skipper or crew because he and his usual crew were over the class weight limit. He said he didn't mind crewing and asked if I'd drive for the summer. I jumped at the opportunity.

John Bertrand: Austin mentioned that winning the Star Worlds was a lifelong dream—30 years in the making. That must feel pretty special for both of you.

John Kostecki: Yeah, he was really pumped. I think this was his first World

Championship, and the Star Worlds is a pretty special one to win. He was definitely thrilled.

John Bertrand: It looked like you only sailed together in five regattas leading up to the Championship.

John Kostecki: Yeah, something like that. Each regatta, we got better and better. We didn't focus too much on the results in those regattas. We were just working on the processes, getting the boat speed right, and staying sharp for the Worlds.

Photo: Will Keyworth

When the Worlds came around, we were going fast and felt confident. We applied the same processes, addressed a few weaknesses, and it all paid off.

John Bertrand: How were you able to sail so consistently? In a fleet of 64 boats, you didn't have any big scores. The starting line was massive, and I assume conservative positioning was key, letting things play out and never taking too many risks.

John Kostecki:
Yes and no. In general, yes, but in the first race of the regatta, we started right at the pin end and won it. Two or three minutes in, we were able to tack and cross the fleet, leading at the first windward mark. That day was really shifty and tricky, though. But in general, yes, we sailed conservatively. We were fast upwind, stuck to the basics, sailed the long tack, and tried to stay on the favored side. It sounds simple, but it worked because we were fast!

John Bertrand: Can you talk about your approach to starting on such a long line?

John Kostecki: In the Star class, they typically raise the orange flag with 10 minutes to go, five minutes before the actual warning. Most of the time, you had enough time to work your way to the end of the line where you wanted to be. It got trickier after a general recall or when they reset the line.
Many of the starts had general recalls, so we'd often hang out above the line in the middle, which gave us the flexibility to bolt to one end or the other when the line reset. We tried to stay as flexible as possible. We also kept an eye on what some of our top competitors were doing and always had that in mind.

WINNING WAYS

John Bertrand: Let's talk about the final race. You covered the first upwind—take us through the rest.

John Kostecki: I think it was the first downwind where we solidified the win. We rounded just ahead of two of the five boats we needed to beat—Will Stout, Danny Cayard, and George Szabo, Guy Avellon. In the previous race, there was a similar wind pattern with a south wind  and lots of shifts. In that race, staying off to the right side of the course on the downwind leg paid off, so I kept that in mind. Our competitors jibed and headed towards the middle of the fleet, while we stayed on the right and found a little more pressure. That allowed us to extend on those two boats and the rest of the fleet.

The Argentine team gained a lot on the final downwind—they're super fast downwind—but we only needed to finish in the top three to win. I knew they would pass us, but we managed to finish 3rd and ahead of Will and Daniel, which secured the championship by 1 point!

John Bertrand: Winning the Star Worlds—where does this rank among all the regattas you've won?

John Kostecki: You're not the first to ask! The trophy is incredible. I don't know the exact year it dates back to—maybe the 1920s—but the names on it are legendary: Lowell North, Malin Burnham, Dennis Conner, Tom Blackaller, and many more. I've been lucky to have had a successful career, and I've honestly lost count of how many world championships I've won. But I'd say this one ranks right up there as one of the best.
It's hard to compare it to something like the Olympics or the Volvo Ocean Race or the America's Cup—they're all so different—but this one is definitely up there. It's a huge win.

John Bertrand: What advice would you give to young sailors who aspire to achieve the level of success that you've had across multiple sailing disciplines?

John Kostecki: My advice would be to just keep at it and try to enjoy it as much as you can. Follow your passion and your heart. That's what I did when I was young—I went where I had the most fun and what inspired me. When you're having fun, you tend to do better. Don't get too focused on the results all the time. Just focus on improving, enjoying the process, and being present in the moment. If you're having fun, success will come.

BOAT TRIM

Boat Speed: A tactician's best friend. Depending on racecourse conditions, boat speed can trump poor tactical choices. The steadier the wind, the more

boat speed comes into play. With great boat speed, you can take less risk.

As a sprouting lad, I wanted to know everything there was to know about a sailboat's hydro and aerodynamics. I began doing something I'd never done before: I paid attention in math class and physics. While it may have been a bit too late for my creatively shaped mind to grasp principles based on Calculus, I got my hands on every book I could find on the subject.

Eventually, I tried to tackle the formulas within C.A. Marchaj's *Sailing Theory and Practice*. Written in 1964, these principles still apply today. This book *almost* changed my life, as I spent my senior year in high school glued to a drafting desk in a special architecture program. I wound up not liking being chained to a desk but have still always been interested in aero/hydrodynamics as they apply to sailboat racing. Let's first take a more scientific look at the variances of boat trim.

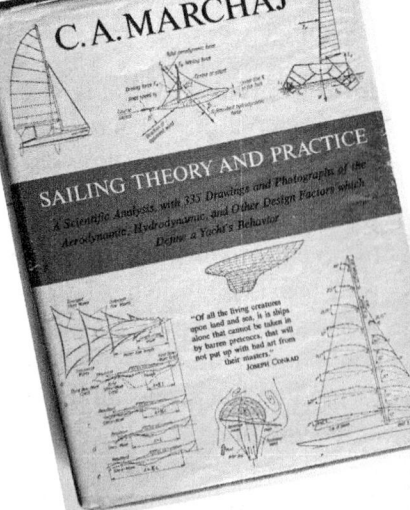

HEEL TRIM

CLOSE HAULED HEEL

The amount of heel you should allow when sailing close hauled again depends upon the boat sailed. It also depends on the strength of the wind. Through powers of observation (fellow sailors flying by), you'll soon learn the ideal amount of heel to achieve maximum upwind speed in various conditions. There are simple devices called inclinometers designed to indicate heel, so you can actually put a number on it. I put that number on the seat of my pants, visual sighting, and feel of the rudder.

Most boats sailing to weather sail best flat. It doesn't make a lot of sense why some boats sail faster with heel. Physics indicated that a blade straight down is going to provide more lift, thus less slippage to leeward. But physics and sailing don't always agree. Sailing with heel is quite different from say, a Thistle in light air to a Laser or Sunfish in heavy, where you want to be like Major Dick Tillman and *"Sail it Flat."* Dick won the first Laser North American titles by doing so.

When I met Dick at the Stephen C. Smith Memorial Regatta, I was still in high school, surprised to have won the regatta. It was my first big win. I did so by reading his book! He probably gave it to me just to make a kid feel good. It was one of the few trophies I wouldn't let my wife throw out, as it reminded me of the day I met Dick. Dick has now passed from cancer, as have many of my sailing friends. Steve Willett, left, gone way too early, within just a few weeks after I took this photo. If you ever have the chance to attend the regatta that run's in Steve's honor in Sacramento, or Stephen C. Smith's honor at Shell Point, FL, the are both raising funds for cancer research.

Okay, back to less serious subjects, like heel trim. On boats such as the MC Scow where there are two canted leeboards, heeling is essential. On this particular craft, you sail with only one blade in the water at a time. As the blade is canted, when you are heeled to that same degree of cant, when heeling at

13 degrees or so, the blade is pointing straight down.

In light air, these boats and all boats need leeward heel, if only to keep the sails full by the magnetic force of the Earth, e.i., gravity. Think about that!

REACHING HEEL

In light air, even on a reach or downwind (where in light air you should not be going dead downwind, but on a broad reach) boats still need leeward heel to keep the sails filled. As soon as there is enough wind to fill the sail without the assistance of gravity, you

should maintain proper heel, which in most boats is flat.

DOWNWIND HEEL

Similarly, in light air, leeward heel will keep the sails filled, particularly on lakes where there is a good bit of motorboat slop. However, once the wind picks up enough to keep the boom flying to the shrouds, you should incorporate a good tilt of heel to weather. This will effectively place the center of effort… the centered power of the sails… more aligned with the center of the boat.

On boats like a Laser, with downwind weather heel, you are also reducing wetted surface. Kids these days sail full tilt to weather even in drifters, holding the boom out by hand if necessary. The act becomes slightly more difficult with age. I've flipped

more times going downwind in light air than in heavy, as I'm heeling to weather so far that the rudder slips out, the boat flipping to windward. More swimming is involved.

FORE/AFT BOAT TRIM

UPWIND

SailCoach Malta

Most sailors pay good attention to heel. Very few pay attention to fore/aft boat trim. When sailing to weather, keeping the boat at least on an even fore/aft keel is worth a few places on the leaderboard.

In light air, you want to shift your weight toward the front of the boat. That's one of the reasons singlehanded sailors walk softly and carry a big stick. Unless you have a super chunky bow, it doesn't matter what boat you're on. Get that weight up toward the mast. It can be the most uncomfortable, cramped position. Combined with the extreme concentration required of light air sailing, you will be reminded that you should have listened to your partner and joined those yoga classes.

In medium air, you don't want to be as extreme as in light, but you still want to keep the bow pressed, the stern from dragging. If you've ever been in a motorboat, setting the course being your excuse, you know that you can push water by sitting on the stern drinking beer. The captain requires you to get another beer from the bow cooler. The boat levels off and planes away at twice the speed. It's like that. Well, maybe that's an extreme example, but let's just say you need to get your tail toward the shroud. In the case you don't have a shroud, get your weight forward, up near the front of the cockpit. Experiment. Find your place in the sun.

Heading upwind in a bit of breeze, the difference is not as critical as in light and medium air on some boats, super critical on others.

On the Flying Scot, you've got a bow like a Saint Bernard, so you need to get the crew just a bit further back, while Skipper can stay even with the mainsheet block. Having your weight centralized will create a more centralized point of "yaw". Separating the crew will have a braking effect. You can wonder about that, all the way back to when you were sitting on a see saw. With you on one end and Joey on the other, the saw of the "yaw" is dampened. Meet Joey in the middle for a bite of his sandwich, and the plank

StFYC Spring Dinghy Weston — Photo: Rick Saez

swings effortlessly.

On the Weta, it doesn't seem to really matter where I'm sitting, fore or aft. The boat is flying and there's no stopping it. In big waves, I try to minimize the boat speed killing effect of chop by sitting further back. Flat water, I'm back up by the shroud, digging the bow in which seems to increase pointing ability.

On the Laser, you're not exactly flying upwind; you're grinding, cracking six knots. The difference between the Laser virtuoso and the out of tune hack? The virtuoso is playing that hiking stick like a violin, fiddling away at the chop. Their body is rocking back heading up the wave and forward diving off the back (sheeting in and out in coordination with the movement).

FORE/AFT TRIM REACHING

Fore/aft trim while reaching generally allows you to get your bum as far back in the boat as you can without dragging the stern. Your exact positioning will either enhance or inhibit the ability to plane. You'll again, generally, initiate the plane by positioning your body further forward, then quickly scooting back once on a plane. This is emphasized if you are surfing. Get way back if you've made a steering error and are about to plow into a wave, filling your cockpit with water.

In high winds, maximum scoot. Keep the boat from braking and you'll keep the boat from breaking. To note: A reinforced seat on your hiking shorts/pants/wetsuit is essential for scooting. You don't want the material to be super gluey. If you want to sail properly by the seat of your pants, they should allow you to slide fore and aft quite freely.

FORE/AFT TRIM DOWNWIND

Sailing downwind as a singlehander, you will really need your booty to be super scooty. It depends upon the wind strength, your boat and your body/crew weight, and the class of boat you're sitting on to determine exactly where you scoot from and to. In breeze and waves, you have to scoot the boot like a butt bothered dog!

A speed puck might come in handy if you don't have a feel for how fast you're going or slowing. I'll give you a ballpark to swing for: plowing into a wave? Scoot back. Dragging stern trying to get the boat planing down a wave? Scoot your tuchas forward.

Plowing into a wave, scoot back, that's common sense. But few sailors have the nerve (the nerve!) to scoot forward to get planing. It's like when you're god forbid, on a motorboat, and the boat wont' plane until someone goes forward for a beer. Again, of a kid, to hand to Mom or Dad. Then the boat takes off!

CENTER/DAGGERBOARD TRIM

UPWIND

Before I forget and lest you do, the first rule of upwind board trim is to put the board down the second you cross the finish line, lest you forget and start the race with it up. Doh! I've done it countless times, the worst when I successfully port tacked the fleet, only to slide into last place before realizing my error. Best to blame that one on the crew.

Note for Centerboard boats only. Another thing to do in preparation for a race is to check and make sure (by turning your boat on its side), that the centerboard when fully down is cocked no further forward than 90 degrees.

For most boats, keep the board down at all times going upwind. Only when your sails are overpowered and you have too much weather helm should you raise the board up a tad, or in a daggerboard's case, pull it up about five inches. Make a mark on the board so you don't guess what magic number that might be.

REACHING

As you want to reduce drag, the board needs to be raised while reaching. How much will be determined by experience and experimentation. You'll still be using the board to reduce lateral slide and propel you forward. A great amount of sideways force is being applied on a reach, but you don't need the boat to be lifting.

If you choose to go to battle with an overtaking boat, or you are trying to overtake another boat, drop the board a bit before loading up.

DOWNWIND

Heading downwind, how little board you can get away with carrying in the water is a balance between drag and stability. Regardless of physics and formulas, a bit of board down helps the boat track. When the breeze picks up, it's best (particularly on a Laser), to put the board down a bit more for control. Too little board and you will likely be in for a death roll and perhaps some new boat parts. There goes that money for a lobster roll. Hopefully, you have dropped enough board to use it for righting purposes, as well as attached a shock cord so you are not swimming for it (they do float, at least on a Laser).

KELP AND WEED

How many times have you used the excuse that kelp and weeds were clinging to your board and rudder? You've gone through days of preparation. Your tactics are sharp. Boat speed, an advantage. Then, while you take your eyes off the water to search for pressure, you hit that dreaded pile of weed thicker than Tommy Chong's stash.

The longer you allow these weeds to smoke up your soak downs, the further behind you'll get. You should no longer concern yourself with where's the pressure. The pressure is happening to your boards and the cassettes that hold them in place. It's not only bad for boat speed, it's bad for the boat.

Those weeds are more clingy than Glenn Close to Michael Douglass in *Fatal Attraction*. You'll also need to clear the rudder somehow. This will require either raising and lowering the rudder, violent wiggles of the stick, or getting your hopefully skinny ass to the back to the stern, clearing by hand. However you manage to do it, cut your losses. Blow those weeds off like a southern lawnscaping leafblowing deity.

At the 505 Worlds in Santa Cruz, efficiently clearing kelp was key to winning. Okay, they were fast, too. Morgan Larsen and Trevor Baylis, convicted boat tinkerers and innovators of stuff, revealed their weapon; a long tubular batten of crime with razor blade attached, aligned to the leading edge of the rudder. Morgan could reach back and clear weed without pulling a wheelie.

SAIL TRIM

Small wonder sailmakers are typically on top of the leaderboard. Classifying them as Pro sailors would not be wrong, as they spend their days testing

Make no mistake about it, this guy, Paul Abdullah, is a pro. If you want to observe sail shape, observe here. A flattened main, full jib provides a more neutral helm. Weather sheet-

sails and seeing how to best trim them; while most of us are behind a desk, pounding nails, ow whatever we do to make ends meet. But basic sail trim can be just as well accomplished by us amateurs as the pros. It's really the sail (and boat) *handling* where the pro's separate themselves from the pack.

Countless books and videos have been produced about sail trim, many giving you more information than you need to get your boat quickly around a racecourse. Read your sailmaker's Rigging and Tuning guide!

Right out of high school I worked as a sailmaker for Hood and Skip Elliot; that was long before computers were used to design and manufacture sails. Still, I've learned a thing or two about sail shape, enough to know when I need flat sail and when full. While it's difficult to write about the shape of a sail… something that comes from years of experience staring at Dacron and Mylar, I'll do my best to share my knowledge. Ask your sailmaker for theirs.

MAIN TRIM – UPWIND

As a singlehanded sail, most boats aside from the ILCA Classes trim their mains in a similar manner. What it really comes down to is leech tension. The stronger the wind, the more you will trim the sail in. That's pretty basic, but you'd be surprised to see how many sailors kill their speed with overtrim. Undertrim will prevent you from pointing, but it's not as bad as overtrim, where you won't be able to point either, because speed creates lift. Water rushing over the daggerboard/centerboard, yes! Paying attention to how close the blocks are separated will pay dividends. Another rule of measure on some boats like the Finn and MC Scow, is where the boom aligns.

Eric Scheidt at Maru Urban Clinics   Photo: Hannah Lee Noll

For example, the corner of the cockpit. Wherever you see the fast guys align the boom end, try to replicate. Do not trim any further inboard than they do.

VANG ON!

The vang plays a key role in flattening the sail, particularly on big belly sails like the mains on a Star or Flying Scot. I leave the vang off up to 8 knots, then crank on as the boat becomes overpowered. It doesn't take much! The thing to remember on boats with the vang mounted to the boat instead of the mast, you have to release the vang before going around the weather mark or risk breaking the boom.

Notice the Star's vang on a track!   Photo: Will Keyworth

On a Weta, you don't have a boom nor vang, so nothing to hit yourself in the head about. You still need to work the mainsheet in a very similar fashion as

On a Weta, you don't have a boom nor vang, so nothing to hit yourself in the head about. You still need to work the mainsheet in a very similar fashion as you would a Laser. That's why whenever Tracy Usher would be handing out the trophies and I took one, he'd always shout, "He's a Laser sailor!" Sailing Lasers has always been a strong foundation for winning in other classes. *"Cheat the nursing home, sail a Laser!"*

CUNNINGHAM

Depending on the main's built in shape, most pointing pundits would tell you to leave the Cunningham off until your start getting overpowered. Tensioning will move the draft, or beer belly of the sail forward, which will impede your ability to point. In breeze, you will be pointing anyway, and bringing the draft forward flattens the sail, opens the leech reducing drag, and increases

Five time Olympian Stu McNay and crew, David Hughes, demonstrating proper sail shape to point high with power through the Tokyo chop.

speed. In most cases, until you are overpowered, Cunningham (or downhaul) should be jack slack.

OUTHAUL

In light air, a flatter sail is generally faster than one full of belly like a pulled pork sandwich. You don't want any vang as you will have enough trouble inducing twist in the leech required to go fast, so tightening the outhaul does the trick. When you really need to slack the outhaul heading upwind is when there is a sea state. You need that belly power to get through the chop. As soon as you're having trouble keeping the boat from heeling past the optimal angle of heel, flatten the sail back out.

In classes where there are multiple sailmakers involved, check your specific tuning guide. For example, a Flying Scot's Madd sail is cut much flatter than a North. The top dogs carry both, or some other make of sail, to use for varied winds and sea states. If those two are the choices, they use the Madd for flat waters and the North for sea states. Sometimes, an older sail is chosen for sea states as they have more belly induced from wear, but you don't see the use of old sails often unless in heavy air to prevent their precious babies from getting ragged like a worn diaper.

How often you upgrade to a new sail depends on the type of cloth and your bank account, mylar requiring less replacement, whereas on Lasers, the top guys change out their sails every few regattas. They can drive a beater of a car and still carry a crisp main. Obviously, they have their priorities straight.

TRAVELER

While not all boats have travelers, for ones that do, in lieu of playing the mainsheet with the vang cranked on hard, keep the mainsheet at optimum tension and play the traveler. The traveler is your insurance when an overpowering gust hits, all puns intended. While it's true that you will still adjust the mainsheet for optimal leech tension and twist as the wind pipes up and down, you will spend a lot more time adjusting the traveler to keep the boat flat and pointing.

Why don't all sailboats have travelers? I suppose they were just designed that way for simplicity Pete's sake.

WINNING WAYS

Peter Commette: *If you have it, use it! Every boat with a traveler is set up differently and has different trade-offs, so consult your class experts and tuning guides for best results. On a Snipe, in light air and flat water the traveler is centered. In light air and chop, sometimes it works to drop the traveler down an inch or two and trim until the leech telltale is on the edge. Many times, for brief but important periods, you can develop better footing power by dropping the traveler 1 mark and sheeting one "click" harder on the mainsheet. This will give you some good power.*

On a Snipe, the traveler is an important control in medium air; reach for it first to depower before reaching for the vang. With the traveler down you can still sheet the main fairly hard to maintain power in the main and headstay tension. The traveler is dropped three to four inches before it's time to rely on the vang to bend the mast. In heavy air, I will drop the traveler as much as 7 marks.

Hal Gilreath and crew rounding to head back upwind, the moment demonstrating how to trim in a sail, with both hands, extending the arms for crew, and for skipper, using tiller hand for optimum speed sheeting.

JIB TRIM

Heading upwind, once the jib comes into play, the first thing you fiddle over is in which position to slide the jib lead. If a jib lead track is present, forward is going to typically be the place to set the lead until the wind picks up, and even then, to keep it forward. I suppose that's why on some boats the top sailors never pull the lead until they sorely need to twist off the leech and depower the jib. They just tell the crew to hike harder. However, a flat boat is a fast boat, so I'm not completely onboard with the forward lead or bust practice. Keeping a uniform jib leech and parallel slot with the main are sound visual guides.

To aid trim and slack, there is a technique for uncleating that if you aren't savvy, might be worth the price of admission. You need to take the pressure off the line when uncleating a cam cleat. That means pulling while uncleating. Big difference! The line comes right out. Yet, if the cleats on a pedestal angled poorly, you're still in danger of not being able to release, flipping when you tack. And when in high winds, if you are having trouble pulling the jib in with just your arms and hands, place your foot on the line and use the weight plus muscle of your leg to trim in that extra bit. Think of me and send donut money each time this helps, if only for my health.

THE SLOT

When trying to obtain optimal efficiency, pay great attention to the flow of air through the slot. If not familiar with the terminology, the slot is the space between the main and the jib when both are trimmed in. Is the jib trimmed in too tight, a closed off slot, choking the flow of air to the lee side of the main? Too far open, and not only are you going to sail poorly to weather, but that boost of laminar flow will dissipate. Joe slow.

Going to weather, you want to pull the jib in as far as possible without closing off the slot. On most boats, overtrim is usually indicated by a curling of the jib's foot, a severe backwinding of the main. Warn your crew with either big biceps or too much coffee, to go easy on the trim, at least until you get the boat up to speed.

Photo: Deb Fewell Durbec

Less experienced crews may not understand what a proper looking slot looks like. You may not understand, either. Should there be a foot of space between the main and jib? More? Less? Depends on the beast. Crewing for a top skipper will give you a solid understanding.

Usually, the top jib leech telltale will stop flying straight back when you over or undertrim, but are they looking up there? Usually, newbie crews will not pull the jib in tight enough. Spinach eating Popeye crews tend to crank the jib in too tight, particularly during a tack (when it's easier to crank). We'll cover that more thoroughly in boat handling, but it never hurts to mention twice that after a tack, you need to under trim both jib and main, and then optimally trim tighter as the boat accelerates, water rushes over the centerboard, i.e., you are moving right along.

Photo: Deb Fewell Durbec

If your mainsail has a window up top with a view of the jib, that's not only for checking whether you're choking the slot (the main backwinding will signal that), but to see if there is proper twist in the jib. This story is told by the telltale. It should be flowing. Adjust if not.

Some teams like to commence "weather sheeting," which entails a slight trim of the jib with the weather jib sheet. Weather sheeting takes the job of the Barber Hauler, who on some boats to the same effect, allowing you to trim the jib in further inboard than where the jib lead is positioned. Instead, you are using the weather jibsheet to haul the jib inboard. This trick enables you to slack the jib sheet a bit to keep that slot open, while bringing the jib more inboard. Per Sean O'Donnell, this has one other beneficial effect; a more powerful jib will reduce your weather helm by placing the center of effort further forward in the boat. It will also keep other teams scratching their heads as you will point higher. With the added power, more water rushing over the centerboard will induce lift.

Jib trim is super important not only for boat speed, but boat direction. When I'm sailing, I'm looking primarily at one thing, and hopefully not the back of my crew's head (have them learn that going upwind, you are always the first to the windward side if it's light). Okay, here we go. I'm looking forward at the lower telltales on the jib. Other than for pressure and where Sid Swashbuckler is headed, that's it! If the jib is not trimmed right, the boat's not trimmed right. It's not pointing in the optimal direction to gain upwind yardage.

If not familiar with proper telltale usage (skip ahead if you are), it's a simple principle. When the telltale on the windward side of the sail is pointed down or unstable, you may be pointing too high. It's okay for it to flop around a little if you're feathering a bit or snaking your way upwind. You don't really need to see it flapping to know that you're too high into the wind. The luffing sail and dimished speed will shout that out. Telltales. These are the things you can do without. Come on, they say. I'm talking to you.

Here's the kicker… when the leeward telltale is pointing any direction but back. If it's hanging straight down, you know you've just been lifted. The more time you take to respond and get it flowing back again, the more stalled both sails will be. Carry on like that and disaster! You're slow and headed in the wrong direction. Once you've corrected your course, you still have to get back up to speed. If it's windy and the lee telltale is hanging, you are over-heeling, with too much feeling (weather helm).

On a Laser, with no jib, you sail more by your Windex wind indicator than your lower main telltale. At least I always have.

Dan Wilson, based out of Alamitos Bay YC, who has spent a lot more time crewing than I have, taught this old dog a new trick. On a Weta, you have to play both sails. Dan's long experience as crew playing the jib paid off. Every time he got lifted, instead of just heading back up, he first cracked off on the jib to get the telltales flowing, then as he headed back up to close hauled, eased it back on until maximum trim was applied.

Just as you don't want to trim the jib before the main when rounding up from a leeward mark, when you get lifted, keeping the jib tight will also prevent you from lifting, braking the rudder. I told Dan there was no way he would beat me in his first race. Of course he did. Dan is seen here with no shoes, crewing on a Coronado 15 in Alamitos Bay, Long Beach, CA.

SAIL TRIM REACHING

WHEN IN DOUBT, LET IT OUT

This generalization mostly applies when on a reach. What it means, is that if you are not sure if you're overtrimmed, ease the sail until it luffs slightly, then trim in until it doesn't. Sometimes at angles of bright sun, you can't see if the telltales are flowing straight back or the lee tale is flopping around stalled. So ease it out. If super light, the crew needs to hold the jib sheet to take weight off the sail and let it fly. Contortionist crews welcome!

OUTHAUL/CUNNINGHAM

On a reach, I don't think it's necessary to bother with the outhaul and downhaul as much as the vang. The twist of your sail is way more important. You can give the main a slight belly through easing the downhaul and outhaul if time and effort allows, but it's not going to give you the same gains you'll benefit from going downwind. In strong breeze, I don't even bother, lest I get into a battle with someone and forget to tighten back up before heading upwind. That's when it will really hurt your speed and ability to keep the boat flat – one in the same.

BOOM VANG

505 Photo: Christophe Favreau

Typically, you will have the top batten in a parallel fashion to the boom. What is meant by this, is if the top batten is hooked inward, pointing to windward of the boom, the vang is strapped in too tight. If anything, you want to have the batten pointing to leeward, the leech of the sail twisting off. By applying too much tension to the vang, you will not only stymie the wind flow but bring the boom down closer to the water. In big breeze, any heel will catch the boom and tip the boat over. Upside down boats are slow.

It's funny how sail shapes and what is determined as optimal can change over the year. In no short fashion changes is the application of vang tension. During my first years of sailing Lasers, we just cranked on the vang on hard before the race began and often let it be for the entire race. You'd get up on the boom and with all your weight push down hard till it was banjo tight.

When I got back into Lasers, racing Masters events on SF Bay, the adjustable vang had just become class legal. I thought it was just to make it easier than placing all your weight on the boom and cranking it. My first regatta at St Fancy, I was to my surprise leading in a heavy air race going to the finish line. I had the vang fully cranked, when Tracy Usher willed one of those wicked Golden Gate gusts to head my way. Even though I had the sail well stalled out by sheeting in pretty hard, just feet from the finish line, the boat spun around and the water grabbed my boom, flipping me over. I flipped it back, but the ebb tide pushed me away from the line. Every time I bore away, I'd flip, maybe five times! I lost count. Mr. Usher crushed past me as he was indeed a Master of these conditions. I still managed to finish in second as a lot of sailors were having issues. I guess my early years of practicing capsizes around alligators finally paid off.

On the Weta Trimaran, reaching involves another sail, the Screecher. I guess you've gathered that by now. Not sure why they call it that, so we usually just call it a kite. The kite easily unfurls going around the weather mark, and if done properly, furls right back up to head back to weather. When not done right, well, another subject to cover in Boat Handling.

The kite's trim on a reach is typically about as tight as you can get it without killing your speed in the lulls, then easing the sheet a foot or two when bearing off in a gust.

Stephanie Taylor with her kite block mounted on the side, while mine is old school on the back. Her kite's shape is better at a deeper angle, but not a tight reach. Kerr Lake, NC. Weta East Coast Championships. Alan Taylor, victor.

Whereas it's important where you place your jib leads in the track if you have one, a much greater difference is felt when placing the location of your kite sheet block. Most people mount the kite sheet block on the side of the tramp to allow the sail to open up more, producing better downwind VMG, but this will be painful on a tight reach in breeze.

Historically, the kite sheet block was mounted on the back of the aka. I believe everyone mounts it on the side now, but those on the West Coast used to mount the block in the back while those on the East on the side. It's a lot windier out West.

To make a short reaching story long, the old dinosaur did not take note of that when borrowing a boat for a regatta back East, and watched boats soak it further downwind. Only when the final leg came into play, a tight reach to the finish, was my block position rewarded. The other sailors could not keep their kites flying. Whichever leg is expected to be on longer, rig for that.

DOWNWIND SAIL TRIM

LIGHT AIR

If the wind is so light that it can't keep the boom out on its own (provided your boat has a boom), you or your crew need to hold the boom out by hand, or if singlehanding, you need to get up by the mast and get the job done on your own.

A boat like a Laser is often sailed with its master up by the dagger, one hand on the boom, the other on the long ass hiking stick, the boat still heeled far to weather in a stretched-out yoga pose I call the Drifter. It's very uncomfortable. If not practiced often enough (sailing in drifter conditions and yoga) good luck walking the next day.

Sailing by the lee in a stay-less boat can be fast. The cool kids are by the lee, reaching, by the lee, in a dance very similar to what Snoop Dog might fancy if he were a sailor. He rides a horse, does the crip walk, hails from Long Beach, so why not? You're in a heavier boat with stays, that's why not.

The biggest mistake people make in light air is to sail the boat dead downwind. Even with everyone on the lee side of the boat to help keep the sail filled, the boom held out by hand particularly in motor boat slop (keep the board down quite a bit in motor boat slop), you need to sail at angles. Otherwise, your downwind run is going to be more painful than that run on sentence. And while you're broad reaching, do so in the direction of wind and out of the lee of boats. If get some real speed going, you can soak it downwind a bit.

I think you can ease the outhaul a bit, and certainly, no Cunningham applied.

MEDIUM AIR

On a traditional boat like a Flying Scot or Thistle, with shrouds and spinnaker, you pretty much sail with the tell tales on the shrouds and masthead fly pointing dead down wind. The main is let out as far as possible, which means at right angles, stopping just short of the shrouds. Again, the Cunningham and outhaul are loosened up quite a bit.

Having a long mainsheet on a shroudless boat (nomostay) lets you test the limits of how far out you can let the main fly. Such boats also do well for a spell when sailed by the lee, particularly if playing the waves.

With a high-performance skiff, F-18, or trimaran like the Weta, the main is trimmed in quite a bit, even more so as the apparent wind increases.

HEAVY AIR MAINSAIL ONLY – One of the misconceptions of sailing in heavy air is that you let the main further out when the wind gets stronger. As already stated, on a shroudless boat you want the main to be let out in most wind at least to right angles of the boat. Of course, with a long enough mainsheet, you could let the sail out to 110 degrees or more, but in heavy air, this would result in a quick wash of the undies. What you want to do on this type of boat and many other high-performance boats as well, is to trim the main in a good twenty degrees from where you would normally set the sail going downwind, sometimes even more. This effectively adds stability to the boat. Along with putting that board down a tad, it helps prevents a death roll to weather.

Trimming in the main in high winds also depowers the main, which you would think might make the boat go a little slower, but it doesn't. The added control allows you to gain VMG, to decrease downwind angles, to point more to the mark (if properly on the long tack).

When conditions warrant hair on the chest (guys only), loosening the Cunningham and outhaul are not essential. Focus on keeping the boat surfing and on a wave, not plowing into one.

DOWNWIND JIB TRIM

If a spinnaker or kite is in use, the jib either needs to be lowered (look around you and you will see what everyone else is doing), or at least attention should be paid to it being not over trimmed one iota. Over trimming will choke off the flow of wind to the spinnaker, where the power delivered is maximized.

DOWNWIND ASYMETRICAL KITE TRIM

Here we go with something I learned in one of Randy Smyth's clinics. He simply sets the kite sheet as loose as he can get away with, and then steers to the tell tales on the kite. I have a problem doing that as I'm pumping the kite to catch a ride on swells, then bearing off to stay on that swell.

Never argue with an Olympic double Silver medalist! Randy Smyth on "Scissors," a boat he designed and made sails for to win the Everglades Challenge. Fast, but not the easist boat to right at night. Google it! Besides the incredible all around sailing skill and craft, I am also drawn to the white sand dunes in the back of this photo, which bring back great memories of Florida Panhandle sailing. More, please!

WINNING WAYS

BOAT HANDLING

When other sailors talk about being out of practice, they're not always talking about a rusty rudder. It's all about making errors when tacking, jibing, or going around the corners. It comes even more into play when interacting with other boats. More critically, responding to dire situations such as a knockdown gust all comes down to boat (and sail) handling. It's the area in sailing where practice really makes perfect.

Photo: Will Keyworth

Andy Burdick: *If you are a mid-fleet sailor and you want to improve - improve your boat handling. If you can do that you will see your results improve. Consistently good tacks and jibes. Good Starts, Good Mark rounding and learning how to stop and start your boat. Boat handling is the key to success in sailboat racing!*

Let's go over some common boat handling situations, why don't we?

HOUSEKEEPING

What do I mean here when I refer to housekeeping? It's not a houseboat. You don't want to be leading the fleet, go to round the weather mark and have your mainsheet knot up. Before any maneuver, particularly rounding a mark, you'd best keep you lines clear and untangled.

If it's windy, some people just throw the line out the back of their boat. I'm not real onboard with that technique, particularly in medium air when adding water weight to the lines is counterproductive. But I will keep the sheets separated and run the main through my hands to clear any knots if I can.

The real kicker screamer, is if you knot up your spinnaker sheet on the take down, so plan to keep house like Alice on the Brady Bunch. You can also knot up the guy when "blowing the guy." Don't blame me. I didn't make the term up. Just in case you're not spinnaker savvy, the guy is the windward sheet that attaches to the pole.

Speaking of the pole, if you're sporting one, that's another thing you need to housekeep so you're not tripping over it or when taking it out for use, poking someone in the eye.

The last thing is probably just keeping the water out of the boat. Make sure those bailers are well lubed. On a Scot, you need a good plastic bottle cut open and a sponge. Lasers, even with the bailer working, you sometimes have to kick the water out. On a boat with open stern like the Weta, water just flows right on out the back.

ROLL TACKING

Singlehanded, one sail

Can you imagine life before roll tacking? I can! What a difference it made. In light air, instead of losing ground, you can gain VMG toward the weather mark performing the roll tack, a technique used where the boat smoothly transitions from one tack to the other by using body movement and the boat's momentum to help change direction. The more you use the tiller to tack, the less effective it becomes. As a singlehander, the roll tack is fairly simple, yet complex in all its steps:

1. The Wind up: Wind like a watch, not the invisible stuff. Have you ever noticed how the best Disney animators (old school) take a character slightly in one direction before zooming off in another? Probably not. A baseball pitcher doesn't just throw the ball. They wind up. Bring your weight inboard to heel the boat to leeward, setting up for the tack. Bear off a tad, loosen the mainsheet about a foot.

2. Initiate the Tack: The key to a good rolling tack is how you use your body to roll the boat, not just the tiller action. Be smooth as you slam your weight to the weather rail and almost dump your tail in the drink. Push the tiller over gradually in the beginning, then more sharply and sheet in. The dagger or centerboard will act as a paddle. If in very light wind, it will propel the boat faster than the wind.

3. The Transition: As the boat passes through the eye of the wind and halfway to the other tack, you should still be fully rolled over, on your ear, with your weight still on what will now be the leeward side, the mainsheet out a bit again. Now comes the big action, the transitive leap to the other side.

4. Full Pop: Now that you are on the high side to weather doing a circus act, slam your donuts down. As you sheet back in, if you hear a "whop" (southern hemisphere) or a "pop' (northern) in the sail, you've done a good job. Whichever hemisphere you're in, make sure you've set your course well onto the new tack. It's better to overtack than under. You can now wave "Later!" to the non-popping weasels.

Now go watch the hundreds of videos on roll tacking, challenge your buddies to a tacking duel practice, and join a clinic to dial it in right.

ROLL TACKING - Light air, with Jib

The only difference when roll tacking with a jib is that you want to backwind the jib to force the bow through the eye (or teeth) of the wind. With a good crew or you (if on a Weta par example), the release and trim of the sheet should be one fell swoop. If it luffs and rattles, like a bad roll of the dice, you're losing everything you've gained. Try not to yell at your crew or curse yourself. Get it right the next tack.

Be careful not to trim all the way in. As mentioned before and with the main, let the boat build speed before going for a harder trim. You can't point until you have lift, water rushing over the board. Nowhere is this truer than on a multihull. .

Tokyo 2020 Olympic Games
© Nikos Alevromytis/International 470 Class Association
Free Editorial Rights

TACKING - HEAVY AIR

Forget the roll unless you're an Olympic caliber sailor. You need to be more concerned with not screwing up the tack, not forgetting to uncleat, not flipping the boat. In this case, you want to make sure that you don't overtack, forcing the boat into a stalled heel. Yet, an undertack will force the boat into irons. Loosening the main before tacking will help with this, as the finish angle of the tack will be less severe and pressurized.

With the Finn, if you don't loosen up the main on a tack you should be an Olympic caliber limbo limbo dancer. On a Weta, you have no boom, which is the best asset of the boat, particularly if your concussion count is high.

WHERE TO TACK

Not right in front of me, I can tell you that!

Where you plan to do the roll tack can be more important than how well you do the roll tack. If the water is smooth, you can do it anywhere at any time, but if there is a good chop or swell running, you need to wait for a smooth patch of water. Of course, you also have to be mindful of other boats and fouling them, as if they have

WINNING WAYS

to alter course, you'll be rolling into a 360.

ROLL Jibe - Light to Medium Air

A "roll jibe" (or "rolling jibe") is a technique used to change the direction of a sailboat when sailing downwind, particularly when sailing in light to moderate winds. It is often used on dinghies, catamarans, and some cruising boats as a smoother, safer way to jibe the boat without having to swing the boom violently across the boat.

Here's how to perform a roll jibe step-by-step:

1. Set Up the Boat: You want the boat to be balanced and under control (as opposed to on the edge of capsize before initiating the jibe, and if windy enough, surfing down a wave.

2. Initiate the Roll: Before you roll the boat, unless up against the shrouds, ease the mainsheet slightly to reduce the power on the main. This makes the boat more responsive to the roll. Heel the boat slightly to leeward. Begin to gradually move the boat to leeward (downwind) by pulling on the tiller or steering wheel slightly to the opposite side of where you want the boat to go. This helps create a small roll of the boat.

3. Roll the Boat! To start the roll, press with your legs if standing, or just shift your weight to windward. This steers the boat into a natural roll. Roll like a donut!

4. Execute the jibe on a wave: Grab the mainsheet or crew, the vang, to swing the boom across. As the boom crosses to the opposite side, give the main a yank to prevent it from catching on any corners. Then press down on the opposite rail to give it a good "cheat and sheet." Don't panic, it's legal and organic!

5. Trim back in: Settle fore/aft and proper heel. Trim the sails on the new tack to control the power and maintain your speed. If a jib is involved, most boats jibe the jib last. Not on my Weta. I don't have a crew, so I prejybe it.

HEAVY AIR GYBING

Roll jibing in heavy air is far more difficult than in light. The main thing is, you want to jibe on a wave, the pressure being lighter on your rig than it would be heading down one. It also helps to throw the main over ahead of the brunt force of the jibe, or at least give the main a good yank with the mainsheet. With crew, grabbing the vang and throwing it over can reduce the shock of it slamming to the other side.

Make sure they don't throw themselves off the boat (Congolese jibe).

Alan Taylor started sailing as a teenager in the late '60s. He got his first Laser (#4621) in 1971. Sailing dinghies on inland lakes in North Carolina, he progressed to the point of being on the podium at most local invitational events and club series races. He started a Sailing Club at NC State University in 1974. After graduation Alan moved to San Francisco, looking for adventure. He discovered he had been a big fish in a small pond! Little did he know what he was up for, when he entered the storied Heavy Weather Slalom. Maybe he thought he knew, but few are prepared for, drum roll...

WINNING WAYS
DEATH ROLL BY LOUDSPEAKER

by Alan Taylor

Alan: It was 1981. I had recently moved to San Francisco from Central North Carolina. Sailing a Laser on a North Carolina lake was vastly different from sailing a Laser on San Francisco Bay. But that's a big part of why I moved, to sail on The Bay.

Peter Commette in Heavy Air Slalom 1981

The Laser Heavy Weather Slalom started in 1974 and had been reported on in numerous sailing publications. It was (and still is) one of the premier events of Laser Sailing. The LHWS was on the schedule so of course I signed up. The buzz of anticipation on the St. Francis YC docks was palatable. The veterans were calm, they'd done this before and knew what to expect. The rest of us were somewhere between "Let's Go" and "What the heck have I gotten myself into?".

The course is two parallel windward / leeward rows of drop buoys. Two boats move into position at the leeward buoys, one on each side. When the horn sounds, boats sail a slalom upwind, cross over to the other row and sail downwind, jibing at each mark. The challenge is to stay upright for two laps. The winner (survivor?) moves on to the next round.

My first race I was paired against Ian Murray, the Australian 18 world champion. Ian was a big guy. I don't know if he had ever sailed a Laser. I was 26 years old, 145 lbs and almost fearless. What the heck. Let's Go!

Most of what I remember was working hard just to get upwind. Downwind was a wild ride with lots of capsizes. For all of us.

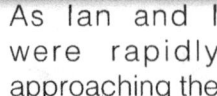

The course was set in front of the St. Francis Yacht Club with spectators lining the porch railings. They also had a loudspeaker to call competitors to the start line.

As Ian and I were rapidly approaching the finish, I glanced back to see him a couple boat lengths behind. Just hang on, almost there. Then I started rolling. You know the Laser roll – to the right, to the left, try to trim the main a little to get back in control while trying to stop that roll. Suddenly the loudspeaker blasts "Looks like Taylor is in trouble!". Voice Of Oz coming down from the sky! Immediate death roll, right there. Fortunately, my bow crossed the finish line just as the mast hit the water. I won my heat, only because I capsized fewer times than Ian did.

Lesson one: Never give up. If you flip, right the boat as quick as you can and keep going. Your competition just might flip as well.

Day 2 I was set to sail against John Bertrand, another world class Laser champion. That day I was more in the "What the heck have I got myself into?" frame of mind. Totally psyched out, I decided to reef the sail. So much for being almost fearless. Naturally, the wind dropped. I was seriously underpowered and finished almost a full leg behind.

The story is well told in Dick Tillman's book, *Laser Sailing*.

Lesson two: Give it 100% or just go home.

Lesson three: When a once in a lifetime opportunity presents itself, go for it. To this day I am glad that I participated in the LHWS. I still smile when I think about that weekend and love to tell the tale. And I still have the T-Shirt.

KINETICS AND PROPULSION

The key to kinetics, or body movements intended to propel the boat forward, and sail movements for propulsion (pumping like a banshee), is the either they have to be done at that right time or at least the right place (when no judges are looking). While that may sound a bit like cheating (it is), illegal kinetics and propulsion are the most oft practiced crimes in sailing. It's not like we're juicing the bat or the body (at least nobody I ever knew).

When sailing upwind, pumping of the torso and rocking the body back and forth as one navigates waves is commonplace. Even in the Olympics or big 420 events, it's commonplace to see the 470 crew out on the wire doing some kind of odd torquing twerking motion. I suppose that's legal under certain conditions. But then, while watching the Marseilles Olympics, a lot of ILCA competitors were flagged by the judges in the lighter conditions, forcing them to exonerate with circles. Like an NBA basketball game, no star treatment!

Photo: Nikos Alevromytis

In the Finn Class at least, they raise a flag when pumping and rocking become legal. Rocking in a Finn is essential for downwind success. Even when that flag is not up, there is still a lot of rock and rolling going on, just not as much. Call it soft rock.

Such devilish self-propulsion acts happened even back in my young heyday, during the O'Day qualifiers. This event, honoring George O'Day, has taken place every year since 1962 when it was sailed on Finns in Long Island Sound. The winner of the final event would be crowned US National Singlehanded Champion, but first you had to beat the best of all singlehanded sailors from every class in your region, mine being the Southeast.

The Florida Yacht Club was the venue. It was the first event I'd sailed in where a judge's boat followed you around the racecourse, making sure that competitors were sailing fairly, not using any type of illegal propulsion. With

Ed Baird, Andy Fox, Rick Merriman and a whole host of other great sailors on the line, I would need to be not only having fun, but on top of my kinetics game. Too much kinetics and you were penalized, too little and you could say goodbye to any chance of winning the regatta and advancing.

The conditions for day one delivered a perfect 10-15 knots, but on Sunday, the wind turned light. My advantage turned disadvantage. Ed Baird and I were neck and neck, yacking away with each other about the diminished conditions. "Hey Ed! I think you're making way."

"Backwards maybe," said Ed. "Bring lunch?"

"Maybe they can just call off the race and hand me the trophy?"

"Not on your life, Buddy."

It was true, we were both hardly making headway downwind, when a couple of the younger sailors rounded the weather mark and started to motor by. Seemed like they were having a lot more fun than we were and making good headway. Sure, they were a spitfire lighter, but we didn't need to check their sail settings; both were rocking like crazy.

The judges were on the water in a keelboat, but they seemed to be off having a bit of lunch, and maybe a few drinks as well. A bit of self-policing was called for. I protested them, but they just gave me the NY salute and kept rocking on. Being from St Pete YC, under Ed's tutelage, he yelled at the young swashbucklers, "Hey Rick! Howard! Knock off the rock n' roll act!"

Even though these were not the words of a proper protest, the kids were Ed's protege's. They quit their shenanigans. However, by that time their lead was solidified, and they crossed 1-2. I had never protested anyone before, but the stakes were high. The winner of that protest would be going to the USYRU Singlehanded Finals. The Elite 8!

The judges listened as all four of us spoke our piece. Then they told us they had already thrown both the kids out. The head judge, Jim Moss, stated that the difference between our rocking and their rocking, is that they were blatantly breaking the rules... that savvy sailors only did it when the judges weren't looking, and not to such a degree. If they weren't looking, how would they know? The key was the degree and blatancy. Rick had already qualified for the Bemis (double-handed), so it was all good by him.

BOAT HANDLING – THE WEATHER MARK

Make sure that you have a mark rounding plan in place well before getting to the weather mark. Is there an offset mark? Write it down on the boat. Which jibe will you be on if the next leg is downwind? If the next leg is a reach, can you fly a kite or will it be too tight? Jibe set or set then jibe? Or just set and jet? You've got to figure all this out *before* you get to the mark. If you don't, the only thing that's going to go downhill is your place in the race.

If you are sailing a spinnaker boat with pole and crew, make sure that you have more than a plan. Have a Playbook. Make sure that everyone is on the same page. This should include the exact order in which things will go down, or up! Speaking here, of course, about raising and dousing the kite. While this is sail handling, it's also boat handling, as your body movements will affect boat speed. Be monkey quick, dog determined, and seal smooth. If you're surfing a wave and on the edge of pandemonium, wait to first get under control before raising more sails.

In all cases, before you get to the mark, do more housekeeping. You or if you have one, your crew, should run your hand through the sheets to make sure they are clear. Most importantly, ease the vang. EASE THE VANG!

Let's break the rounding down again for various situations. The goal is to round the mark quickly and headed on the fastest course for the next mark, and then and only then setting the boat up for optimum speed. If you have extra hands (a crew), they might be able to work on the finite adjustments, but even they may have their hands full flying sails (spinnaker up, jib down in some boats). Whether you relax the sail with secondary controls (Cunningham, outhaul) before or after rounding will depend on how tight your course is as you approach the mark. Set your course *first*. I think that's common sense, but sailors don't always have it in the heat of battle.

Light air- main only

If by common example, you are rounding the mark to port, there is no offset mark and your best heading is downwind on starboard tack right off the bat, you want to get around that mark focused primarily on carrying that wind in your sail as far downwind as possible, but never dead downwind. It's a much more delicate operation. If you've got a little puff, it's possible to get into a by-the-lee position and jibe away from disturbed air behind, but in most cases, you'll want to carry the wind into a broad reach position.

You'll be more concerned with keeping wind in your sail than using windward heel to assist tiller movement.

Medium air main only

In moderate conditions, with no offset mark, provided you don't have rusty blocks and the main sheet knotted, the main should ease on its own. Let it release so you can bear off – with minimal rudder resistance (braking) – and get into a downwind position as quickly as possible. The wider an arc you swing, the more VMG you will lose, so swing it and send it! Release the sheet and get your butt outboard, producing a sharp weather heel to assist steering into a downwind position. Heel the boat to weather. Heel the boat to weather. Heel the boat to weather.

Heavy air - main only

There's no magic involved… every little thing you do in medium air gets amplified in heavy air. With greater pressure on the rudder, the act of releasing sheet becomes paramount to allow you to bear off, as this is what is putting

the pressure on your blades. However, heeling the boat to weather will become more difficult, requiring greater effort. Don't throw yourself off the boat in the process. Check those hiking strap lines in preparation!

A bonus move for any boat? Timing your rounding so that you are bearing off on a swell. To begin your downwind journey surfing is far better than stuffing it and filling the boat with water, even if with a self-bailing cockpit. Stuffing slow. Surfing a ball. Just make sure you get the boat flat and down first, or you'll be one edge like these kids.

Random but applicable note; keep your eyes wide open for any boats flipping in front of you! To avoid punching through their bottom or running somebody over, sometimes there is no other solution than to stop your boat by flipping over yourself.

Main & Jib Only boats (no spinnaker or A sail)

Light air - jib

Similar to the mainsail only boats, try to keep the jib full and flying as you round the weather mark. As crew, assist the main on its outward journey. Once on course, trim the jib on the looser side and pay close attention to the tell tales. Don't choke it. A broad reach will be much faster and make gains over the dead downwinders if it's too light to gain any advantage by going wing-on-wing.

Medium air - jib

Get around the mark using the same technique as with mainsail only. Release the jib after the main if not in unison to make it easier to bear off. If the mark is dead downwind, get the whisker pole out or find a crew with long arms. It's time to go wing on wing. Make sure they bloop the jib a little, not hold it dead flat to the wind.

Heavy air - jib

Ask the skipper if they want to go wing on wing or head back to the dock. Sometimes it's more important to keep the weight back in the boat than to fiddle with a pole, so if going wing-on-wing, wait until the boat is on a plane before going forward to set.

Main, Jib, with Asymmetrical kite

Light air

Get the gennaker, screecher, kite, or what is categorized as an A sail out as smoothly as possible. Most often, I'll pull an A sail out from its furl just before or in the act of rounding the mark, keeping the sail filled nicely. With a crew, it's not as important to get it out in advance, but if singlehanded on a boat like the Weta, you should get it out and just let it flap.

Having the A sail out early enables you to release the main and jib as you round. The A sail will fill as you get onto a reach. It's the most powerful sail you've got now and will help turn the boat downwind. Once you're on that reach, then use your speed and any apparent wind you can muster to bear off to an optimal VMG angle. Don't soak it downwind right off the bat or you'll kill your speed. You'll get passed quicker than slippety slick. However, they who do manage to eventually soak it lower while carrying speed will be first to the downwind mark.

Don't make a bunch of jerky movements with the sheets or with body motions, either. Don't rock the boat. It's okay to allow the boat to heel a bit to leeward, keeping the sails full by gravity.

Medium air - A sail

Similar to rounding with just the main, you'll want to get the main out and pressure off the tiller and heel the boat to windward, or at least keep your weight outboard, and let the main out first followed quickly by an approximate jib set. Don't worry about setting the jib perfectly. To have the jib luff is better than stalling. Get that A sail out quickly to power up your horses. Build the apparent wind and get onto an optimal angle and racecourse position amongst your opponents as quickly as you can. Then get the board up and futz with the incremental sail adjustments.

Heavy air - A sail

If you're paying attention to the sea or lake state, you can get the boat surfing even without the A sail, but get it set quickly. It will fill a lot faster if you unfurl on a reach before heading downwind, but if the breeze is on, get your boat well positioned on a wave (can you hear the Beach Boys anthem?) and your body in a good position both fore/aft and outboard for weather heel.

In real heavy air, I'll get the board partway up before getting the kite out. I'll also keep the main in much further than normal.

With Old School Spinnaker

Light air - spinnaker

In most boats it's worth setting the pole before rounding (unless you are planning to jibeset). But again, don't head dead down wind. A broad reach at maximum should be your heading. Be smooth as Exlax. Once the spinnaker is hoisted, lower the jib. As you've got all the time in the world in light air to correct poor hoist technique, for more on sequencing, let's go to the more difficult set in medium air.

Medium air - spinnaker

Adding to the simpler sequencing of bearing away from the weather mark, a smooth set involves perfect coordination between skipper and crew like none other to gain advantage. It also involves a ton of preparation and practice. Packing your kite right is not as important as packing a parachute, unless you like winning races. Get in a few practice sets before the race begins to iron out your packing errors if you've made them, as well as to preset the pole height. Set all turning block ratchets according to the wind as well.

Crewing for Dave Rink, checking his Playbook for spinnaker success. Christina Angeles is showing me the old school ropes long forgotten using A-sails! MarkJump Photography

The spinnaker halyard, sheets, and guy should be out of the guy hook before you round. If not a dreaded jibe set, and with no traffic coming that might force you to tack, pre-set the pole before rounding. Having that pole setting weight forward is not favorable heading downwind, whereas when still going to weather, it won't make much difference in medium air. You can also send crew forward to put the pole on while heading to the offset mark if one is set.

When the crew pulls the pole out from the bottom of the boat, the tail end goes straight up, as opposed to straight back into the skipper or third crew's eye. Sounds like a good name for a band.

Every skipper has their preference as to who does what on the hoist. You may be sailing with three on board as well, but surely someone is being tasked with hoisting. If this is the skipper, as in Dave's regimen, it's a standing two-handed operation with the tiller between the knees while the crew is setting the pole. He also takes both spinnaker guy and sheet in hand, flying it until all is settled. Then, I suppose if he doesn't trust the crew (me), he hangs onto the guy and hands the sheet off to the crew. However it's done, practice it over and over and do it the same way each time.

From that point on, it's a lot up to the skipper to adjust to wind shifts and maintain a steady course, keeping the chute full. Every time I see a chute collapse, I think, "Skipper!" It's not always Gilligan's fault.

Heavy air - Spinnaker

Adding again to the now more difficult sequencing of bearing away from the weather mark, perhaps the most screwed up maneuver in all of sailboat racing is the raising of the spinnaker in breeze (a close second, the douse). At the top of the list of perils comes the shrimping of the kite. There are other ways to blow the hoist, but this for me shrimping the kite has always followed a very successful weather leg. We Bubba Gumped it. Skipper again! You didn't have a good game plan for Maryanne.

Don't think they got the spinnaker doused "Justin Time."

What other ways are there to tank your race? You can send the halyard up the mast, attach the halyard to the clew, and hourglass it every time. The windier it is, the more likely to enforce bad behaviors. Even Ginger knows that.

Once again, in heavy air, don't be in a rush to hoist the spinnaker. Get the boat heading downwind and planing. Then hoist the spinnaker at the crest of a wave heading down it, not when plowing into the next one, particularly on a swamp-able boat like a Thistle.

Remember, the little things like bagging the main, getting the jib set perfectly, and the board up should be secondary to getting on the right course with that main the boat level and settled. As well, optimal weight distribution to promote planing will avoid an instant douche into a wave, as if done right, you should be accelerating around the mark. Done wrong, and... mayhem.

PARIS OLYMPICS   Int'l 470 Class Association Photos: Nikos Alevromytis

ROUNDING THE REACHING JIBE MARK

The most important thing in all winds when rounding the reaching mark is to be smooth. A good roll jibe will get you around safely. Similar to rounding the leeward mark, you want to approach the mark wide and take it close on the downwind side. Since your sails and boom will be on the mark side on the approach, jibing wide then rounding close will reduce the risk of hitting the mark. Tactically speaking, you want to shut the door on anyone trying to take an inside path, i.e., your wind. By taking the mark close on the lee side, this door should be shut.

Before approaching the reaching mark, take a good look ahead. If leading your fleet in a multi-class regatta, note how the other boats are handling the rounding. Is the course running evenly, or will you have to douse, furl? Is the mark set in a wind shadow or area of less (or more) wind? This will determine if you need to sail high or low of the rhumb line, the straightest course to the next mark. If the mark is set in less wind, come out of the mark higher than the rhumb line. If in more, grab some insurance and head low. Some might differ in opinion on that as it opens the door to people rolling over you, but given fleet spacing, I'm always trying to gain downwind yards in the puffs so I can head up in the lulls. Nothing and everything to do with boat handling.

Ken Early and Pascal Tetard (FR) make their way around the jibe mark without running anyone over. Not sure why they sent me this photo as that's not me flipped. Only thing that didn't go upside down or turn inside out in the event for me.

ROUNDING THE LEEWARD MARK

HANDLING THE MAIN

If one area could be pinpointed where most gains in racing after the start have been made, it is in rounding the leeward mark. I'm not just talking about establishing an overlap. If I've blown it, and been outfoxed by somebody like

Andy Squirrel, I'm swinging wide (if I've not sandwiched myself like Whimpy Tuesday), then coming in with speed closer to the mark than Andy. Maybe Andy was bagging his nuts with one hand, while I was using two hands to haul in the mainsheet. Optimally, you want to come out of there with clear air and freedom to tack, rather than pinned down in some hedgehog's shadow.

I also want to make sure I've remembered to lower the board. Ha! You don't need to worry so much about main downhaul as you do about pre-adjusting the outhaul, though both can be adjusted after rounding the mark. As already horse beaten, having the draft further back in your sail can help you point higher. But in breeze, I crank it all on ahead of time, as heeling far over isn't fast.

The lighter the wind, the more you should heel the boat to leeward, assisting the rudder to round the boat up with least resistance. Swing wide on the approach if no other boats are around so that you position yourself as close to the mark on the other side as possible, without hitting it. Again, I'm using both hands without dropping the stick. Here's how most top guns do it:

Grab the hiking stick near the end to give you more leverage. Assuming you are rounding to port (it's not a starboard chosen gate), grab the sheet with your left hand near the block and bring that sheet above your head to the sky. Once your arm is fully extended, grab the sheet with your right claw, hiking stick in hand, and pull upward with the stick just until you can get your left hand back to the cleat to pull more sheet. Repeat until nearly sheeted all the way in, then use your left hand to adjust to optimal leech tension.

ROUNDING WITH JIB

Here's the catch if you have a jib, and make sure you instruct this kindly to your crew before they get it wrong, as they most often will. Do not, and I repeat, do not, okay louder now. DO NOT pull the jib in before rounding the leeward mark. You can trim it in *as* you round the mark, but not beforehand. A jib trimmed before the mark will hinder you from pivoting around the centerboard, braking the boat as you try to use the rudder to counter the imbalance. Let the main do the heavy lifting. Even the best skippers have gotten this wrong when performing as crew. By heeling the boat over and bringing in the main before the jib, you'll ease right on up.

FURLING

With a furling kite like on the Weta, it's important not to overstand the mark. Approaching the mark on a tight reach makes the rounding much more difficult. You want to time it just right so that during the last yards or meters in the zone, you are heading downwind. This takes the pressure off the kite, ensuring an error-free, tight furl. Blow that furl, leave any bit of sail flapping in the wind, and it will at minimum impede your progress with drag. In stronger breeze, the kite will unfurl.

In this worst-case scenario, you need to bite the bullet. Head back downwind, do a proper furl, and head back up. Consider it a penalty stroke. You've dropped the ball in the drink.

Of course, if you have a forward douse type of A sail, you don't have to worry and can douse at the last second. There is no furl to foil. The good guys do it even while rounding the mark at the last second. Those guys are not reading this book.

DOUSING

Photo: Deb Fewell Durbec

Rounding the leeward mark with a spinnaker is a game within a game. If you douse too early, you can get outfoxed and out squirreled, limping your way around the mark which is notoriously a zone of disturbed air. However, coming in to the mark cold is a lot safer than coming in late and hot with no overlap. Your first greeting from scowling skippers will be, "NO ROOM!" Then, as you may blow the douse, you will blow the rounding. Even without the impending penalty turn(s), you're going to give a lot more places away than if you come in cold. Of course, if you have great skipper/crew coordination, are well practiced at the maneuver, the risks can be rewarding.

Jibe douse or douse jibe? That's a decision you need to make early. Create a takedown sequence plan, practice it, and try not to deviate. It's more important if you have more downwind legs to sail (you're on your first lap) to get it doused on the port side of the boat.

CREWING

WINNING WAYS

Mike Wright crewing for Stephanie Taylor, getting ready for racing adventure at the Gorge.

One of the best ways to gain racing experience is to crew for an experienced skipper. It's like putting in your time on an apprenticeship. Dave Rink crewed for Sean O'Donnell for a long time before buying a boat and taking over the skipper role. It wasn't long before he was taking home the hardware. Sean truly believes that Dave will soon win a National Championship, and that journey began by dedicating time to crewing.

Even after you've owned your own boat and skippered for quite a while, crewing for skippers who consistently finish at the top of the fleet will make you a better skipper. You will not only improve your tactics but learn all sorts of things such as the secrets to successful spinnaker launch and takedowns. Put in your time and hey, they may buy you dinner and put you up at the Four Seasons. Right.

HOW MANY CREW?

In most classes of boat, you must determine the amount of crew to carry before the first race begins. One crew or two live crew? To swap out a child on drifter Saturday and a Sumo wrestler on dogs off chains Sunday in most all classes, not allowed. If the weather is variable, a good approach is to crew up for the middle ground. On a Weta, people go two up if it's windy or they want to race in that division, or one up below 25 knots for speed.

WHEN CREWING, DO THIS

Aside from your main responsibility of trimming sails (do that well), and looking out for pressure and other boats, you're also responsible for balancing the boat. Having done a lot of "Social Sails" where the crew is inexperienced, the first thing they do when tacking is head for the high side, blocking the skipper's view. This makes Skipper grumpy, but unless roll tacking (rarely done in Social Sails), he kindly instructs them to let the skipper cross first, then to focus on keeping the boat at a proper heel (unless it's a game on breeze... then get the heck to the high side and hike your ass off... don't forget to uncleat the jib!). Even with a roll tack, the crew still needs to allow the skipper to be in a position where they can view the jib telltale and boats crossing ahead. So yeah, be the boat balancer. Sit on the low side, sit in the middle, lean in, arch back, whatever you have to do to make skipper not grumpy.

PARIS OLYMPICS Int'l 470 Class Association Photo: Nikos Alevromytis

Tom Pace: If you want to sail, let alone race - and still be happy - communication, positive interaction, and seamlessness with your crew will decide if you win or lose. I may use a full 'military voice' and seem harsh at times, but as long as both crew and skipper understand all that's in play, the on-water successes continue to happen. For some, it's a Captain Bligh mentality. For me, it is collaborative. I'm all ears to what's happening in and out of the boat. I support my crew, and appreciate their time spent trying to get wins for all of us.

Before the races that day, go over who is responsible for what, in sequence. "Ok... so many feet ahead of the about weather mark, helm will call the bear away and the command to the first ease of the main and jib..." On performance and foiling craft, this would be a vocal reminder to be a small bit above the layline in order to foot a little passing the weather mark en route to the offset .. and to ease the cunningham/boom vang/main sheet for fastest power as you approach the offset. Plan it all out ahead of race day. Practice going through each and every procedure beforehand, so that when you're getting close to the mark or approaching any maneuver, there's no panic; just smooth execution.

The skipper can clearly see the chessboard heading upwind, but it's important that the crew be the fly's eyes when going downwind. Keep your helmsman focused on driving on every downwind lump and making the boat glide best possible with most minimal tiller movement possible. The crew should constantly feed the helmsman ALL the info of what boat behind has breeze, what tack they are on, and what should be your boat's best angle to get to the bottom mark. Decide well before the bottom which gate to take, which side of the course you want to play on the next uphill, set up the rounding to go wide at the entry, tight to the mark and upwind angle on the exit of the rounding. Rah!

FLYING THE KITE

The trimming of the spinnaker or A sail is pretty straightforward. When in doubt, let it out... until the sail curls as if to collapse. Sheet in until it doesn't. Repeat. Sounds easy, right? Takes a great amount of concentration. You are now the boat's engine. Don't let it sputter.

If on a spinnaker boat, equally important to trimming the spinnaker sheet is to set the pole properly. It should be preset to the approximate height during pre-race practice, but as wind strengths change, you will probably have to tweak this. It's a minor advantage to have it perfectly set so that the two clews are even on the horizon with each other (if the boat were sailing with on an even keel). More importantly, the pole and attached *guy* (the innuendos are endless here, especially after a few drinks), should be pulled back as far as possible without collapsing the chute.

THE SKIPPER-CREW RELATIONSHIP

The success of most skippers relies upon how whether they sail in lockstep with their crew, or if that relationship is *rocky motley*. If you want a crew dedicated to race with you, your attitude needs to be like a NASA crew aiming for the moon; lock step.

It's tough finding a dedicated crew. As soon as they become so well trained they can not only perform their crew duties flawlessly, but call tactics as well, they are often off and running in their own boat, and knowing your every secret. There is certainly nothing wrong with this. It builds the fleet and makes you both (or all three) better sailors.

The less successful skipper is the one who is always fishing for a crew. They show up at a regatta and ask around, often left with the guy down at the bait shop that doesn't know the short end of a jib sheet, or worse (sometimes better!) three sheets to the wind. If they get lucky, they conjure up a hot shot from the Junior program, but even the best pick will still need to jive with your personality. If you keep looking for crew, that might not be your strong point.

The last type of crew is the family crew. Whether it is wife, brother, sister, son or daughter —wait, I've left out parent here – that relationship takes on additional layers. Hopefully, the bond grows stronger through sailing. As a skipper, you certainly don't want to be looking for more family. In particular, many of the most successful husband-wife relationships have either benefited from weekend after weekend close quarters, or wound up in divorce. Certainly, you don't want to force your kids into crewing for you. If they're willing to, the end goal should be to eventually crew for them. (Warning: they may kick you off the boat).

Jo Giltinan 18 Footers Photo: Christophe Favreau

For the most successful skipper/crew relationships in sailing, you need to look at the dynamic duo from Down Under: Peter Burling and Blair Tuke. This relationship has long endured partly due to winning (nearly everything), but also to their camaraderie. Moreso, it is Burling's calm demeanor that keeps them on top. That's key. Don't rub your crew the wrong way. Don't be a Captain Bligh (or Madame Skullcrusher)!

Annie Gardner: *Communication is crucial to success. Leaning how to relay info without too many words is always my goal with new crew. On fast boats like the F18 or Nacra you don't have time for a conversation. Figuring out your own way to relay info is a good tool. With a new crew I like to start with some sort of team building exercise. Leadership trickles down so showing strength, admitting mistakes, modeling the way to show how to balance hard work with having fun, celebrating small victories like doing a maneuver well, and being a gracious loser to a team that sailed better, all are examples of how to get the crew to respect you so that when you ask for more, they are ready and willing to give it.*

GOOD RECOVERY

Peter Commette

I didn't handle it so well in the beginning when we first started sailing together. The occasional flying off the handle would not fly. After we won Snipe Nationals with Connie as crew in '96, we put the boats away to focus on raising kids and my law practice. They weren't into sports. And then, lo and behold, one day my oldest daughter said, "Oh, I'd like to crew for you, Daddy." One by one, they all said, "Oh, yeah, yeah, that's what I was thinking of!" That's what I want to do!" And so, I spent the following years until the youngest went to college with my kids as crew. Connie went off to crew for Augie's father, Gonzolo Diaz.

After Connie had experienced what a gentleman Mr. Gonzolo Diaz was (at least he behaved well when with her, she would now no longer allow me to sail on an emotional roller coaster. She not only was embarrassed by me when I got mad and screamed. She was also embarrassed by me when I got really excited, and especially when demonstrative to anybody on the racecourse. And with my kids, the worst thing a dad can hear is, "Dad, you're embarrassing me." So, Connie really started to get me in line.

"Peter, I've had it. I've had it with you. This is what I've learned from the old man. And this is what you're going to start doing, or I'm no longer going to sail with you." And the old man system was no matter what was going on, no matter how screwed up things were, it didn't matter. The only thing I'm allowed to say after a disaster is, "Good recovery." That's it. And so, I've gone from a screaming maniac to, "Good recovery."

"Keep pushing! You gotta keep pushing! You gotta keep pushing!"

Going into the last race of the 2008 Don Q, it was Ernesto Rodriquez in first, Connie and I were in second and Augie Diaz was in third in a no-drop series. (Easier math; good for me!) I boned the start and the first leg. I said to Connie that we lost the series and maybe even third. She never accepts that sort of talk. "I've seen you come back from worse positions. Keep your head in it and keep pushing!"

We kept pushing. Picked off a boat here, a boat there. Finally, we got into a good groove, pulling ourselves into maybe fifth at the last leeward mark. At this point, Augie is winning the race and had to put one boat in between him and us, and Ernesto was in fourth, so Augie had his points on Ernesto, too. Because of where Augie was, we needed to be in second with a boat in between Ernesto and us, to win the regatta. What Augie didn't know was his math was off. We had heard the number for the boat in second place that last leg called over at the start. He never returned. OCS! He only counted in Augie's mind.

Rounding that last leeward mark, I recognized the type of condition on Biscayne Bay we call "The Old Man Highway," after Augie's dad. When the wind is from a certain direction, you can really hit a big shift and favorable current out on the left. We sent it. Tacked at the leeward mark. Banged the left corner hard. Easy strategy, born out of desperation.

Coming back on port for the finish, we get ahead of Ernesto. Augie still was in first with the OCS boat behind him. But Ernesto had worked into being the next boat behind us, coming up to his last tack to port to the finish. We needed that point. We had to wait until his last tack and then go back to screw him up to get a boat back in between him and us. Problem: the boats on the edges; at least one would probably get by us, giving Augie the point he didn't know he needed.

So, while we are setting ourselves up to go back after Ernesto, I tell Connie the plan, but I think we've lost it. Connie goes, "Oh, come on, Peter! You never know what can happen! Ernesto could fall out of the boat." I set us up, Ernesto made his last tack to the finish, missed his hiking strap, and fell out of the boat! Augie won the race, we crossed the line in third, but second to cross was the OCS boat. We won! I tear up when I think about this race and how Connie and I worked together. Same thing when thinking of the fun miles under my belt with my daughters... lucky guy!). I love this story, particularly, because it was the last major regatta that Connie and I won together... so far.

On the racecourse, give up on the emotional roller coasters but never give up on a race!

CHANGING OF THE GUARD

Like I wrote, I didn't grow up in any Junior YC program. My program consisted of sailing camp and taking a course at the Red Cross with Dad. At age 16, we started winning the Barefoot Sailing Club races in the 470, but to win any kind of regional regatta, I  decided there was something I needed to do, and it was tougher than a Ronstan block. I had to kick Dad off the boat.

He was pretty upset about it, rightly so, but was getting older (50!); not agile enough for the trapeze. He gave it his best, but tacking was like the changing of the guard at Buckingham Palace. Dad had fought in D-Day, had liberated Camp Ebensee in Austria, and was a true war hero as the "Hawkeye" in Patton's Army. But when it came to tacking, he needed specific Red Cross Sailing commands: "Ready to tack? Hard to lee!" By that time, on Lake Lanier, the header would have already passed. With my new crew, Chris Downing, it was just, "Tacking!"

Looking back on it, failing to timely tack on a header paled in comparison with a timely attack on the enemy in WWII. Being a teenager, you could not have told there was any difference. As soon as I could drive, I was on a tear to reach my target – beat Ed Baird! Aside from eventually beating Ed Baird (in a Laser, not the 470), I wish today that I had not kicked Dad off the boat, had stuck with the Snipe and learned the ropes, not become entangled by them. At least I wasn't engaged in foiling. Who knows, it might have existed!

Chris and I were the same age, 16. He had been crewing for another ancient 470 sailor (probably not even age 40 but you know how teenagers are), so we joined forces and together started to do a lot better. I don't think Dad talked to me for a year. It was a tough pill to swallow, sailboat racing retirement by child enforcement, but he still measured the other boats and slipped the paper under my door, with the end notes: Spreader bar, two degree further aft. *PRACTICE!* It was a tough time between us, but what teenager/parent relationship isn't?

THISTLE TIME

I got my crewing chops in on a Thistle under the tutelage of Johnny Sinclair. Johnny raced Lasers as did everyone, but he was the James Dean of Thistle sailing. He came from a long bloodline of Thistle greats and goats.

This photo of his Johnny Sinclair's father, Sinny, chilling on "Sinbad," hanging above the fireplace on the Lake Lanier SC wall.

Looking for some sailors to test out sails from his new loft, Harold Gilreath gave me a Thistle. All I had to do was dig it out from under a pile of leaves, torch off the old paint, sand, and paint anew. It was a woodie, mast and all, a real project boat. "Put some hair on your chest. Sail a Thistle," Harold would tell me. But it was true. There is no better boat for light air on Lake Lanier like the Thistle, hair or no hair.

The difference between a wood boat and a fiberglass Thistle seemed to be vast, but this was later proven to be something dancing in my head. Once I had replaced the wooden mast with an aluminum Proctor, the boat did okay for me. Bleeding sweat and tears over a classic, wood boat is something everyone should have to go through as a life ordeal. I never quite did his sails justice, though I do have a few trophies that tell otherwise. For some reason, I can only remember the races I lost.

With Lee Estes as my crew (an MC Scow National Champion and mentor), we had a real shot at winning our first major Thistle regatta, right near where I live now at LNYC. We had the lead over icon Ed Harrel with one race to go on Sunday. To beat Ed would be amazing. I'd come home with so much hair on my chest, I'd look like Wolverine. Instead, being the showoff I was, we flew the spinnaker right from the club dock. Just in front of the club house, a gust hit and we swamped. No air bags and too young to drink, there was nothing iconic about this. We missed the last race.

Just to illustrate the difference between a wooden and fiberglass Thistle, I do remember winning one Thistle regatta, the Orange Peel at Florida Yacht Club. It was one of the largest events of the year. Andy Fox, a Laser sailing friend at the time and Thistle National Champion, promised his crew that he'd crew for them one regatta a year. Luckily for me, they picked this one. Andy lent me his fiberglass boat.

Abdullah & Co. after killing the 2025 Orange Peel Perpetual trophy.

With Chris and a girlfriend as my crew, our only goal was to have fun, mix it up a bit on the racecourse, and eat the most peeled fancy yacht club shrimp Saturday night. This put my name on the biggest perpetual trophy I've seen short of the America's Cup. We like to do things big in the South.

Fast forward many years later, I returned to the Old Goat at LLSC, another prominent Thistle regatta. With Lee as my crew on his fiberglass boat, we stunk up the lake, but it was amazing to see old friends, who remembered me as the kid with the soot face, who got too close to the start boat canon. The regatta was won by the legendary Burke brothers, in wooden Thistle #1.

BREAKDOWN PARTY
by Paul Abdullah

At the 2024 Thistle Nationals in Toms River, NJ, we had just completed the second day of racing and while sailing in with the spinnaker up in 18kts, we attempted to jibe but were hit with a puff and had to wave it off. On the second attempt, the boom came over and immediately we broke the port side middle and lower diamonds. The mast started to bend to starboard and we quickly unloaded the sails by heading up and getting the mainsail and spin down.

Once things calmed down on the boat panic set in about how we could continue competing in the regatta for the remainder of the week. We got a tow from an RC support boat and once we hit shore, I started to put a plan together. I was able to secure spare diamonds from Mike Ingham. Fortunately, I got to him before others did because there were other boats that needed repair. I had broken diamonds before and knew how to go about taking them off and assembling the new parts using the sockets and flaring tool.

The group of competitors formed an assembly line and I was able to get my rig back together and the rest of the crowd did as well. Once the rig was back up, we noticed it wasn't perfectly straight but we could continue in the regatta. Even after our near disaster we were able to continue our solid performance with finishes of 14-2-2-2-2-2-3 to seal the win. We couldn't have done it without Mike and other friends in the Thistle family.

FINAL WORD

Getting old sucks, but I was cheating the nursing home by getting back to sailing Lasers in what they still call the SF Bay Area. I wasn't as good at as some of the guys like Tracy Usher and Peter Vassella, but I was keeping in shape training for triathlons, and with my weight and height advantage, I'd always be up there in the top five. Laser Master's events or otherwise, it was more of a fight against the raw elements than the competition (my favorite Mark Twain quote: the coldest winter I ever spent was a Summer in San Francisco). Even in the open events where we sailed against the young hot shots, the top places always went to the silver sailors. I even managed a silver medal at the Senior Games in Sailing at age 50. They AARP carded me.

All my years of windsurfing and crashing started to add up to neck pain (wearing a ten-pound camera on my head, perhaps?). With a Groupon coupon, I decided to visit a chiropractor. He turned out to be a giant Samoan guy, who cracked my neck all right. He also severed my phrenic nerves. The phrenic nerves control the diaphragm. At least my neck pain was gone. Life took a deep dive. One lung down, breathing and the ability to hike not overrated, I went from first at Midwinters to dead last in the spring.

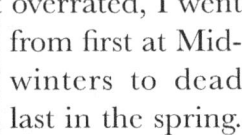

I went from mtn biking 30 miles one day and swimming a mile the next to not being able to swim a lap. I tried to windsurf, fell off and almost drowned. To watch Davo blaze off on the horizon and win by a mile was a hard pill to swallow, but at the same time I marveled, *that used to be me!*

After doing everything I could for three years to recover, nothing was working. I had to sell my boat to pay for medical expenses.

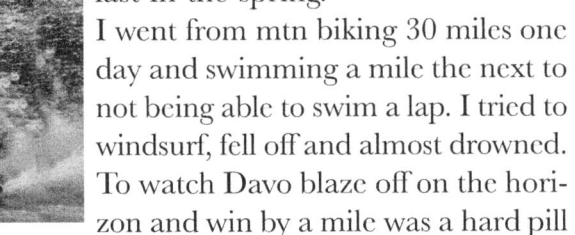

Fast forward three years later, the doctors were about to write me off, when gradually, my right lung came back to life. I knew it had, as that was when Davo lent me his boat and I won the Weta

WINNING WAYS

Nationals at Cascade Locks (Columbia River Gorge), in what was the windiest regatta I've ever sailed: 3 days straight of Hot n' Now 25 gusting to 40 naut conditions! It wasn't against Davo, it wasn't winning Laser Nationals or an Olympic medal, but it wasn't simple, either. After what I'd been through, it was the greatest thrill of victory I could possibly imagine.

I retired from Weta racing in 2020 after several other health challenges, but I still get out on the lake and the Med when the water is flat, still have fun on the new version of the Windsurfer LT. As far as my racing days go, they're pretty much over, but at least I lived to tell and write about it.

Achieving results in sailing comes down to more than eating donuts. Much like playing a musical instrument, with practice comes mastery, and with mastery comes mindless play. Both talented musicians and masters of boat racing often talk about a Zen state. They're best sailing up the racecourse completely zoned in, thinking but not thinking. Like the Chicago song, whether it's a Saturday or Sunday afternoon, they're *groovin'*. There is simply no other way to get groovin' than to get out there and race.

I hope you've enjoyed this book. If it improves your results or just gives you a break from scrolling, please write a kind review for it on Amazon!

Check out my sailing blog The Long Tack on Substack, https://thelongtack.substack.com

Travels through France with the wonderdog, Toby. www.travelswithtoby.com

and The Hemingway Trilogy on Amazon.

ACKNOWLEDGMENTS

I would like to thank all of the great story contributors to this book. I'd like to give special thanks to Dick Lamb, whom as first reader, spent countless hours advising on word choice. I also would like to express special thanks to the class organizations for their photography contributions, including the International 420 and 470 Class (Dimitris Dimou), International 505 Class, Melges Boat Works (Morgan Kinney), the SoCal Lido Fleet (Bruce Cooper, Ullman Sails), Maru Urban Clinics, SailCoach Clinics, and a great deal of gratitude to the contributing photographers. Google, find their Instagrams, and hire!

Christophe Favreau was the first photographer to kindly offer his incredible imagery to this book. After telling him that I'd rather be sailing than shooting it, he was happy to help other sailors and give exposure to the International 505 Class (who sends him to cover their Worlds and shoots as staff for a French Voiler magazine). Christophe has been covering sailing events for over twenty years. He loves the 505's and 18 Footers!

Hannah Lee Noll is a prolific sailing media professional and the founder of WindDance Creative, a creative agency specializing in storytelling, social media, and photography for global sailing brands like NY Yacht Club, Bacardi Cup, Harken, Melges, and US Sailing Team. Her photos of Maru Urban Clinics exemplify her dedication to the growth of the sport. Her contributions have been recognized with multiple leadership awards including induction into the College Sailing Hall of Fame for student leadership. As a competitive sailor, Hannah has won regional and national championships. She races scows, Melges 24s, J/70s, Snipes, Etchells, and Melges 15s.

Will Keyworth is an Annapolis, MD based Nautical Photographer with decades of on water experience. Will's love of photography and sailing both go back his early years growing up on the Chesapeake Bay. He spent 38 years sailmaker and professional sailboat racer competing in championship events around the globe. Will's love of photography followed him through his adventures and became a new career after his retirement in 2020. His photography comes to life through the keen eye of a sailor/racer and he has become a highly sought sailing event photographer up and down the east coast capturing the sailing action at local, national and world championship events.

Lexi Pline has been taking photos since she first picked up a camera in middle school, and hasn't stopped since. She currently works in Media and Communications for US Sailing, where she runs the social channels, shoots regattas and writes stories; as well as a freelance news photographer. Lexi has been awarded the National YoungArts Award in Photography two years in a row (2014-2015. Lexi is also an avid sailor, and an alumni of the Boston University Sailing Team. When not out shooting great photos, you can find her out sailing.

WINNING WAYS

Andrea Lelli is a sailor, photographer, and boatbuilder with a deep passion for high-performance sailing. After competing in the 420 class until 2016, Andrea transitioned into leadership roles within the class association, serving as secretary and later as president until 2024. While pursuing a degree in aerospace engineering, Andrea developed a strong interest in sailing photography, capturing national and international regattas. Now based in Southampton, UK, Andrea works as a boatbuilder and technician at the SailGP Technologies yard.

Nikos Alevromytis was born in Athens, Greece, and brings us his many great artistic sailing images of major events, including the Tokyo and Japan Olympic Games for 470 class. He has also covered the 2017 470 World Championship in Thessaloniki, the 2017 Open European Optimist Championship in Burgas, the 2018 470 Open European Championships, and the 2018 Hempel World Sailing Cup for the 470 class.

Deb Fewell Durbec not only cleans up beaches, she cleans up with the photos at a great many Thistle and Snipe regattas held at Florida YC. She's pretty shy (but not shy with sharing her photos with us!), so I'll post a photo here of what must be her Thistle sailing son. He rips!

John Cole was introduced to the magic of sailing and photography when he was nine years old. For the past five decades his love for being on the water, with a camera always at the ready, has been his passion, therapy, and profession. His journeys have taken him to 34 countries, most of which involved being at the helm of some sort of watercraft. John was a professional charter captain for ten years, "somewhat retired" as Senior Ops manager for photography at Disney's theme parks.

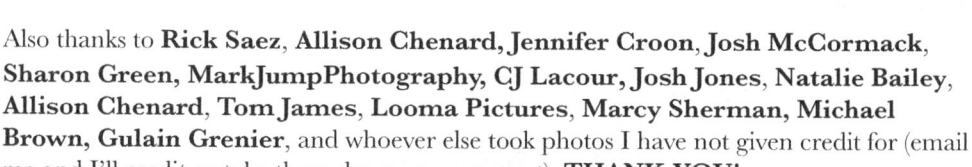

Brian McDonald: Surfer, skater, swimmer, paddler, photographer, former US Windsurfing National Champion, and member of the Collegiate Sailing HOF (Stanford). Mechanical engineer. @sailing314 Instagram.

Also thanks to **Rick Saez, Allison Chenard, Jennifer Croon, Josh McCormack, Sharon Green, MarkJumpPhotography, CJ Lacour, Josh Jones, Natalie Bailey, Allison Chenard, Tom James, Looma Pictures, Marcy Sherman, Michael Brown, Gulain Grenier,** and whoever else took photos I have not given credit for (email me and I'll credit or take them down upon request). **THANK YOU!**

Made in United States
Orlando, FL
30 March 2025

59981857R00164